COMMUNITY WITHOUT CONSENT

RE-MAPPING THE TRANSNATIONAL
A Dartmouth Series in American Studies

SERIES EDITOR
Donald E. Pease
Avalon Foundation Chair of Humanities
Founding Director of the Futures of American Studies Institute
Dartmouth College

The emergence of Transnational American Studies in the wake of the Cold War marks the most significant reconfiguration of American Studies since its inception. The shock waves generated by a newly globalized world order demanded an understanding of America's embeddedness within global and local processes rather than scholarly reaffirmations of its splendid isolation. The series Re-Mapping the Transnational seeks to foster the cross-national dialogues needed to sustain the vitality of this emergent field. To advance a truly comparativist understanding of this scholarly endeavor, Dartmouth College Press welcomes monographs from scholars both inside and outside the United States.

For a complete list of books available in this series, see www.upne.com.

Zachary McLeod Hutchins, editor, *Community without Consent: New Perspectives on the Stamp Act*
Kate A. Baldwin, *The Racial Imaginary of the Cold War Kitchen: From Sokol'niki Park to Chicago's South Side*
Yuan Shu and Donald E. Pease, *American Studies as Transnational Practice: Turning toward the Transpacific*
Melissa M. Adams-Campbell, *New World Courtships: Transatlantic Alternatives to Companionate Marriage*
David LaRocca and Ricardo Miguel-Alfonso, editors, *A Power to Translate the World: New Essays on Emerson and International Culture*
Elèna Mortara, *Writing for Justice: Victor Séjour, the Mortara Case, and the Age of Transatlantic Emancipations*
Rob Kroes, *Prison Area, Independence Valley: American Paradoxes in Political Life and Popular Culture*
Etsuko Taketani, *The Black Pacific Narrative: Geographic Imaginings of Race and Empire between the World Wars*

ZACHARY MCLEOD HUTCHINS, EDITOR

COMMUNITY WITHOUT CONSENT

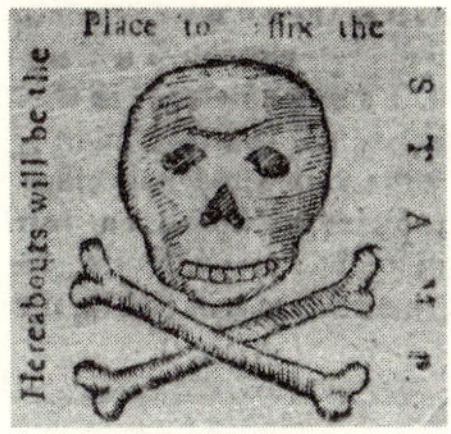

New Perspectives on the Stamp Act

DARTMOUTH COLLEGE PRESS
HANOVER, NEW HAMPSHIRE

Dartmouth College Press
An imprint of University Press of New England
www.upne.com

Manufactured in the United States of America
Designed by Doug Tifft
Typeset in Sabon and Scala Sans by Integrated Publishing Solutions

Library of Congress Cataloging-in-Publication Data
Community without consent: new perspectives on the Stamp Act / edited by Zachary McLeod Hutchins.
pages cm. — (Re-mapping the transnational : a Dartmouth series in American studies)
Includes bibliographical references and index.
ISBN 978-1-61168-881-8 (cloth : alk. paper) — ISBN 978-1-61168-882-5 (pbk. : alk. paper) — ISBN 978-1-61168-952-5 (ebook)
1. Great Britain. Stamp Act (1765) 2. Taxation—Political aspects—United States—History—18th century. 3. United States—History—Colonial period, ca. 1600–1775. 4. Protest movements—United States—History—18th century. 5. Riots—United States—History—18th century. 6. United States—History—Revolution, 1775–1783—Causes. 7. Great Britain—Relations—United States. 8. United States—Relations—Great Britain. I. Hutchins, Zachary McLeod.
E215.2.C66 2016
973.2′7—dc23 2015034442

Chapter 5 was published previously and is reprinted here, by permission, from *Early American Literature*, Vol. 50, Number 3, (2015).

5 4 3 2 1

CONTENTS

ACKNOWLEDGMENTS

I remember, as a boy, standing on a stepladder hauled through the morning mist every April by my father, Kenneth Hutchins, so that I could see an orderly line of soldiers in the scarlet uniforms of British regulars march across the green at Minuteman National Park, where they would be routed and slain by a ragtag mob of minutemen. My fascination with the colonial period was born on those battlefields and during the long summer afternoons I spent staring at poster-sized copies of both the Declaration of Independence and the Constitution of the United States of America, which had been framed by my mother. She wanted me to be a dentist or a doctor, but her passion for American literature and history seduced me into the occupational briar patch that is the humanities. My contributions to this volume are dedicated to Priscilla Glass Hutchins.

Of course, my language and ideas here make up only a small fraction of a larger whole, and working with the contributors to this volume—Pat Mullins, Molly Perry, Gil Gigliotti, Caroline Wigginton, Alex Jablonski, Todd Thompson, and Clay Zuba—has been both humbling and extremely gratifying. As we hashed out our ideas in person, at the 2014 convention of the American Society for Eighteenth-Century Studies, I quickly came to understand why scholars sometimes characterize the development of a book as organic; I could not have asked for a more collegial and generous group of scholars with which to collaborate. Other colleagues, at Colorado State University and elsewhere, have offered their time, expertise, and encouragement liberally. I am particularly beholden to Ellen Brinks, Roze Hentschell, Louann Reid, Ben Park, Christopher Jones, Jill Rudy, Brian Roberts, Jamin Rowan, Phil Snyder, and Tim Marr: their advice, feedback, and support have been invaluable.

And, finally, I am deeply indebted to the staff at Dartmouth College Press. Much of what is good about this book can be attributed to the expert guidance of Donald Pease, the Solomonic wisdom of Richard Pult, and the critiques submitted by anonymous readers they selected. Thanks also are due to Amanda Dupuis and Mary Becker, whose copyediting was incisive but judicious and saved the collection from condemnation by the grammar gods. Any lingering errors or linguistic infelicities are, alas, my own.

ZACHARY MCLEOD HUTCHINS

INTRODUCTION: THE STAMP ACT, FROM BEGINNING TO END

THE INDIVIDUAL MANDATE PROVISION of the 2010 Affordable Care Act requires that every citizen of the United States maintain minimum, essential health insurance coverage or pay a penalty. When the constitutionality of this provision was challenged Chief Justice John Roberts, delivering the decision of the Supreme Court, declared that the individual mandate "may for constitutional purposes be considered a tax, not a penalty."[1] In their jointly authored dissent to this majority opinion, Justices Antonin Scalia, Anthony Kennedy, Clarence Thomas, and Samuel Alito reject this characterization of the penalty and suggest that in declaring the mandate a tax Roberts has arrogated to the Court rights belonging to the legislative branch of government:

> Judicial tax-writing is particularly troubling. Taxes have never been popular, see, *e.g.*, Stamp Act of 1765, and in part for that reason, the Constitution requires tax increases to originate in the House of Representatives. See Art. I, §7, cl. 1. That is to say, they must originate in the legislative body most accountable to the people, where legislators must weigh the need for the tax against the terrible price they might pay at their next election, which is never more than two years off. . . . We have no doubt that Congress knew precisely what it was doing when it rejected an earlier version of this legislation that imposed a tax instead of a requirement-with-penalty.[2]

This dissent portrays the opinion of the Court as a failure of republican processes and representative government. Scalia, Kennedy, Thomas, and Alito allege that judges appointed for life and thus unaccountable to voters have imposed a new tax on U.S. citizens. If Supreme Court justices—appointed by the president, who is in turn elected by electoral college members chosen by voters—represent the will of the people, they do so at multiple removes, not directly but virtually. To characterize the Stamp Act as analogous to the tax upheld or created by Chief Justice Roberts is, thus, to summon up that familiar specter of tyranny: taxation without representation.

Conservative lawmakers such as U.S. Senator Rand Paul have pointed to this passage of the dissent as a call to action, framing their fight against the Affordable Care Act as the beginning of an impending ideological revolution just as the Stamp Act Crisis was, in the enduring words of Edmund and Helen Morgan, a "Prologue to Revolution."[3] But the Stamp Act Crisis marked not so much the beginning of American nationalism as the decline of British nationalism in the Americas; it was a conflict that unraveled the fictions endowing nations with agency and investing them with authority. Despite the absence of American members, Parliament insisted that colonial interests had been virtually represented throughout the legislative process that produced the Stamp Act: a position that only called attention to the artificiality of all representative systems of government. During the long eighteenth century, when power shifted from monarchs to legislative bodies putatively representing the interests of an absent and therefore imaginary populace, nations were gradually recognized as contingent institutions predicated on the belief of individuals that these disembodied entities existed and acted on their behalf, in their collective interest. The failure of these representative systems in the Stamp Act Crisis and other eighteenth-century political conflicts revealed what Jacqueline Rose has termed the "fantasmatic" authority of legislatures and, thus, nations.[4] The dissent of Scalia, Kennedy, Thomas, and Alito suggests that the Affordable Care Act is a new legislative failure that should once again remind the inhabitants of North America of the fantasmatic nature of power derived by virtual representation. Because it was followed, ten years later, by shots fired in Lexington and Concord, the Stamp Act of 1765 may represent the most famous breakdown in representative government, and the legacy of this tax, which inspired both the colonial rejection of tautological British nationalism and, paradoxically, the rise of American nationalism, is still under construction.[5]

Since the period of civic unrest caused by the Stamp Act and Townshend Duties was followed by the American War of Independence, scholars almost always characterize the colonial response to these tariffs as the beginning of that conflict, and there are good reasons for this scholarly consensus.[6] To historians writing with the burden of historical awareness, rebellion and the establishment of a new, North American state can seem like inevitable outcomes of Prime Minister George Grenville's decision to pay down British debt incurred on the American front of the Seven Years' War by taxing colonists unrepresented in Parliament. Yet in 1765 Grenville himself—and most of his contemporaries, on both sides of the Atlantic—clearly saw the Stamp Act as a piece of legislation signifying the end of an old war rather than the beginning of a new one. Indeed, the act's first sentence announces that revenue generated by "*certain stamp duties, and other duties, in the* British *colonies and plantations in* America" will be applied "*towards further defraying the expences of defending, protecting, and securing the same*."[7] Despite this invitation to read the Stamp Act as a conclusion to the Seven Years' War, students of Britain's role in that global struggle almost never mention this by-product of the conflict, and chroniclers of the French and Indian War, its North American front, have likewise rarely devoted serious attention to its legislative denouement.[8] Again, there are good reasons for omitting discussion of the Stamp Act from accounts of the French and Indian War, including the fact that stamp duties never generated enough revenue to pay down war debt. But the scholarly consensus identifying reactions to the Stamp Act as a beginning of the American Revolution rather than an end to the French and Indian War also attests to the persistently seductive sway of nationalist paradigms in the academy.

To speak of the transatlantic taxation debates of the 1760s as a beginning is to elide from history those "British *colonies and plantations*" in the Western Hemisphere that refused to join the thirteen colonies cum United States in their fight for independence. Inhabitants of the Leeward Islands of St. Kitts and Nevis violently opposed the Stamp Act but make no appearance in most accounts of colonial resistance to the duty because their defiance was not a prologue to revolution: their participation in protests against the new tax does not fit our preferred narrative of incipient nationalism.[9] Yet resistance did not always lead to revolution, and acquiescence to the Stamp Act's provisions did not necessarily preclude incorporation into the new nation-state produced by rebellion; residents of Georgia both purchased stamps authorizing the passage of their vessels in 1766 and signed the Declaration of Independence a decade later.[10] Although the Stamp Act applied to almost thirty British colonies, we regularly and arbitrarily limit our discussion of the statute to its effect on the thirteen colonies that would eventually form a political union, rather than the larger group of twenty-six that *already* shared political ties to Great Britain. The Stamp Act riots and the American Revolution were discontinuous, if sequential, events, but because scholars have generally embraced national identity as a meaningful signifier, they regularly link the two causally. By ignoring taxpayers in Georgia and tax protestors in Nevis, we present the Stamp Act as an irresistibly unifying moment that suggests both the inevitability and the desirability of an American national identity.

However, if we think of the transatlantic tax debates as a conclusion to the Seven Years' War instead of a prelude to the American War of Independence, their significance vis-à-vis the utility and necessity of nationalism is reversed. Rather than reading the Stamp Act as a catalyst spurring colonial unification and the adoption of an American identity eventually inseparable from allegiance to the United States, we might view the duty's passage as an event revealing the insufficiency of British national identity as a force ensuring social cohesion.[11] In 1753, just before the French and Indian War, Robert Darcy, Earl of Holderness, wrote to each colonial governor on behalf of King George II, urging "that all his provinces in America should be aiding and assisting each other, in case of any invasion, . . . and in case you shall be informed . . . of any hostile attempts, you are immediately to assemble the general assembly within your government, and lay before them, the necessity of a mutual assistance."[12] Holderness calls on national identity—loyalty to King and Crown—as an inducement to unifying action, but colonial legislatures largely rejected this appeal to their shared Britishness as a motivation for cooperation. As Brendan McConville attests, the inhabitants of North America loved the idea of a king, "but they did not share a universal understanding of his nature, political patriarchy, the British constitution, or even whether they lived under an imperial, British, English, or customary constitution."[13] Seven decades after the Glorious Revolution, the British monarch's abdication of absolute authority to Parliament invited colonists to question the location and the nature of the state's power.[14] Holderness's letter marked the first moment when a British monarch asked his American subjects to act in concert, exposing this fragmented understanding of the state and the frailty of British national identity abroad.[15] Further, the failures and peccadilloes of His Majesty's soldiers during the French and Indian War, including the imperial disdain for colonial war heroes such as George Washington, exacerbated these rifts by forcing individuals born on opposite sides of the Atlantic, with diverging understandings of and commitments to the Kingdom of Great Britain, to cooperate in close proximity.[16] Predicated on the transparent fiction of colonists' virtual representation in Parliament, the Stamp Act deepened divisions exposed by the French and Indian War and thrust into view the artificial, subjective nature of the modern state as an institution grounded in fantasy.

Collectively, the essays in this volume interrogate the utility of American nationalism and national identity as lenses through which to view a tax levied against the inhabitants of geographical areas that comprise, today, more than a dozen different nations.[17] Even the Stamp Act itself acknowledged the existence of competing national identities among British subjects in the Western Hemisphere, punishing individuals whose linguistic preferences identified them with competing nationalisms by stipulating that for documents written "in any other than the *English* language, a stamp duty of double the amount of the respective duties before charged thereon" should be paid.[18] Although the essays in this volume are all written in English (and may, thus, reflect the success of imperial policies promoting linguistic and cultural homogenization), they interrogate the actions and language of eighteenth-century men and women born in France, Africa, the Caribbean, and elsewhere, restoring an awareness of the linguistic and cultural diversity within the umbrella of eighteenth-century British identity, diversity that the Stamp Act sought to suppress through taxation and that the nationalist thrust of scholarship on the duty has further obscured.

Each chapter has been grouped in one of four topically related clusters. The essays in part I, "Ritual Responses to the Stamp Act," examine the use of ceremony and pageantry to subvert the norms of British national identity through the formation of counterpublics.[19] That these temporarily unifying acts of resistance did not necessarily lead to the establishment of a permanent American identity or nation is the argument of chapter 1, "The Sermon That Didn't Start the Revolution: Jonathan Mayhew's Role in the Stamp Act Riots," by J. Patrick Mullins. As Mullins explains, early Loyalist historians chronicling the American War of Independence blamed Boston minister Jonathan Mayhew for inciting mob violence that destroyed the papers and damaged the dwellings of Thomas Hutchinson, William Story, and Benjamin Hallowell in a sermon preached the day before, on August 25, 1765. Because this Boston riot served as a precedent informing similar scenes of destruction in each of the other thirteen North American colonies, historians in both the eighteenth and twentieth centuries have characterized Mayhew's sermon as an originary moment for the American Revolution. While he acknowledges that Mayhew promoted Whig ideology during his tenure in the pulpit, Mullins effectively decouples this prominent preacher from the 1765 violence against royal officials by providing an alternative explanation for the origins and motives of the mob that attacked Hutchinson and by documenting Mayhew's insistence on the duty of restraint in effecting political change. The ritual gathering of Mayhew's nouveau riche congregation did not lead to the coarse behavior and wanton demolition of the Hutchinson mob, Mullins argues, much less the American Revolution. Indeed, Mullins remakes Mayhew's supposedly incendiary sermon into a cautionary tale that illustrates the challenges of assigning causality in a complex chain of historical events, even when those events are separated by a single day rather than the decade that passed between Mayhew's death in July 1766 and passage of the Declaration of Independence.

In chapter 2, "Buried Liberties and Hanging Effigies: Imperial Persuasion, Intimidation, and Performance during the Stamp Act Crisis," Molly Perry picks up where Mullins leaves off, with the Boston riots that devastated Hutchinson's home. Unlike the signers of the Declaration, Perry reminds us, participants in mob violence did not affix their names to lists or provide other guarantees of their commitment to the anti-stamp cause. The participation of individuals on the edge of crowds was often fleeting, no more than a "Huzzah" in passing or an involuntary, coerced inclusion in rituals (such as the impression of counter-stamps on paper goods bought at market). Furthermore, even the most ardent opponents of parliamentary authority regularly oscillated from postures of resistance to declarations of support; for most of the faceless individuals who participated in the hanging of effigies, the burning of stamps, and the tolling of church bells mourning liberty's death, affiliation with the anti-stamp cause was contingent and temporary, not a commitment that would carry over to the founding of a new nation. And yet, if the crowds were faceless, their shifting racial composition signaled an awareness of the need to demonstrate performatively an awareness that the British body politic could not yet accommodate the presence of Native Americans, Africans, or women. The picture of white male colonial solidarity that emerged from accounts of colonial protest would eventually be codified in the new nation, Perry contends, even though not all of the individuals who participated in those protests persisted in their opposition to English authority during the Revolution.

The essays in part II, "The Poetics of Taxation," examine verse inspired by the Stamp Act. In chapter 3, "'Daring to Try the King's Patience?': (Futile?) Resistance versus Insatiability in *Fabula Neoterica*," Gilbert Gigliotti translates and analyzes a 1765 neo-Latin newspaper poem whose anonymous author struggles to balance the competing values of duty and freedom in the context of the Stamp Act. In his tale of the confrontation between a colonial mouse and the royal British lion, Gigliotti's poet speaks through classical language and allusion to the educated white men who will come to make up Perry's body politic, voicing dissatisfaction with both the insanity of parliamentary schemes for virtual representation and the presumption of colonists who would instruct imperial superiors on how best to govern. The poem wavers, throwing its support behind each side in turn, unable to find an acceptable resolution to the conflict. This indeterminacy and the poet's unwillingness to commit to either side of a disappointing binary, Gigliotti declares, speaks to a desire for further dialogue between Crown and colonies rather than a hasty and premature ending to the conflict. The poet asserts his privilege and social power in the form of his poetry but cannot dredge, from the classical tradition on which he draws, a solution to the crisis, only a plea for reason and restraint.

Whereas Gigliotti's poet speaks to a transatlantic and imperial public, the subject of chapter 4 offers a decidedly localized and domestic response to the Stamp Act Crisis. In "Letters from a Woman in Pennsylvania, or Elizabeth Graeme Fergusson Dreams of John Dickinson," Caroline Wigginton recovers an unpublished poem in which Fergusson imagines an alternative history for the origins of John Dickinson's influential *Letters from a Farmer in Pennsylvania* (1767–68). Fergusson's verses recount a dream in which an angelic William Penn descends from heaven and delivers a scroll containing the language of *Letters* to Fergusson; she, in turn, gives the scroll to Dickinson, who reads the heavenly message to the masses. In this poetic counterfactual, Wigginton suggests, Fergusson recenters an imperial struggle over the Stamp Act and parliamentary authority around the domestic concerns of heterosocial communities rather than the proto-national fraternity of countrymen on whom Dickinson calls. In the joint agricultural labors of men, women, and children, Fergusson locates a solution for residents of Pennsylvania's fertile landscape; hers is an answer that pointedly ignores Caribbean islands dependent on imported goods because she envisions the conflict through a local lens. The Stamp Act, Wigginton reminds us, was legislation that excited discussion between familial communities and women as well as a continent of angry white men.

The essays in part III, "The Levy and the Slave," revisit the Whiggish characterization of taxation without representation as a condition equivalent to slavery. Chapter 5, "The Slave Narrative and the Stamp Act, or Letters from Two American Farmers in Pennsylvania," turns from Fergusson's poem to another work of literature inspired by Dickinson's *Letters from a Farmer in Pennsylvania*: J. Hector St. John de Crèvecoeur's *Letters from an American Farmer*. Crèvecoeur provides a Tory rebuttal to Dickinson's denunciation of the Stamp Act and Townshend Duties, insisting that parliamentary authority has protected the colonies and that taxes have civilized the inhabitants of an otherwise backward and savage land. If the colonists are slaves, Crèvecoeur insists, they are not slaves by law but Aristotelian slaves by nature, unfit to govern themselves. Then, to demonstrate the difference between the political threats of which Dickinson speaks and the bodily horrors of human trafficking, Crèvecoeur depicts a gruesome scene of torture in which an enslaved African pleads first for water and then for death from a South Carolina crow cage. Crèvecoeur implies that until colonists stop condemning kidnapped Africans to live gibbeting or face that punishment themselves, from the British crown, their hypocritical cries of slavery will continue to ring hollow.

The legal status of slaves—both the peasants of Poland and the Africans laboring on Caribbean and South Carolina plantations—was used as a foil by Dickinson and other legal theorists attempting to articulate the rights and responsibilities of British subjects. In chapter 6, "'Providence never designed us for Negroes': Slavery and British Subjecthood in the Stamp Act Crisis, 1764–1766," Alexander Jablonski examines competing constructions of what it meant to be a British subject. Both colonists and metropolitan commentators agreed that subjecthood was shaped by a number of factors, including ancestry, race, and the performance of character; racialized peoples or individuals lacking in courage and resolve could not qualify themselves to receive the rights of British subjecthood. Accordingly, London writers alleging that colonists were unfit to be subjects emphasized the degenerative influence of North American climates and the specter of creolization. North American colonists, for their part, reciprocally accused their Caribbean counterparts of accepting parliamentary tyranny with more meekness than enslaved Africans accepted the tyranny of the lash; Caribbean slaves and slave owners thus became foils of character and race, Jablonski contends, whose submission marked them as unworthy of the rights fought for and won by British subjects. Colonists construed their performance of rebellion and resistance to tyranny as a sign of their own racial purity and admirable character, proof that they merited the legal protections secured by their virtuous English ancestors.

The essays in part IV, "Indians across the Atlantic," also address allegations of creolization, but the focus in these chapters is on Native, rather than African, bodies. In chapter 7, "'Homespun,' 'Indian Corn,' and the '*indigestible* . . . Stamp Act': An Empire of Stereotype in Franklin's Letters to the London Press," Todd Thompson shows how Benjamin Franklin used Native foods as an acknowledgment of cultural differences between England and its American colonies, while challenging the accompanying claims that these differences signaled the inferiority of colonial creoles. Franklin differentiates English nationalism from British identity, arguing that American, Irish, Scottish, and Welsh subjects of the British Empire have been alienated by a prideful English insistence that provincial customs—the consumption of hominy, for example—mark these subjects as backward and uncivilized yokels. Rather than reject maize and other markers of colonial creolization, Franklin embraces this Native marker of racial difference and insists that the British imperial project accept putatively inferior peoples as full partners of the English. Updating his earlier "Join, or Die" cartoon in a new image circulated to members of Parliament, "Magna Britannia: her Colonies Reduc'd," Franklin visually depicts Virginia, Pennsylvania, and other colonies estranged by the Stamp Act as the severed limbs of a personified British Empire; Franklin, as Thompson explains, warns that England cannot survive without its North American partners in trade and must subdue English nationalism in the service of strengthening a transatlantic coalition, even if that means accepting American creoles as full and equal participants in the imperial enterprise.

In chapter 8, "Redness and the Contest of Anglo-American Empires," Clay Zuba surveys the archive of eighteenth-century political cartoons to track representations of colonial British America as one or more Native bodies during the Stamp Act Crisis and surrounding decades. He finds that a metropolitan attempt to signal the inferiority and dependence of American colonies—by representing the colonies as Native creoles—compelled diasporic colonists to assert racial purity by conforming to European cultural norms even as it unintentionally contributed to colonists' growing sense of a shared identity distinct from that of British metropolitans. Colonial adaptations of metropolitan prints stripped the American Indian of Native artifacts and dark skin, but they largely accepted the Indian as a visual representation of North American identity. The figure of the red Indian thus obstructed the inclusion of British colonists in a larger category of national identity, registering a rupture in the compatibility of nation and empire. The English could pursue empire or nationalism, Zuba suggests, but not both. Most specific provisions of the Stamp Act begin with the phrase "For every skin or piece of vellum," but the duty and discourse surrounding its implementation clearly did not apply to *every* skin in the same manner; for individual and collective bodies pejoratively identified with red or black skin, the Stamp Act was a reminder of the political and economic advantages of whiteness in the eighteenth-century Atlantic.[20]

The afterword revisits this idea of a colonial corpus, emphasizing the corporatist understanding that animated collective action during the Stamp Act Crisis. Before the Declaration enshrined a liberal emphasis on individual rights in American culture, British colonists understood the corporation as a locus of rights and responsibilities and acted on corporatist principles in their protest against parliamentary tyranny. This forgotten aspect of North American history seems particularly relevant today, in the wake of recent decisions by the U.S. Supreme Court on the constitutionality of the Affordable Care Act and other bills, decisions that have awarded the rights of free speech and religious freedom to corporations. Two hundred and fifty years after its passage, the Stamp Act continues to inform a nation and a national tradition gradually revealed by the slow dissolution of British nationalism in the riots and rituals it inspired.[21]

Notes

1. John Roberts, "Opinion of the Court," *National Federation of Independent Business v Scofield*, http://www.supremecourt.gov/opinions/11pdf/11–393c3a2.pdf, p. 35 (accessed 2 October 2014).

2. Antonin Scalia, Anthony Kennedy, Clarence Thomas, and Samuel Alito, "Scalia, Kennedy, Thomas, and Alito, JJ., dissenting," *National Federation of Independent Business v Scofield*, http://www.supremecourt.gov/opinions/11pdf/11–393c3a2.pdf, pp. 24–25 (accessed 2 October 2014).

3. Rand Paul, "Obamacare Is Not Constitutional," *National Review Online*, 28 June 2012, http://www.nationalreview.com/articles/304386/obamacare-not-constitutional-sen-rand-paul (accessed 5 October 2014); Edmund S. Morgan and Helen M. Morgan, *The Stamp Act Crisis: Prologue to Revolution*, 3d ed. (Chapel Hill: University of North Carolina Press, 1995).

4. Jacqueline Rose, *States of Fantasy* (New York: Oxford University Press, 1996), 9.

5. The central premise of the Stamp Act, that colonists will pay taxes because they are British and that they are British because Parliament has decreed that they are subject to taxation (and what other pretense could there be for identifying residents of Quebec or Florida, so recently seized from France and Spain, as British?), is tautological. Wai Chee Dimock exposes the rhetorical slipperiness of nationalism, arguing that states are "fabricated things, with an identity all too prominent but no less spurious. They are not natural subjects, even though some of us make them look as if they were, as if each were some kind of personality. . . . Personification of this sort turns a territorial unit into the prime agent of history. It turns scholars into partisan specialists, trained to do no more than show how that agent works. And, for American studies, it leads to this automatic assumption—to study the United States, we need go no farther than the United States—surely a tautology if ever there is one." See Wai Chee Dimock, "War in Several Tongues: Nations, Languages, Genres," in *Globalizing American Studies*, ed. Brian T. Edwards and Dilip Parameshwar Gaonkar (Chicago: University of Chicago Press, 2010), 270–71.

6. Most accounts of the Stamp Act's implementation and revocation situate those events as preliminary steps in creating the United States of America. Among many others, see Peter David Garner Thomas, *British Politics and the Stamp Act Crisis: The*

First Phase of the American Revolution (New York: Clarendon Press, 1975); Harry M. Ward, *The American Revolution: Nationhood Achieved, 1763–1788* (New York: St. Martin's Press, 1995); John Ferling, *A Leap in the Dark: The Struggle to Create the American Republic* (New York: Oxford University Press, 2003); Robert Middlekauff, *The Glorious Cause: The American Revolution, 1763–1789*, 2d ed. (New York: Oxford University Press, 2005); and Gary B. Nash, *The Unknown American Revolution: The Unruly Birth of Democracy and the Struggle to Create America* (New York: Viking, 2005).

7. "The Stamp Act, March 22, 1765," in Edmund S. Morgan, ed., *Prologue to Revolution: Sources and Documents on the Stamp Act Crisis, 1764–1766* (Chapel Hill: University of North Carolina Press, 1959), 35.

8. Fred Anderson, *Crucible of War: The Seven Years' War and the Fate of Empire in British North America, 1754–1766* (New York: Alfred A. Knopf, 2000), is the obvious exception to this rule; he devotes several excellent chapters to the Stamp Act and its repeal. Among the many histories of the French and Indian War that ignore the Stamp Act or treat it only cursorily are Robert Leckie, *"A Few Acres of Snow": The Saga of the French and Indian Wars* (New York: John Wiley, 1999); William R. Nester, *The First Global War: Britain, France, and the Fate of North America, 1756–1775* (Westport, CT: Praeger, 2000); Stephen Brumwell, *The British Soldier and War in the Americas, 1755–1763* (New York: Cambridge University Press, 2002); Matthew C. Ward, *Breaking the Backcountry: The Seven Years' War in Virginia and Pennsylvania, 1754–1765* (Pittsburgh: University of Pittsburgh Press, 2003); William M. Fowler, Jr., *Empires at War: The French and Indian War and the Struggle for North America, 1754–1763* (New York: Walker, 2005); and Walter R. Borneman, *The French and Indian War: Deciding the Fate of North America* (New York: HarperCollins, 2006).

9. Andrew Jackson O'Shaughnessy, *An Empire Divided: The American Revolution and the British Caribbean* (Philadelphia: University of Pennsylvania Press, 2000), 98–101.

10. Morgan and Morgan, *The Stamp Act Crisis*, 172.

11. As Philip Gould notes, both colonial critics and colonial supporters of Parliament struggled to maintain and articulate a sense of British identity: "notwithstanding the image we have of the Loyalists as the true American Anglophiles, the Revolution actually complicated and often problematized their identification with English culture." See Philip Gould, *Writing the Rebellion: Loyalists and the Literature of Politics in British America* (New York: Oxford University Press, 2013), 8.

12. *America's Founding Charters: Primary Documents of Colonial and Revolutionary Era Governance*, ed. John L. Wakelyn (Westport, CT: Greenwood Press, 2006), 368.

13. Brendan McConville, *The King's Three Faces: The Rise and Fall of Royal America, 1688–1776* (Chapel Hill: University of North Carolina Press, 2006), 9.

14. As Eric Nelson suggests, the American Revolution and, later, the installation of George Washington as president was, in part, an attempt to relocate the state's authority in the prerogative of a monarchical, bodied presence. See Eric Nelson, *The Royalist Revolution: Monarchy and the American Founding* (Cambridge, MA: Harvard University Press, 2014).

15. Even as the lackluster response to Holderness's appeal revealed the relative

weakness of nationalist sentiment in colonial North America, Linda Colley argues that the inclusion of Scottish Highlanders in the British Army units fighting the French and Indian War served to strengthen a sense of British national identity for the Scots and English. See Linda Colley, *Britons: Forging the Nation, 1707–1837* (New Haven, CT: Yale University Press, 1992), 103.

16. See Alan Rogers, *Empire and Liberty: American Resistance to British Authority, 1755–1763* (Berkeley: University of California Press, 1974); Douglas Edward Leach, *Roots of Conflict: British Armed Forces and Colonial Americans, 1677–1763* (Chapel Hill: University of North Carolina Press, 1986), 76–166; Francis Jennings, *Empire of Fortune: Crowns, Colonies, and Tribes in the Seven Years' War in America* (New York: Norton, 1988), 204–22. For a contrasting view that emphasizes the achievements and relative restraint of the British regulars during the French and Indian War, see Stephen Brumwell, *Redcoats: The British Soldier and War in the Americas, 1755–1763* (New York: Cambridge University Press, 2002). T. H. Breen and others have argued that the French and Indian War pushed colonists to self-identify as British with increasing fervor, but as Anderson argues, that nationalistic fervor swelled four years into the conflict, in 1758, and was driven by the empowerment of a popular William Pitt; British nationalism in colonial North American would again wane after his descent from power in 1761, and Pitt would side with the colonists in criticizing the Stamp Act. See T. H. Breen, "An Empire of Goods: The Anglicization of Colonial America, 1690–1776," *Journal of British Studies* 25.4 (1986): 467–99; and Anderson, *Crucible of War*, 219–31, 698–701.

17. In 1765 the "British *colonies and plantations in* America" included land now claimed by Antigua and Barbuda, the Bahamas, Barbados, Belize, Canada, Dominica, Grenada, Honduras, Jamaica, Nicaragua, St. Christopher and Nevis, St. Vincent and the Grenadines, Trinidad and Tobago, and the United States.

18. "The Stamp Act, March 22, 1765," 41.

19. As Michael Warner argues, "Counterpublics are 'counter' to the extent that they try to supply different ways of imagining stranger sociability and its reflexivity; as publics they remain oriented to stranger circulation in a way that is not just strategic but constitutive of membership and its affects." British subjects in America imagined new ways of constructing a constitutive sociability—through ritual and performance—not necessarily recognized as legitimating discourse by the imperial public within which they circulated. See Michael Warner, *Publics and Counterpublics* (New York: Zone Books, 2002), 121–22.

20. "The Stamp Act, March 22, 1765," 36–40.

21. See David Waldstreicher, *In the Midst of Perpetual Fetes: The Making of American Nationalism, 1776–1820* (Chapel Hill: University of North Carolina Press, 1997), 1–3, 24–30.

[1]

RITUAL RESPONSES TO THE STAMP ACT

[1]

J. PATRICK MULLINS

THE SERMON THAT DIDN'T START THE REVOLUTION: JONATHAN MAYHEW'S ROLE IN THE BOSTON STAMP ACT RIOTS

ON JANUARY 30, 1750, Jonathan Mayhew, pastor of the Congregational meetinghouse in Boston's West End neighborhood, offered a performance from his pulpit that historian Bernard Bailyn dubbed "the most famous sermon preached in pre-Revolutionary America." Published as *A Discourse Concerning Unlimited Submission and Non-Resistance to the Higher Powers*, the sermon pronounced the doctrine of unconditional obedience to monarchs to be "as great *treason* as ever man uttered; it is treason,—not against one *single* man, but the state—against the whole body politic;—'tis treason against mankind:—'tis treason against common sense—'tis treason against GOD." Mayhew's widely reprinted sermon resonated with many Yankee Congregationalists and reverberated into the future. Academic historians have long acknowledged the importance of clergy—particularly New England's Congregational clergy—in popularizing Whig political theory and mobilizing the people to revolutionary action. But Mayhew looms foremost among these "pulpit politicians," not least because he helped radicalize his fellow clergy. Delivering the Massachusetts Election Sermon in May 1765 to Governor Francis Bernard and the newly elected provincial assembly on the eve of the Stamp Act Crisis, Boston pastor Andrew Eliot echoed his friend Mayhew's *Discourse* when he styled submission to tyranny as "a crime . . . an offense against the state . . . an offense against mankind . . . an offense against God."[1]

Giving Real Whig political principles such as popular sovereignty, consensual government, and the right of resistance a theological foundation with a biblical sanction, Mayhew's political sermons won over the laity as well as the clergy. Fifteen-year-old John Adams embraced the *Discourse* as his political "Chatechism." As an old man, Adams informed his fellow retired president Thomas Jefferson that he had read and reread this sermon "till the Substance of it was incorporated into my Nature and indelibly grafted on my Memory." The radical Whig principles that Mayhew popularized through his spoken and printed sermons of the 1750s and early 1760s shaped the political outlook of many young Yankee gentlemen who would go on to provide the leadership for New England's opposition to Crown policy during the Imperial Crisis of 1765–1775, among them two signers of the Declaration of Independence, Robert Treat Paine and Adams himself. "If the orators on the 4th of July really wish to investigate the principles and feelings which produced the Revolution," Adams wrote in 1818, "they ought to study . . . Dr. Mayhew's sermon on passive obedience and non-resistance." The retired president also maintained that Mayhew helped radicalize "the common people" by opposing the attempted introduction of a colonial bishop in the early 1760s, thereby directing ordinary folks to "close thinking on the constitutional authority of parliament over the colonies."[2]

Aggressively using pulpit and press to popularize Real Whig principles among clergy and laity, gentry and common folk, Mayhew helped prepare New England's cultural ground for a radical popular reaction against British imperial innovations, beginning with the Stamp Act and culminating in the Revolutionary War. Whether he would have welcomed the Revolution as the fulfillment of his professed political views, we can never know: Mayhew died three months shy of his forty-sixth birthday, four months after repeal of the Stamp Act, and almost exactly ten years before Congress approved the Declaration of Independence. In any event, Mayhew persisted in public memory as a progenitor of the Revolution, thanks primarily to John Adams's efforts at memorialization. Paradoxically, over his last year of life, Mayhew was astonished by the intensity of public anger against the Stamp Act and terrified that the crisis would lead to an armed insurrection against Britain. Although Bailyn styles Mayhew as the "pre-eminent spokesman in the colonies for everything that was new, bold, and radically nonconformist in church and state," the pastor considered himself a conservative champion of Low Church Protestantism, the Glorious Revolution, and the British Constitution. Throughout his career as a pulpit activist, Mayhew aimed to inform his hearers and readers of their rights and threats to their rights, that they might preserve their civil and religious liberty within New England's traditional institutions as well as the British Empire. But the public did not always extract from his sermons the lessons he intended. In warning New Englanders against the looming menace represented by an episcopate on the one hand and the Sugar Act on the other hand, Mayhew inadvertently helped generate the cultural conditions for civil war during the Stamp Act Crisis.[3]

If the body of Mayhew's political sermons and pamphlets laid the philosophical groundwork for the American Revolution in general and the Stamp Act Crisis in particular, commentators most commonly cite two individual performances as evidence of this influence. While academic historians like Bailyn have joined Adams in assessing the 1750 *Discourse Concerning Unlimited Submission* as an ideological starting point for the Revolution, there is a long tradition of commentary—from Mayhew's eighteenth-century acquaintances to twenty-first-century scholars—crediting another untitled and unpublished sermon from August 25, 1765, as the immediate inspiration for mob violence against British crown officials in Boston at the beginning of the Stamp Act Crisis.

The Boston Stamp Act riots that began on August 14, 1765, were low-grade in their violence and destructiveness. As Molly Perry observes in the following chapter, the kind of crowd action that occurred on August 14 fell within a long English tradition of plebeian ritual protest that reaffirmed Crown authority even as it challenged policy. The galvanizing moment that lent the Stamp Act Crisis its proto-revolutionary cast came on August 26, when Bostonians attacked and ransacked the private home of Thomas Hutchinson, lieutenant governor and chief justice of the Province of Massachusetts-Bay. Bailyn described this riot as "more violent than any yet seen in America, more violent indeed than any that would be seen in the entire course of the Revolution." Urban mobs imitated the example set by Boston in colonial cities up and down the Atlantic seaboard, from an assault upon the royal governor's home in New York City to raucous protests in Charleston, South Carolina. While the Boston riot of August 14 was clearly organized to prevent enforcement of the Stamp Act, the August 26 riot and its sources and objectives have proved harder to explain. Hutchinson cited the attack as an example of "how easily the people may be deluded, enflamed, and carried away with madness against an innocent man," and Boston's Tories—principally Rev. Henry Caner and Hutchinson himself—blamed Mayhew's August 25 sermon for enflaming the people and sending a mob out into the streets to wreak havoc.[4]

Academic historians have adopted a more nuanced version of this Tory thesis that the Hutchinson riot was a direct result of Mayhew's demagoguery. In his analysis of Mayhew's role in the Stamp Act riots, Bailyn makes Mayhew's sermon an object lesson in the law of unintended consequences. He concludes that "while there is no indication that Mayhew deliberately sought to incite his audience to violence there can also be no question that he had endorsed the most radical line of resistance to Parliament's taxation." Many scholars have built upon Bailyn's position, arguing that Mayhew's radical assertions and heated rhetoric in the sermon on August 25 inadvertently incited the riot of August 26 and thereby set colonial opposition to the Stamp Act in a menacingly revolutionary direction. "The experience of most popular leaders and the lesson they derived from the uprisings of 1765," Pauline Maier has observed, "were personified in the plight of Boston's radical minister Jonathan Mayhew," specifically the question of how to prevent tyranny without unleashing mob violence. Harry Stout relates that the August 26 riot occurred "at least partly in response to an inflammatory sermon by Jonathan Mayhew." According to Stout, Mayhew was contrite, but he gave Boston Whigs "an unforgettable look at the popular power unleashed in part by their own libertarian rhetoric." More recently James Byrd has contended that clergymen "did their share to fuel the violent reaction to the Stamp Act," as in the case of Mayhew's "rabble-rousing sermon" that incited the Hutchinson riot, leaving "Mayhew regretting the wrath his sermon had provoked." Byrd concludes from this example that sermons "could be more politically subversive than even preachers realized."[5]

While several scholars have adopted this neo-Tory interpretation of the Hutchinson riot, they have relied heavily upon accusations made by Mayhew's enemies in 1760s Boston and have assumed a causal connection between the sermon and the riot without taking pains to substantiate it. A closer examination of the available evidence suggests that Mayhew's sermon of August 25, 1765, likely had little if anything to do with the riot of August 26. The rioters were historic agents in their own right, marching out that night less as wild-eyed zealots doing the Lord's work on the orders of Pastor Mayhew than as shrewd men who knew they shared the same interest in free trade as the Loyal Nine, a secret society of Boston businessmen with whom the rioters collaborated in extralegal action to stop implementation of the Stamp Act as well as writs-of-assistance prosecutions under the Sugar Act. The West Church divine did, however, contribute indirectly to the Stamp Act riots as a highly effective popularizer of Whig political principles within New England political culture. Mayhew's role in the Stamp Act riots was not that of malicious puppeteer, as Hutchinson would have it, but as the reaper of a cultural whirlwind he had sown for many years before that fateful August night.

Historians have generally assumed that the August 26 riot was, like the riot of August 14, a protest against the Stamp Act and that it targeted Thomas Hutchinson because the common people mistook him for a champion of the Stamp Act. Hutchinson himself promoted this conclusion publicly. Appearing before the assembled Superior Court of Massachusetts, tearful and in rags, the day after his home's destruction, the chief justice intoned, "I call my *Maker* to my witness, that I never, in New England or Old, in Great Britain or America, neither directly nor indirectly, was aiding, assisting, or supporting, in the least promoting or encouraging what is commonly called the Stamp Act; but on the contrary, did all in my power, and strove as much as in me lay, to prevent it." Hutchinson viewed himself as a sincere but misunderstood Yankee patriot whose motives and actions had been distorted in the public mind by demagogues like James Otis, Jr., and Dr. Mayhew. Hutchinson had, indeed, opposed passage of the Stamp Act in July 1764 with a pamphlet explaining that the proposed tax was bad policy for the empire. However, he avoided any suggestion that Parliament lacked the authority to tax the colonies, believing that the colonies' traditional immunity from parliamentary taxation was at best a privilege rather than a natural right. In the fall of 1764, when colonial assemblies mobilized to petition Parliament against the tax, Lieutenant Governor Hutchinson maneuvered successfully to ensure that the petition sent to Parliament by the Massachusetts General Court that November would make strictly prudential arguments against the Stamp Act and refrain from the kind of forceful affirmations of natural rights and constitutional limits favored by Otis and the other "friends of liberty" in the provincial House of Representatives. Following passage of the Stamp Act in March 1765, Hutchinson advocated colonial obedience to the Stamp Act as the law of the land, and rumors spread that he had secretly lobbied the British government for passage of the Stamp Act from the beginning. It did not help his reputation that his brother-in-law and the provincial secretary for Massachusetts, Andrew Oliver, received a royal commission as a stamp distributor.[6]

While Hutchinson was no devotee of the Stamp Act, Jonathan Mayhew was no despiser of Thomas Hutchinson. The clergyman, who had long collaborated amicably with Hutchinson on the Harvard College Board of Overseers, admired Hutchinson and kept a portrait of the lieutenant governor in his home. On May 16, 1765, he sent to his London friend, the merchant and philanthropist Thomas Hollis, a copy of Hutchinson's *History of Massachusetts-Bay*, which he had praised to Hollis in December 1764 as "judicious and impartial," often "very full in the principles of liberty, civil and religious." Bailyn concluded that Mayhew was one of a minority of Bostonians who believed Hutchinson truly had his country's best interests at heart. The clergyman dreaded the scheduled implementation of the Stamp Act on November 1, 1765, but did not blame Hutchinson for this sword dangling over the province. In an apologetic letter to Hutchinson following the August 26 riot, Mayhew claimed that, when he heard the lieutenant governor spoken of in private company as a supporter of the Stamp Act, "I have as often taken the Liberty to say, I had heard you express yourself in a manner that strongly implied the contrary; which I did with a view to remove those prejudices which I perceived some persons had against you in that respect." Mayhew opposed the Stamp Act, but he believed that Hutchinson did as well.[7]

On August 8, 1765, Mayhew shared his thoughts about the Stamp Act in a letter to Thomas Hollis. He wrote, anxiously:

> The Colonies are universally and greatly alarmed at the Measures lately taken respecting them. These Measures appear to me extremely hard and injurious. If long persisted in, they will at best greatly cramp, and retard the population of, the Colonies, to the very essential detriment of the Mother country. And what may, in time, be the consequence of raising a general and great disaffection in the people of this large Continent, no one can certainly foresee. But you and I, Sir, are at least clear in this point, that no people are under a *religious obligation* to be slaves, if they are able to set themselves at liberty.[8]

Mayhew shared the popular aggravation at the Stamp Act and affirmed his long-standing rejection of the Tory principles of passive obedience and non-resistance to tyranny, but he played no direct role in the burst of popular anger in Boston on August 14, which caught him by surprise. "When I last wrote," Mayhew informed Hollis on August 19, "I did not think the spirit of opposition to the Stamp-Act would break out so soon, in any open Acts of Violence, as it has done."[9]

On August 14, Bostonians woke to find Andrew Oliver, provincial secretary and prospective stamp distributor, hanging in effigy from an elm tree (which would come to be celebrated as the Liberty Tree) in downtown Boston. "By his Side hung a Boot, out of which the De[vi]l made his appearance with his fork," and the boot had a green sole, a "punning device" on the names of Sir George Grenville (often spelled Greenville) and the Earl of Bute, two British statesmen widely blamed for the Stamp Act. "Some thousands of people went that day to see it," Mayhew wrote Hollis on August 19, "and it seemed to give general satisfaction to the people." At sundown, the crowd demolished the new stamp office, sawed off the head of the Oliver effigy, and then burned the wood and the effigies near Oliver's house, "amidst loud acclamations." Later that night, Mayhew related, some members of the crowd invaded and sacked Oliver's private residence. On August 15, Oliver promised to renounce his commission as stamp agent, which, "it is supposed, was the only thing that prevented his House being torn down the next Night." That evening, the mob marched to the home of Thomas Hutchinson and called on him to deny that he encouraged passage of the Stamp Act. Mayhew reported that, upon arrival of the mob, Hutchinson concealed himself, "and they departed without doing any Mischief."[10]

Mayhew concluded from the urban unrest of the preceding days that any attempt to enforce the Stamp Act would provoke armed resistance in the colonies. In his letter to Hollis, Mayhew wrote that American hatred of the Stamp Act was so intense and so universal that "I am satisfied it will never be carried into execution, unless it is done at the point of the Sword, by a large army, or rather by a number of considerable ones, at least one in each Colony; there being about sixty thousand fighting men in this Province only: And it is given out by many, that they will spend their last blood in this cause." Mayhew added that he was stating only the facts of the case, not his evaluation of them, but he wrote that Britain would be foolish to wage war to enforce "this odious tax." Such a war between Britain and the colonies would result in either America's destruction or America's independence, either of which would be detrimental to both Britain and America. "God forbid there should be an intire Breach between them," he told Hollis, "which might prove very fatal to both!"[11]

As Maier has observed, Mayhew—like eighteenth-century Whigs in both America and Britain—adhered to an "ideology of resistance and restraint" that affirmed the right of resistance to an oppressive government while insisting that such resistance was justified only once all non-violent means of redress had been exhausted. The pastor feared a fratricidal civil war between the colonies and their mother country, but he also feared the subjugation of the colonies by a corrupt British government. How to preserve liberty while also upholding civil peace and the rule of law was the fundamental dilemma confronting the "friends of liberty" in Massachusetts and the other colonies. The consensus among colonial Whigs was, minimally, to inform the people of their natural and constitutional rights and the danger posed to those rights by the Stamp Act. Mayhew later explained to his parishioner Richard Clarke that, for weeks before the August 26 riot, he had been "solicited by different persons to preach upon that subject [of the Stamp Act], as one who was a known friend to liberty." His unnamed gadflies questioned Mayhew's commitment to the cause of civil liberty, and this was "a reproach, which I knew not well how to bear," so he resolved to address the current crisis in broadly abstract terms with a sermon on the timely subject of civil liberty. He would put the genteel ritual of the Sunday sermon in service to the cause, but it was the plebeian ritual of the Liberty Tree protest and the popular enthusiasm it sparked which moved Mayhew to action. "You know well, sir," he wrote Clarke on September 3, "the general temper of the town, Province, and all the colonies, then and now, respecting the Stamp-act. . . . I was far too carried away in the common current." For fifteen years, Mayhew had been one of the intellectual leaders of New England. In preparing his sermon against the Stamp Act, though, he was acting on the direction of the laity, and not so much shaping public opinion as explicating in theological terms what most Bostonians already believed to be true.[12]

On Sunday afternoon, August 25, the pastor gave a sermon before his West Church congregation on Paul's Epistle to the Galatians, speaking from the twelfth and thirteenth verses of the fifth chapter on the nature and value of civil liberty. Posterity can never know with certainty what he said on that occasion because Mayhew did not read his sermon from manuscript. He delivered it *ex tempore* from rough notes, which no longer exist. But within the next two weeks, Mayhew wrote out a ten-page memorandum of the sermon based on his notes and memory. If his representation of the sermon in this memorandum is to be accepted as true, then the performance conveyed both the Whig belief in the right of resistance and an accompanying argument for the duty of restraint. Mayhew argued that individuals "give up some part of their natural liberty, or the right which they have in a state of nature, to act as they please, each individual for himself." He said of civil liberty: "It supposeth the restraint of laws, some persons to govern, and some to be governed. For people do not enjoy civil liberty, where each individual does what is right in his own eyes, without any regard to others. This is a State of anarchy & confusion; as distant from a state of civil liberty, as slavery itself, in which it often terminates, one extreme leading to another, seemingly the most opposite thereto."[13] Individual liberty can be made compatible with subjection to law under civil government, the pastor explained, when the laws "are made by common consent & choice; that all have some hand in framing them, at least by their representatives, chosen to act for them, if not in their own persons." If people are "governed contrary to, or independently of, their own will & consent," then they are "in a state of slavery." Moreover, the colonists should be considered slaves rather than freemen "if they are to possess no property, nor to enjoy the fruits of their own labor, but by the mere precarious pleasure of the mother, or of a distant legislature, in which they neither are, nor can be represented."[14]

Having distinguished civil liberty from slavery, Mayhew then carefully distinguished it from anarchy as well. He reminded the congregation that, while the apostle Paul told the Galatians that they had been "called unto liberty," he also cautioned them, "Only use not liberty for an occasion to the flesh." As examples of abusers of liberty, he cited those who "disregard the wholesome laws of Society, made for the preservation of the order and common good thereof," "who causelessly & maliciously speak evil of their rulers; endeavouring to make them appear odious or contemptible, or to weaken their influence, and proper authority, in their several stations," and "who cause factions, or insurrections against the government, under which they live; & who rebel against, or resist their lawful rulers, in the due discharge of their offices." Laws contrary to popular consent nullified civil liberty, but so did the lawlessness of violent crowds. Having made clear that he was no advocate of mob rule, Mayhew then addressed the touchy subject of resistance to oppressive laws like the Stamp Act. When "a nation is something actually abused by their rulers to a great degree," he observed, the question naturally arises "whether passive obedience and non-resistance were the duty of such a people; or whether opposing such rulers, and the execution of unrighteous & oppressive laws, could properly be accounted using liberty for an occasion to the flesh?" Mayhew wrote that this question "was answered in the negative, for the following reasons," and then abruptly concluded the memorandum reconstructing his August 25 sermon.[15]

On the evening of August 26, an unspecified "number of rude Fellows" —in the words of the *Boston Gazette*—rallied around a bonfire on Boston's King Street and formed a mass of indignation. The mob divided into two teams. One of them entered and damaged the home of William Story, deputy registrar of the vice-admiralty court, and the other targeted the home of Benjamin Hallowell, comptroller of customs. The mob then re-formed and marched to Hutchinson's three-story Palladian mansion. The young lawyer Josiah Quincy, Jr., an eyewitness to the riot, documented this attack in a diary entry a day later, on August 27. As the crowd surged into his house, Hutchinson fled with his daughter, and Quincy believed that Hutchinson's life would have been forfeit had he not made this escape. The "Rage-intoxicated Rabble," Quincy recalled, swept into house and destroyed or stole everything of value. But they did not stop there. Over hours of steady work, the rioters inflicted structural damage on the house, pulling down interior walls and devoting three hours to the removal of its cupola. They left little more than a shell behind and then regrouped to march upon the home of Charles Paxton, surveyor of customs for the Port of Boston, but broke off that final attack with the approach of daylight. Hutchinson later estimated the damage to his home and goods at 2,200 pounds sterling. The following morning, a disheveled and haggard Hutchinson appeared at the Massachusetts Superior Court in session to take his place with his fellow judges. Associating the riot of August 26 with the riot of August 14, the chief justice, like Quincy and most Bostonians, took for granted that the attack was directed against him as a wrongly accused champion of the Stamp Act. Privately, Hutchinson would soon come to think somewhat differently on this point.[16]

As morning broke and thousands of Bostonians gathered to witness the shattered ruins of the Hutchinson manor house, rumors hummed like summer bees. What motivated such a riot, unprecedented in its destructiveness? As the *Boston Gazette* noted, "The true Causes of this notorious Riot are not yet known." While its original source remains uncertain, one rumor had it that Dr. Mayhew's sermon on the subject of liberty, preached the afternoon preceding the riot, stirred the Boston canaille to their anarchic work. Before the day was over, Mayhew dashed off a private letter to Hutchinson, offering him "condolence, on account of the almost unparall'd outrages committed on your house the last evening." The minister insisted vehemently, "God is my witness, that from the bottom of my heart, I detest these proceedings." He understood, though, that some of his "numerous and causeless enemies" claimed that he approved the rioting and "had indeed encouraged them in a Sermon which I preached the last Lord's day on Gal. 5. 12, 13."[17] Defending himself against the smear, Mayhew wrote emphatically:

> This I absolutely deny. I did indeed express myself strongly in favor of civil & religious liberty, [as I hope I shall ever continue to do;] and spoke of the late Stamp Act as a great grievance, likely to prove detrimental in a high degree, both to the Colonies, and to the Mother Country; which, I believe, is the Sense of almost every person of understanding in the Plantations; And, particularly, I have heard your Honor speak to the same Purpose. But then, as my text led me to do, I cautioned my Hearers very particularly against the abuses of liberty; and intimated my hopes, that no persons among ourselves had encouraged the bringing of such a burden on their country, notwithstanding it had been strongly suspected. . . . And, in truth, I had rather

lose my hand than be an encourager of such outrages as were committed last night.[18]

Standing on his reputation for truthfulness, even to the point of indiscretion, he begged Hutchinson to believe him and disregard the accusations made against him.

A few days later, Richard Clarke—a wealthy merchant and full member of the West Church—expressed to Mayhew his offense at the language of the August 25 sermon, apparently accepting the rumor that it had touched off the August 26 riot. Anxious that he may have tipped the balance of Whig values too much toward resistance in his last sermon, Mayhew then tipped it back toward restraint. On the next Sabbath, September 1, he gave a sermon to the West Church denouncing the August 26 riot in such strong language that some "friends of liberty" considered Mayhew a traitor to the cause and gave him reason for concern about the security of his own person and property. "I still love liberty as much as ever," he told Clarke, and seems to have contended similarly in the September 1 sermon, "but have apprehensions of the greatest inconveniences likely to follow on a forceable, violent opposition to an act of parliament; which I consider, in some sort, as proclaiming war against Great Britain." Clarke did not attend that service, however; as Mayhew feared, the merchant had already decided to withdraw his family from membership in the West Church, and he did not return to the fold. Sometime between August 27 and September 3, Mayhew composed his memorandum of the August 25 sermon, for circulation among his friends, in an effort to combat the allegation of incitement to riot—a felony under English law—and stanch the hemorrhaging of his public honor.[19]

The divine wrote Clarke a long and rather abject apologia for his alleged role in the riot that destroyed Hutchinson's home. He denied the rumor that his August 25 sermon argued for violent resistance to the Stamp Act. Although "composed in a high strain of liberty," he was certain that "no person could, without abusing & perverting it, take encouragement from it to go to mobbing, or to commit some abominable outrages as were lately committed, in defiance of the laws of God and man. I did, in the most formal, express manner, discountenance everything of that kind." Mayhew reminded Clarke, as a witness to the August 25 sermon, that he concluded the sermon with an exhortation to the people not to "use any method, for the defense of our rights & privileges, besides those which are honest & honourable." Considering all of the caveats he offered in his sermon about the abuse of liberty, Mayhew told Clarke, "[I]t is humbly conceived the author ought in common justice to be acquitted, as no encourager of mobs and riots."[20] Still, he confessed:

> I readily acknowledge, what I was not so well aware of before, that it was a very unfortunate time to preach a sermon, the chief aim of which was to show the importance of Liberty, when people were before so generally apprehensive of the danger of losing it. They certainly needed rather to be moderated and pacified, to the contrary: And I would freely give all that I have in the world, rather than have preached that sermon; tho' I am well assured, it was very generally liked and commended by the hearers at the time of it.[21]

Mayhew noted to Clarke that "some persons beside yourself had, thro' mistake, and others through malice, represented my discourse in that odious light," to the extent that he felt compelled to defend his performance in the September 1 sermon. He fell short, though, of accepting responsibility for touching off the riot of August 26, even as an unintended consequence of his forceful oratory. Despite Mayhew's long and heartfelt letter, Clarke did not reconcile with his pastor or return to the West Church. He would, as a consignee for the tea destroyed in the Boston Tea Party, become hated in the city and emigrate to England in 1774 as a Loyalist exile.

The clergyman's private efforts at self-justification did not quash the allegation of incitement. Rev. Henry Caner, the rector of King's Chapel in Boston and another future Loyalist exile, wrote Thomas Secker, the archbishop of Canterbury, about the affair on September 5, 1765. According to Caner, the day before the Hutchinson riot, Mayhew "distinguished himself in the pulpit upon this Occasion (it is said) in One of the most seditious Sermons ever delivered, advising the people to stand up for their rights to the last drop of their Blood." Caner was not a witness to the sermon and did not cite his source, but the accusation stuck. The Anglican clergyman was the main propagator, perhaps even the originator, of the incitement accusation, and Mayhew appears to have suspected as much. On the same day that Caner wrote the archbishop, Mayhew wrote Caner cordially that he feared Rev. East Apthorp, former parson of Christ Church in Cambridge, thought poorly of his character due to their public debate in the early 1760s over Anglican efforts to convert New England's Congregationalists and introduce a colonial bishop. Mayhew could have said the same of Caner himself. In his 1763 pamphlet, *A Candid Examination of Dr. Mayhew's Observations*, Caner had defended Apthorp against Mayhew's critique of Anglican proselytization, denounced Mayhew personally for theological heterodoxy, rejected claims by Congregationalists to religious liberty, and asserted British authority over the colonies in the broadest terms. Mayhew's published response reaffirmed the autonomy of New England institutions under the British Empire. "I must first defend our *laws* themselves against his bold attacks," he wrote of Caner in 1763, "before I defend our *churches* by them." Caner had a long-standing grudge against Mayhew and ample motivation to put the worst possible construction on the August 25 sermon. When Mayhew remarked in his August 27 letter to Hutchinson that the accusation of incitement had been made maliciously by his "numerous and causeless enemies," he may well have had Caner specifically in mind. Mayhew's aggressive opposition to the agenda of High Church Anglican clergy before the Stamp Act Crisis had made enemies of Apthorp, Caner, and Archbishop Secker, and the allegation of incitement to riot left him vulnerable to a legal reprisal. In the fall of 1765, Thomas Hollis informed Mayhew of rumors that the archbishop of Canterbury was considering bringing Mayhew to London for prosecution in an ecclesiastical court.[22]

Mayhew's efforts to smooth things over with Clarke, Hutchinson, and Caner came to nothing. His private missive of August 27 did not succeed in convincing Hutchinson that the sermon on Galatians had "cautioned my Hearers very particularly against the abuses of liberty." On October 3, 1765, Hutchinson said of Mayhew in a letter to Rev. Apthorp that "Sunday the 25th of August, notice being given that he was to preach a political discourse, he had a crowded audience, which he entertained from this text, 'I would they were even cut off which trouble you for, brethren, ye have been called unto liberty'. Here he stopped, the remainder of the sentence [regarding not using liberty as a pretext for licentiousness] not being to his purpose."[23] Hutchinson was persuaded that Mayhew intentionally incited the people to violence. The question of Mayhew's motivation remains.

Years later, from his grim London exile, Hutchinson repeated this charge of incitement in the third volume of his *History of Massachusetts-Bay*, published forty-eight years following his death in 1780. He claimed that Mayhew had preached, on August 25, 1765, a sermon "from these words, 'I would they were even cut off which trouble you'. The text alone, without a comment, delivered from the pulpit at that time, might be construed by some of the auditory into an approbation of the prevailing irregularities." Again, Hutchinson suggested that Mayhew had omitted the following verse, forbidding the abuse of liberty as "an occasion to the flesh," which, "if properly enforced, would have been sufficient to have kept the people within proper bounds." Hutchinson added that one man "who had a chief hand in the outrages that soon followed" attested during subsequent incarceration that "he was excited to them by this sermon, and thought that he was doing God service." Hutchinson's reputation for rigorous scholarship notwithstanding, he never identified the rioter who claimed to have been motivated by the sermon, nor has any affidavit to that effect materialized.[24]

From what motivation did Hutchinson think Mayhew had inflamed the mob? Having leveled the incitement allegation in his October 3 letter to Apthorp, Hutchinson repeated it in an October 5 letter to Francis Bernard, the royal governor of Massachusetts. Mayhew not only had incited the mob with his sermon of August 25, Hutchinson claimed, but had intended Governor Bernard, not Hutchinson, to be the victim of its wrath. "The D[octor's] venomous arrows were aimed at you," Hutchinson wrote privately to Bernard, but "I had the misfortune to be grievously wounded by his random shot." Why might Hutchinson propose with such assurance that Mayhew had intentionally targeted Bernard? This peculiar, enigmatic claim by the chief justice must be understood in the context of a largely forgotten scandal that he and the governor recalled all too keenly.[25]

In November 1761, Mayhew remarked to a friend his understanding that Governor Bernard had accepted a two-dollar tip for receiving a petition. When the rumor got back to Bernard, William Story bet the governor that Mayhew would retract the story when confronted. The incident turned into an ugly confrontation between Mayhew and Bernard in which both men stood on their honor, each refusing the other satisfaction. Hutchinson and Andrew Oliver served as witnesses to the confrontation between Bernard and Mayhew, and Hutchinson acted as the governor's second in this affair of honor. After a few months of contention, the governor and clergyman returned to their respective corners without bloodshed or legal action but never resolved their quarrel. The two men bore an animus against one another, fed by the partisan bickering between Bernard's ruling faction and the political opposition led by James Otis, Jr. Hutchinson concluded not only that Mayhew gave his August 25 sermon with the intent to incite the mob to riot, but that the governor was the intended target. In a master plan for revenge, Hutchinson believed, the crafty clergyman had used the Stamp Act as a pretext for a personally motivated reprisal. Perhaps Hutchinson's bizarre theory of the riot sprang to mind from the coincidence that Bernard's supporters in the old quarrel with Mayhew—namely, Story, Oliver, and Hutchinson—had also been victimized by the Stamp Act riots.[26]

But the August Stamp Act riots in Boston and, later, throughout the colonies filled Mayhew with dread. On September 26, 1765, he anxiously wrote Thomas Hollis:

> You can hardly conceive how the minds of people in the colonies are inflamed by the late Parliamentary regulations, particularly the Stamp-Act. The violent Measures which have been taken already in most of them, to make the Stamp-Officers resign their posts, and many other things, confirm me in the opinion which I intimated to you in the last, That this Act will never be carried into execution, without the effusion of much blood: For it is the general voice of the people, that they had rather die by the sword, than submit to such slavery as they conceive they shall be under, by submitting to such a kind of taxation.[27]

Mayhew's fear that colonial opposition would lead to bloody warfare was not a conservative reaction against the riot of August 26; he had expressed similar concerns to Hollis on August 19. On October 1, the day the Stamp Act Congress convened in New York City, Mayhew again conveyed to Hollis his concerns that the crisis would end in a revolutionary war. He wrote: "For my own part, I have both privately and publicly delivered my opinion of the inexpediency and great danger of any *forcible*, *riotous* and *illegal* proceedings, in opposition to parliamentary authority, even though the Colonies should be oppressed. *We are not able to contend in this way with Great Britain*. But far the greater part of the People in the Colonies seem at present resolved to *run all hazzards* rather than submit: For they say nothing worse can happen to us than such slavery."[28] In the weeks preceding and following the August 26 riot, he sounded nothing like the Mayhew of Hutchinson's Tory imagination: a conniving demagogue and irresponsible incendiary who had intentionally unleashed mob violence against Crown authority. The context provided by Mayhew's private letters to Hollis just before and just after the August 26 riot, and to Clarke and Hutchinson immediately after the riot, belie the claims of his Tory contemporaries, and of modern historians like Stout and Byrd, that his sermon was "inflammatory."

By January 7, 1766, the West Church divine was near despair that Britain would enforce the Stamp Act at the cost of "the destruction of the Colonies." He told Hollis that he feared for "the whole British empire," which was being led to ruination by "a pensioned, bribed H[ouse] of C[ommo]ns and H[ouse] of L[ords]." Seven days later, William Pitt returned to the House of Commons and took up the colonial cause. An astonishing reversal of fortune ensued. After fierce debates, Parliament repealed the Stamp Act, and King George III approved the repeal bill on March 18. News of the reversal reached Boston by one of John Hancock's ships in the earliest hours of May 17. Six days later, in a thanksgiving sermon titled *The Snare Broken*, Mayhew told his congregation, "I now partake no less in your common joy, on account of the REPEAL of that act; whereby these colonies are emancipated from a slavish, inglorious bondage; are re-instated in the enjoyment of their ancient rights and privileges, and a foundation is laid for lasting harmony between Great Britain and them, to their mutual advantage." Since August 14, 1765, Mayhew had experienced intensifying anxiety, worrying that the Stamp Act Crisis would result in war and the subjugation of the colonies. News of repeal lifted that hefty psychic yoke, and his thanksgiving sermon expressed enormous relief and unfeigned joy that America had avoided such a doom.[29]

In *The Snare Broken*, Mayhew sought to reestablish balance between the Whig values of resistance and restraint. He reasserted the claim of his August 25 sermon, that the Stamp Act was a menace to the natural and civil rights of American colonists. But he opposed "any methods of opposition to that measure, on the part of the colonies, besides those of humble petitioning." He attributed the successful repeal of the Stamp Act to the non-importation of British goods by colonial merchants, the eloquence of Pitt on behalf of the colonies in the House of Commons, and the rationality and sound judgment of king and Parliament. The pastor's faith in the justice of the British Constitution had been reaffirmed, and he used the occasion to urge reconciliation with Britain and a return to law and order. In a final attempt to clear himself of the Tory charge of inciting the August 26 riot, Mayhew added: "I take for granted, that we are all perfectly agreed in condemning the riotous and felonious proceedings of certain *men of Belial*, as they have been justly called, who had the effrontery to cloke their rapacious violences with the pretext of zeal for liberty." While he condemned the Hutchinson riot and urged the common folk to return to their normal, peaceable course of daily business now that the crisis was past, he did not hesitate to reaffirm the Whig principles of his August 25 sermon, exhorting the colonists to remain protective of their rights and vigilant against future British encroachments upon them. The Mayhew of May 23, 1766, was not quite the anti-populist reactionary—chastened and tormented by the violence he unintentionally unleashed—limned by modern scholar Alan Heimert.[30]

Four months after delivering *The Snare Broken*, the forty-five-year-old clergyman died of complications from a massive stroke. On August 27,

1767, the second anniversary of the Hutchinson riot, Mayhew's friend, Congregational minister Andrew Eliot, challenged the lingering Tory smears against a fallen divine who could no longer defend himself. In a private letter to Hollis, Eliot, an eyewitness to the Hutchinson attack, described it as "a scene of riot, drunkenness, profaneness and robbery." Against Hutchinson's claim that Mayhew had approved of the attack on Provincial Secretary Andrew Oliver's house on August 14, Eliot maintained:

> The Doctor preached a sermon on liberty, but said not one word of the attack on the Secretary. The next day was the 26th of August. Some malevolent persons charged the riot of that evening upon the Doctor, though the plan was laid before, and it is questioned whether one of the rioters had ever heard of the Doctor's sermon. The Doctor's tender spirit was much moved with such a report. He preached the next Sunday a sermon against abusing liberty to licentiousness. Some now charged him with contradiction. He thought of himself as much injured, as he undoubtedly was. "Of the 14th of August, I choose to say nothing," said he to A.E., not long before his much to be lamented departure, "the proceedings of the 26th I abhor, from my very soul."[31]

The *Boston Gazette*, on September 3, 1765, had observed that most Bostonians "seem dispos'd to discriminate" between the raucous protest of August 14 and the destructive mobbing of August 26, "judging them to proceed from very *different* Motives, as their conduct was most evidently *different*." If Mayhew did indeed abhor August 26 but privately approve August 14, he well reflected public opinion on this point, as he did in the August 25 sermon as well as *The Snare Broken*, which proved the most popular and widely reprinted pamphlet on the repeal of the Stamp Act in the colonies.[32]

As the Revolutionary War wound down and the cause of the Loyalists was lost, the deceased pastor's reputation again came under fire from his Tory critics. The unsubstantiated claims of Caner and Hutchinson provided a foundation for the Tory interpretation of the Stamp Act riots formalized by Peter Oliver, brother of Andrew Oliver, who replaced his brother-in-law Hutchinson as Massachusetts chief justice before following him into exile in London. In his 1781 tract, *Origin and Progress of the American Revolution*, Oliver argued that the Revolution resulted from manipulation of the common people by ambitious demagogues, James Otis, Jr., foremost among them. Oliver maintained that Otis found help in this work from three Congregational ministers in Boston: Samuel

Cooper, Charles Chauncy, and Jonathan Mayhew. Together, they formed a "sacerdotal Triumvirate" responsible for "encouraging Seditions & Riots, until those lesser Offences were absorbed in Rebellion." In Oliver's *Origin and Progress*, Mayhew's reputation as an incendiary pivoted upon his role in the riot of August 26, 1765. From his London exile, the embittered Loyalist wrote:

> And it was remarked, that on the day preceeding the Destruction of Mr. *Hutchinson*'s House, he preached so seditious a Sermon, that some of his Auditors, who were of the Mob, declared, whilst the Doctor was delivering it they could scarce contain themselves from going out of the Assembly & beginning their Work. However, when the Villainy was perpetrated, he felt some severe Girds of what is vulgarly called Conscience; but he found, too late, that his Words were too hard of Digestion to be ate.[33]

Oliver embellished the allegations of Caner and Hutchinson while providing no evidence to support them.

A central point on which the Tory interpretation—and the variations on that interpretation offered by academic historians—hinges is the nature of the audience Mayhew addressed on August 25. Regardless of whether the sermon could be constructed as favoring violence, as Mayhew insisted it could not, his Tory critics claimed that among the auditors of the West Church on that Sabbath day were people of the lower ranks of society who presumably could be expected to act impulsively and violently when offered a biblical sanction to do so. Hutchinson, Oliver, and the modern historians who built upon their claims never substantiated the key contention that participants in the August 26 riot had also been present at the August 25 sermon. Mayhew insisted he did not know anyone involved in the riot, and Eliot, who was present at the assault on Hutchinson's home, privately expressed doubt that any of the participants had heard Mayhew's sermon.[34]

Scholars have described the sermon as "inflammatory" and "rabble-rousing," but this characterization seems to rely mainly upon the claims of Mayhew's Tory critics, none of whom heard or read the sermon themselves. Mayhew's memorandum of the sermon certainly did not offer any arguments or statements of principle that his parishioners had not heard from his pulpit before; his affirmations of the right of resistance and taxation by consent in the August 25 sermon were familiar to readers and hearers of his previous political sermons, such as the 1750 *Discourse Concerning Unlimited Submission* and the Massachusetts Election Sermon of 1754. It is unlikely that any West Church members, including

Richard Clarke, would have found the contentions of this sermon shocking or inflammatory in content.

It is possible, though, that Mayhew's audience experienced his delivery of the spoken sermon as inflammatory in style and tone. Scholars of early New England sermon literature such as Stout and Meredith Neuman have argued that the meaning of a sermon in its cultural context does not rely wholly upon the meaning intended by the sermonizer, but also upon the meanings given it by his audience, particularly as reconstructed in the private notes that some lay auditors took during and after that day's worship service. As Neuman explains, both speaking the sermon and listening to the sermon are required for "the production of a communal sermon culture." This body of scholarship undercuts the top-down view implicit in some intellectual and religious histories insisting that the laity passively accepted the contentions of their pastor in eighteenth-century New England and understood each sermon as he meant it to be understood. Indeed, Neuman contends, "the laity, their responses, their misinterpretations, their applications, and their doubts all help to shape the ministers' preaching, whether spoken or published." And this was clearly the case with the August 25 sermon in the West Church. Mayhew related to Clarke that he composed and delivered the sermon at the request of and under pressure from the laity. To determine whether a spoken sermon might have served as an inspiration for members of the audience to take action, as was allegedly the case with Mayhew's August 25 sermon, a historian would have to reconstruct how its auditors may have experienced oral delivery of the sermon aurally (including its pitch and cadence), what thoughts and feelings they came away with from the service, what they chose to remember from the sermon, and how they integrated those selected lessons with their existing knowledge and then applied it to action.[35]

To answer the question of whether Mayhew's hearers in the pews and gallery of the West Church on August 25 might have viewed his sermon as inflammatory (or been inspired by it to violent action), historians must consider not simply the content of the sermon, as conveyed plausibly by the pastor's memorandum, but also the laity's experience of Mayhew's performance from the pulpit. In the absence of sermon notes or remarks about the performance in personal diaries and letters, the lived experience of Mayhew's August 25 sermon must remain tantalizingly elusive. One cannot even say for certain how Richard Clarke and his family heard and interpreted the sermon in the ephemeral moment. If Clarke was offended by what he heard on August 25, he did not say so to the clergyman that day. Clarke expressed his offense to Mayhew only a few days later, when his pastor visited the Clarke family home, after the Hutchinson riot and after rumors began to circulate that the sermon had inspired the riot. Clarke almost certainly reinterpreted the performance in light of the riot, and it is possible that he found it offensive only after the fact and not at the moment that he experienced it. If Caner was indeed the one person most responsible for propagating the accusation of incitement in the week following the riot, one should note that Clarke's home was directly across School Street from King's Chapel, he was acquainted with Caner, and Caner was friends with Clarke's son-in-law, the artist John Singleton Copley. Whether Clarke concluded on his own that Mayhew's sermon had provoked the riot or whether Caner poured poison in his ear is impossible to say. And only Clarke could say for himself whether he responded positively to the sermon in the moment and became aggravated with his minister's performance retrospectively.[36]

Other than Mayhew and Clarke themselves, we do not know, and perhaps can never know, just who was present in the West Church on August 25, let alone how auditors experienced and interpreted the sermon, and what thoughts or actions it may have prompted. In 1765, the West End meetinghouse hosted one of the three largest congregations in Boston, with about 150 heads of household admitted to full church membership. Also boasting one of the richest congregations, the West Church was certainly not one regularly attended by "the rabble." In 1737, merchant Harrison Gray and other members of Boston's commercial nouveau riche founded the meetinghouse in the West End, a new neighborhood of Boston on which they stamped their own imprint. Seeking a minister who was liberal in temperament, rationalist in theology, and genteel in style, Deacon Gray approached Mayhew, a recent graduate of Harvard College, and the congregation elected him pastor on March 6, 1747, by a vote of forty-four to two. At fifteen pounds per week, plus rent and firewood, the West Church deacons provided Mayhew with one of the most generous salaries among Boston clergy. They could well afford to. Historian John Corrigan identified eighty-six full members of the West Church in 1765. According to town assessment records, twelve of the eighty-six parishioners fell within the top 9.6 percent of taxpayers in Boston, while another five members ranked in the top 12 percent. The extensive property holdings of West Church congregants reinforce an image of the August 25 sermon as a sober ritual in which a rationalist pastor engaged his genteel audience, not the fist-pounding, rabble-rousing, blood-curdling spectacle depicted by Hutchinson, Caner, and Oliver.[37]

Moreover, from his election as pastor in March 1747 by an almost unanimous vote until Clarke's departure in August 1765, Mayhew maintained unity within his congregation. While Clarke broke fellowship in protest over the August 25 sermon, this was not the case with the other full members of the West Church, including future Loyalist exiles such as Harrison Gray and his son, Thomas Flucker, Samuel Quincy, and Clarke's own nephew, Isaac Winslow. They maintained membership in the West Church congregation alongside such future revolutionaries as Paul Revere, Samuel Alleyne Otis (brother of James Otis, Jr.), and the publishers of the *Boston Gazette*, Benjamin Edes and John Gill. One may reasonably infer from the lack of additional defections during the Stamp Act Crisis that Mayhew's other parishioners did not blame the August 25 sermon for the August 26 riot, as Clarke did. We currently lack the evidence to know just what they thought of this episode, but Mayhew's feedback on the sermon before the riot left him "well assured, it was very generally liked and commended by the hearers at the time of it."[38]

The West Church congregation was wealthy and genteel, but it could still have been the case that some Bostonians of the lower social ranks did hear Mayhew speak that day. Hutchinson claimed that the church was particularly crowded on August 25, since it was known that Mayhew intended to give a political sermon addressing the Stamp Act Crisis. There may have been some members of lower social rank in attendance that Sunday who were not full church members and had not frequented Mayhew's services before, but evidence is required to substantiate this claim by Hutchinson and Oliver, who were not witnesses and did not cite their sources. We can only speculate about just who attended the service and how they reacted to the sermon, or how Mayhew delivered the sermon and what it sounded like. To determine the substance of the August 25 performance, in the light of other evidence and reliable testimony, we must still rely primarily upon the sermon memorandum.

It is a problematic document, to be sure, written by Mayhew after the riot in an attempt at self-justification to his friends. But we can reasonably accept that the memorandum does indeed convey the content of the sermon as delivered originally. Mayhew included in his letter to Clarke substantial quotations, in an effort to "remind you" of what he really said earlier that week. He understood well that Clarke would know if those quotations did not reflect the actual content of the original sermon, and Mayhew's quotations in the letter correspond accurately with what he wrote in the memorandum. While we can definitively identify only Clarke as a witness to the original performance, it is almost certain that the friends with whom Mayhew shared his memorandum included other men who were present in the pews that day, and they too would have known if the memorandum was not essentially the same as the sermon he delivered on August 25. There is, moreover, Mayhew's reputation for candor, even to a fault. In 1762, Connecticut clergyman Rev. Ezra Stiles remarked in his private notebook: "*Mayhew* is the most open and honest and undisguised of the American Divines; he is learned and you are in no doubt whether you have his honest and full Opinion, tho Error, and yet he will be found very nearly right." Mayhew had much to prove in the wake of the incitement accusation, but his reputation for honesty and integrity further supports the memorandum as a reliable representation of his August 25 sermon.[39]

Even if some Bostonians "who were of the mob" attended the sermon and were inspired by it to strike against Hutchinson, the Hutchinson riot could still not be explained as a religiously inspired spontaneous uprising. Protesters had pelted Hutchinson and Sheriff Stephen Greenleaf with rocks when the officers tried to disperse the demonstration of August 14, and they had marched on Hutchinson's home the following day. When the mob took action again on August 26, it demonstrated considerable discipline, organization, and calculation in selecting the homes of Story, Hallowell, Hutchinson, and Paxton for attack. The rioters systematically destroyed the public papers in these homes and labored methodically to demolish the Hutchinson mansion, actions which imply planning well in advance of the sermon. In the absence of substantiation, the Tory argument that Mayhew's sermon on Sunday caused a riot on Monday amounts to little more than a temptingly simple but fallacious claim of *post hoc, ergo propter hoc*.[40]

Historians may never provide a fully satisfactory explanation for the August 26 riot, because few participants have been identified and the ringleaders were never unmasked. The behavior of the crowd, however, suggests their motivation. On the day following the attack, Hutchinson claimed he was being punished as an encourager of the Stamp Act; August 26, then, should be considered a continuation and intensification of the protest against the Stamp Act on August 14, which included riotous damage to Andrew Oliver's home and a march to Hutchinson's home. But Hutchinson was not the only victim of the mob on August 26—he was preceded by Story and Hallowell and almost succeeded by Paxton. The riot was a broadside against the principal Crown officers of the province (with the exception of the royal governor). It could make sense to intimidate Andrew Oliver (as a prospective stamp distributor) and Thomas

Hutchinson (as a would-be advocate for passage of the act, committed publicly to enforcing the law of the land), but the targeting of all of these Crown officers suggests a motive other than a scheme to prevent implementation of the Stamp Act.

Since the fall of 1760, town and provincial politics had become toxic due to partisan conflict over the constitutionality and use of general search warrants known as writs of assistance. As the new governor of Massachusetts, Francis Bernard had arrived from England with instructions from the Privy Council to begin rigorous prosecution of local merchants who violated the Navigation Acts. Charles Paxton, surveyor of customs for the Port of Boston, assisted the governor ably in the seizure of ships and confiscation of their contraband cargoes, beginning with the goods of John Erving, a member of the provincial council. Represented by James Otis, Jr., an organization of import merchants called the Boston Society for Encouraging Trade and Commerce brought suit against Paxton. Among the sixty-four litigants were four members of Mayhew's West Church congregation, namely Melatiah Bourne, Thomas Greene, Joseph Scott, and Richard Clarke. Bernard appointed Lieutenant Governor Thomas Hutchinson as the new chief justice of the Massachusetts Superior Court with an assurance that he would uphold the contested constitutionality of writs of assistance. In February 1761, Otis made his case against writs of assistance before the court. Chief Justice Hutchinson delivered a ruling supporting the use of these writs in November 1761, and Paxton had resumed his "customs racketeering" by that December. The Sugar Act of 1764 further empowered customs officers to hunt down smugglers with writs of assistance and created vice-admiralty courts to secure convictions, without fear of nullification by sympathetic colonial juries. In Massachusetts, Governor Bernard's policy of ruthless enforcement of the Sugar Act fell to Hutchinson (as both lieutenant governor and chief justice), Paxton (as surveyor of customs), William Story (as deputy registrar of the vice-admiralty court), and Benjamin Hallowell (as comptroller of customs for the Port of Boston). It was no curious happenstance that the mob specifically targeted the homes of Paxton, Story, Hallowell, and Hutchinson on August 26, 1765. Violence against this particular quartet strongly suggests opposition to the Sugar Act.[41] The Boston Stamp Act riot of August 26 likely had little to do with the Stamp Act, and the economic interests of the laity—not the theology of the West Church clergyman—prompted its organization and sanctioned its violence.

Two years earlier, the merchant Briggs Hallowell had been allowed by a clerk of the Board of Trade in London to peruse depositions—sworn before and signed by Chief Justice Hutchinson—providing evidence of smuggling by specific Boston traders. In the summer of 1765, printed copies of Hallowell's testimony were circulating in town, adding fuel to the fire of indignation against customs racketeering in general and Hutchinson's contribution to this practice in particular. As Hutchinson himself noted in his *History of Massachusetts-Bay*, Hallowell's testament "brought, though without reason, the resentment of the merchants against the persons who, by their office, were obliged to administer the oaths, as well as against the officers of the customs and admiralty, who had made the depositions." Boston merchants (unspecified in Hutchinson's account) then "contrived a riot, which, after some small efforts against such officers, was to spend its principal force against the lieutenant-governor." That the mercantile interest—from wealthy merchants and shipmasters down to shopkeepers, clerks, able seamen, longshoremen, and rope makers—might resort to extralegal violence against Crown-appointed customs racketeers was more understandable than Hutchinson allowed, in light of the turmoil of the preceding years.[42]

The campaign by Governor Bernard and his principal officers to suppress smuggling had been a source of escalating aggravation for the people of Boston, whose economic well-being depended heavily upon illegal commerce with non-British markets, particularly the French and Dutch West Indies. Enforcement of the Navigation Acts and the Sugar Act threatened those Yankees who made their livelihood directly or indirectly from the shipping trade, as well as consumers of cheap contraband goods. With both Sugar Act prosecutions and implementation of the Stamp Act bearing down on Boston in the summer of 1765, nine middling businessmen formed a shadowy social club to organize political opposition to these menacing British measures. Calling themselves the Loyal Nine (and by December 1765, the Sons of Liberty), they met in the second floor counting room of Chase and Speakman's distillery on Hanover Square. Most of them were artisans and shopkeepers on the rise, like distiller Thomas Chase, braziers John Smith and Samuel Cleverly, painter Thomas Crafts, jeweler George Trott, and Benjamin Edes, printer of the *Boston Gazette* (and a full member of Mayhew's congregation). Others were more closely aligned with the mercantile interest, like Henry Bass, a merchant and relation of Samuel Adams, shipmaster Joseph Field, and John Avery, a merchant and distiller who served as the club secretary. One of the merchants who sued Paxton in 1761 to stop the use of writs of assistance, Avery was building a fortune by importing black slaves and cheap molasses from the West Indies and then distilling the molasses into rum for export. Such prosperous men—and the poorer folk who made the rope and sails, unloaded the cargoes, manned the ships, and worked the distilleries—had much to lose from a successful suppression of smuggling by the governor's officers.[43]

The Loyal Nine orchestrated the Liberty Tree protest on August 14, which took place just around the corner from their meeting place on Hanover Square in Boston's South End. To a street gang—the South End Mob, led by its shoemaker "captain" Ebenezer Mackintosh—they left the dirtier work of raising the effigies, fending off Sheriff Greenleaf, parading the effigies through town, dismantling Andrew Oliver's stamp office, and then burning the timber with the effigies in a bonfire on Fort Hill. As Perry notes in the following chapter, this carnivalesque ritual fell into the category of non-violent plebian protest known as "rough music," meant to bring in line those who violated community norms of behavior, as Oliver would have done had he begun enforcing the Stamp Act. Perhaps the Loyal Nine would have been content with the August 14 protest had it ended with the bonfire, but the close proximity of Oliver's house to Fort Hill proved too tempting to the crowd. Mackintosh's mob changed the script that the Nine had presumably written for them, directing their aggravation against Oliver's home and then pelting Hutchinson and Greenleaf with rocks when they intervened. Rough music then turned to riot, though a gentle one compared with the havoc of August 26. To what degree the Loyal Nine had a hand in the attack upon Oliver's home that evening remains unclear, but most Bostonians applauded the August 14 protest, riotous though it was, and Mayhew declined to criticize it.[44]

The connection between August 14 and August 26 also remains a mystery. The identities of the Hutchinson rioters (with the exception of its leader, Mackintosh) remained the town's most closely guarded secret. For information on their identities, Governor Bernard offered a reward of three hundred pounds sterling—as historian Gary Nash notes, the equivalent of "an artisan's wages for four years or more"—and yet no one came forward to collect it. The "rude Fellows" who rioted on August 26 were not mere robbers or vandals, let alone religious enthusiasts whipped into a pious frenzy at the West Church. While the historic record does not specify particular participants and their motives, it does indicate that—as on August 14—the South End Mob (and not West End parishioners) provided the main body of the rioters. Thanks to their regimentation by Captain Mackintosh and his lieutenants, the rioters displayed "almost military precision," in Nash's words, as they went about their mission of destruction and chastisement. The *Boston Gazette*, in its report on the August 26 riot, noted that the mob's first victim was William Story, and their target was the office in his home where he stored the records of the vice-admiralty court. "They enter'd the Office and destroyed the Papers therein, many of them being the Property of Mr. Story, but most of them the Files and Records of the Office," the newspaper relates. The mob also took care to destroy the public and private papers of Hallowell and Hutchinson. In addition to intimidating the Crown officers who had long tormented Boston's merchants, the enraged rioters aimed to eliminate any legal documents that could be used to prosecute violators of the Sugar and Navigation Acts. If their motive was drunken plunder, why specifically and repeatedly target legal papers for destruction?[45]

In light of such considerations, the attack on Hutchinson's house does not seem such a mystery after all. The August 26 riot was not a "random shot" fired by Mayhew against Bernard out of personal pique, as Hutchinson believed. It was a targeted strike aimed against the Crown's power to enforce trade regulations and collect customs, an objective that benefited warehouse laborers, rope makers, and mariners—along with Avery and his merchant friends. This alignment of commercial interests does not necessarily mean that the rioters were acting on direct orders from the Loyal Nine. Encouraged by public approbation of the August 14 riot, the South End Mob might have decided to take the next step on their own, in a direction they imagined the town-born would similarly approve. Such New Left scholars as Nash and Alfred Young have characterized Mackintosh as the prime mover of the Stamp Act riots and argued that the rioters were not only historical agents in their own right but a revolutionary vanguard advancing an egalitarian agenda, to the dismay of the merchants who lost control of them. In destroying Oliver's carriage and pulling down Hutchinson's cupola, the Boston proletarians were venting long-standing resentment of the wealth piled up by an elite few while poorer folk endured an economic depression. Notably, Mayhew's August 25 sermon does not figure at all in this interpretation of the Stamp Act Riots.[46]

There is a more nuanced position between the New Left thesis and the view of Bailyn, Maier, Byrd, Edmund Morgan, and other historians that the August 26 rioters took their marching orders from Mayhew or the Loyal Nine or both. Rather than an example of history from the top down or from the bottom up, the Hutchinson riot might best be understood as a collaboration between the middling businessmen of the Loyal Nine and the struggling workingmen of the South End Mob. Their interrelation comes more easily if one understands the society of 1760s Boston less in terms of horizontal classes—as one finds in the analysis of Nash and Young—than in terms of vertical interests. As self-conscious as the merchants were of their wealth and the workingmen were of their poverty, both groups viewed themselves as part of a vertically aligned mercantile interest benefiting from the importation of cheap goods from outside the British Empire, and they shared a compelling motive to stop the Bernard-Hutchinson-Oliver faction from enforcing Crown policy, even if it required methods rougher than rough music.[47]

Considering the high level of secrecy practiced by both the Loyal Nine and the South End Mob, one cannot say for certain whether Mackintosh launched the attacks of August 26 at the behest of the Loyal Nine or to what degree they approved of his destructiveness. After Andrew Oliver's ritualized public resignation as stamp tax agent under the Liberty Tree on December 17, 1765, however, the Nine apparently felt such relief about this final triumph over local officialdom that they let their discretion lapse. In his diary entry for December 19, 1765, John Adams recorded that Thomas Crafts and Thomas Chase "gave me a particular Account of the Proceedings of the Sons of Liberty on Tuesday last." On the same day, Henry Bass wrote to Samuel Savage explaining how the Loyal Nine orchestrated the resignation. Bass urged his father-in-law in a postscript to "keep this a profound Secret." "We do every thing in order to keep this and the first Affair Private," Bass wrote, and "are not a little pleas'd to hear that McIntosh has the Credit of the whole Affair." In coming to grips with the proto-revolutionary violence of August 26, historians must, as Richard Beeman put it, acknowledge "the autonomous power of ordinary people, properly organized"—including the role the Loyal Nine seems to have played in organizing that power properly.[48]

Without resort to the sermonizing of Jonathan Mayhew, the Stamp Act riots of August 1765 can be explained compellingly as a defense of colonial property rights and freedom of trade against both the Sugar and Stamp Acts by a covertly coordinated effort of middling businessmen and the Boston "street." Some modern scholars have built upon the old Tory interpretation to contend that Mayhew unintentionally instigated the Hutchinson riot, as he did not realize the motivational power of his own religiously charged rhetoric or the full depth of popular anger against the ruling elites. But Mayhew's controversial sermon of August 25, 1765, likely played little if any role in motivating the riot of August 26. And even if it could be demonstrated that some participants in the riot had been motivated by the sermon, the riot likely still would have taken place when and how it actually did without Mayhew's preaching. The rioters acted on their own interests and were not in need of a clergyman to wind them up like tin soldiers and set them on the march. Mayhew did not incite the August 26 riot any more than he had the riot of August 14: both caught him by surprise.

As scholars who take the role of religious and political ideas in human motivation seriously, it is understandable that Bailyn, Maier, and Byrd might be inclined to believe Hutchinson's accusation that a sermon by a celebrated intellectual leader started the most destructive colonial riot and, over the long run, helped set the colonies on a course toward revolutionary violence. Exploding that accusation and replacing it with a more plausible explanation for the Boston Stamp Act riots does not require, however, minimizing the role of religious and political ideas generally or the pulpit activism of Mayhew, particularly in the origins of the American Revolution. Bailyn, Maier, and Byrd are right to characterize the Stamp Act Crisis as the result, in part, of a preexisting ideology—put in place to a great degree by Mayhew—which served as a prerequisite for the backroom politics of the Loyal Nine and the street brawling of the South End Mob.

Mayhew's political sermons of the 1750s and 1760s popularized radical Whig principles such as consensual government and the right of resistance in New England's political culture, preparing the cultural context in which the Boston Stamp Act riots could occur. His criticism of the early 1760s, against High Church Anglican clergymen like Henry Caner and East Apthorp seeking to convert Congregationalists and establish a colonial episcopate, had agitated the common people against British threats to their religious liberty. And his spoken and written sermons shaped the political thinking of many leading figures in Boston society, from emerging Patriots such as John Adams and Andrew Eliot to members of his own congregation, like Paul Revere and Samuel Otis. Through an effective use of pulpit and press, Mayhew had already done much to whip New Englanders into a state of anxiety about the security of their rights before news of the Stamp Act arrived in the Port of Boston. Nevertheless, during the Stamp Act Crisis, Mayhew criticized in his letters to Thomas Hollis the folly of New Englanders for their willingness to wage war against Britain. He never recognized the role he played—over a long career of ideological activism—in generating so intense a public response to the Stamp Act. Mayhew may be considered an intellectual father to the Sons of Liberty, but they were children he never acknowledged as his own, birthed long before the August 25 sermon that Hutchinson and modern historians have blamed for inciting violent rebellion in the colonies.

Notes

1. Bernard Bailyn, ed., *Pamphlets of the American Revolution, 1750–1776* (Cambridge, MA: Harvard University Press, 1965), 204, 237–238n; Lester J. Cappon, ed., *The Adams-Jefferson Letters: The Complete Correspondence between Thomas Jefferson and John and Abigail Adams*, vol. II (Chapel Hill: University of North Carolina Press, 1999), 527; Bernard Bailyn, *Faces of Revolution: Personalities and Themes in the Struggle for American Independence* (New York: Vintage, 1992), 113. For a sampling of recent scholarship that credits the clergy with the popularization of Whig political ideas and the mobilization of general public opposition to British authority, or more generally the political use of religiously based and biblically framed political rhetoric before and during the Revolution, consider James B. Bell, *A War of Religion: Dissenters, Anglicans, and the American Revolution* (Houndsmills: Palgrave Macmillan, 2008); Thomas S. Kidd, *God of Liberty: A Religious History of the American Revolution* (New York: Basic Books, 2010); Eran Shalev, *American Zion: The Old Testament as a Political Text from the Revolution to the Civil War* (New Haven, CT: Yale University Press, 2013), ch. 1; T. H. Breen, *American Insurgents, American Patriots: The Revolution of the People* (New York: Hill & Wang, 2010), ch. 9; and Dustin Gish and Daniel Kinghard, eds., *Resistance to Tyrants, Obedience to God: Reason, Religion, and Republicanism at the American Founding* (Lanham, MD: Lexington Books, 2013), 1–15, 105–124.

2. Cappon, ed., *The Adams-Jefferson Letters*, 527.

3. Bailyn, *Pamphlets of the American Revolution*, 210; for the thesis that Mayhew played a central role in the intellectual origins of the American Revolution, see John Patrick Mullins, *Father of Liberty: Jonathan Mayhew and the Intellectual Origins of the American Revolution* (PhD diss., University of Kentucky, 2005).

4. Bernard Bailyn, *The Ordeal of Thomas Hutchinson* (Cambridge, MA: Harvard University Press, 1973), 35–38; for the thesis that mob violence was routine in the American colonies before 1765, and even considered a legitimate component of the British constitution, see also Pauline Maier, *From Resistance to Revolution: Colonial Radicals and the Development of American Opposition to Britain, 1765–1776* (New York: W. W. Norton, 1991 [1972]), ch. 1.

5. Bailyn, *Faces of Revolution*, 127, 128, 132, 133; Maier, *From Resistance to Revolution*, 48; Harry S. Stout, *The New England Soul: Preaching and Religious Culture in Colonial New England* (New York: Oxford University Press, 1986), 263; James P. Byrd, *Sacred Scripture, Sacred War: The Bible and the American Revolution* (New York: Oxford University Press, 2013), 29–30. See also Dirk Hoerder, "Boston Leaders and Boston Crowds, 1765–1776," in *The American Revolution: Explorations in the History of American Radicalism*, ed. Alfred F. Young (DeKalb: Northern Illinois University Press, 1976), 244.

6. Bailyn, *Ordeal of Thomas Hutchinson*, 36, 62–66; Andrew Stephen Walmsley, *Thomas Hutchinson and the Origins of the American Revolution* (New York: New

York University Press, 1999), 59–63; Richard Archer, *As If an Enemy's Country: The British Occupation of Boston and the Origins of Revolution* (Oxford: Oxford University Press, 2010), 18–19.

7. Bernhard Knollenberg, ed., "Thomas Hollis and Jonathan Mayhew: Their Correspondence, 1759–1766," *Proceedings of the Massachusetts Historical Society*, 3d ser., vol. 69 (October 1947–May 1950), 162–163, 169; Bailyn, *Faces of Revolution*, 45; Jonathan Mayhew Papers, Folder no. 91, Bortman Collection, Boston University.

8. Knollenberg, "Thomas Hollis and Jonathan Mayhew," 173.

9. Ibid., 175.

10. Ibid., 174–175.

11. Ibid., 175–176.

12. Maier, *From Resistance to Revolution*, 27–29, 38, 60; Jonathan Mayhew, "Letter of Rev. Jonathan Mayhew to Richard Clarke, 1765," *The New-England Historical and Genealogical Register*, vol. 46 (Boston: New England Historic Genealogical Society, 1892), 17.

13. Mayhew Papers, Folder no. 91.

14. Ibid.

15. Ibid.

16. *Boston Gazette, or Country Journal*, September 2, 1765; Josiah Quincy, Jr., *Reports of Cases Argued and Adjudged in the Superior Court of Judicature of the Province of Massachusetts Bay Between 1761 and 1772* (Boston, Little and Brown, 1865), 168–173; Walmsley, *Thomas Hutchinson and the Origins of the American Revolution*, 66–69; Bailyn, *Ordeal of Thomas Hutchinson*, 35.

17. *Boston Gazette, and Country Journal*, September 3, 1765; Mayhew Papers, Folder no. 91.

18. Mayhew Papers, Folder no. 91 (bracketed material in the original).

19. Bernard Bailyn, "Religion and Revolution: Three Biographical Studies," *Perspectives in American History*, 4 (1970): 116–117; Mayhew Papers, Folder no. 91; Mayhew, "Letter from Mayhew to Clarke," 19.

20. Mayhew, "Letter from Mayhew to Clarke," 16–19.

21. Mayhew, "Letter from Mayhew to Clarke," 17.

22. Mayhew, "Letter from Mayhew to Clarke," 15; Charles W. Akers, *Called unto Liberty: A Life of Jonathan Mayhew, 1720–1766* (Cambridge, MA: Harvard University Press, 1964), 205, 210; Mayhew Papers, Folder no. 91; for Henry Caner's critique of Mayhew's arguments regarding the Bishop controversy, see [Henry Caner], *A Candid Examination of Dr. Mayhew's Observations on the Charter and Conduct of the Society for the propagation of the Gospel in Foreign Parts, To which is Added, A Letter to a Friend, Containing a Short Vindication of the Said Society against the Mistakes and Misrepresentations of the Doctor in his Observations on the Conduct of that Society, by One of its Members* (Boston: Thomas and John Fleet, Green and Russell, Edes and Gill, 1763); for Mayhew's response to Caner, see Jonathan Mayhew, *A Defence of the Observations on the Charter and Conduct of the Society for the Propagation of the Gospel in Foreign Parts, Against an Anonymous Pamphlet Falsely Intitled, A Candid Examination of Dr. Mayhew's Observations, &c., and also Against The Letter to a Friend Annexed Thereto, Said to Contain a Short Vindication of said*

Society, by One of its Members (Boston: R. and S. Draper, Edes and Gill, and T. and J. Fleet, 1763), esp. 54–55.

23. Mayhew Papers, Folder no. 91.

24. Thomas Hutchinson, *The History the Province of Massachusetts-Bay From 1749 to 1774, Comprising a Detailed Narrative of the Origin and Early Stages of the American Revolution* (London: John Murray, 1898), 123; Maier, *From Resistance to Revolution*, 60; Hoerder, "Boston Leaders and Boston Crowds," 244.

25. Akers, *Called unto Liberty*, 206n.

26. For the quarrel over the two-dollar gratuity and the conflict between Mayhew and Bernard that followed, see J. Patrick Mullins, "'A Kind of War, Tho' Hitherto an Un-Bloody One': Jonathan Mayhew, Francis Bernard, and the Indian Affair," *Massachusetts Historical Review*, 2 (2009): 27–56; see also Colin Nicolson, *The "Infamas Govener": Francis Bernard and the Origins of the American Revolution* (Boston: Northeastern University Press, 2000), 77.

27. Knollenberg, "Thomas Hollis and Jonathan Mayhew," 178.

28. Ibid., 176, 180–181.

29. Jonathan Mayhew, *The Snare Broken, A Thanksgiving-Discourse, Preached at the Desire of the West Church, in Boston, N.E., Friday May 23, 1766, Occasioned by the Repeal of the Stamp-Act* (Boston: R. and S. Draper, Edes and Gill, 1766), 2–3.

30. Ibid., 6–9, 13–14, 19–21, 33–36, 38–42; Alan Heimert, *Religion and the American Mind: From the Great Awakening to the Revolution* (Cambridge, MA: Harvard University Press, 1966), 259–261, 274–275, 280, 290–293; for other account of Mayhew moving toward a more conservative position in *The Snare Broken*, see Bailyn, "Religion and Revolution," 121; see also Maier, *From Resistance to Revolution*, 60.

31. Andrew Eliot, "Letters from Andrew Eliot to Thomas Hollis," *Collections of the Massachusetts Historical Society*, 4th ser., vol. 4 (Boston: Massachusetts Historical Society, 1858), 407; Edmund S. Morgan, "Thomas Hutchinson and the Stamp Act," *New England Quarterly* (December 1948): 471.

32. *Boston Gazette, and Country Journal*, September 3, 1765.

33. Douglas Adair and John A. Schutz, ed., *Peter Oliver's Origin and Progress of the American Revolution: A Tory View* (San Marino, CA: Huntington Library, 1961), 44; Morgan, "Thomas Hutchinson and the Stamp Act," 471.

34. Hutchinson, *History the Province of Massachusetts-Bay*, 123; Adair and Schutz, *Peter Oliver's Origin and Progress of the American Revolution*, 44; Eliot, "Letters from Eliot to Hollis," 407.

35. Meredith Marie Neuman, *Jeremiah's Scribes: Creating Sermon Literature in Puritan New England* (Philadelphia: University of Pennsylvania Press, 2013), x, 8–9, 63, 98. For the evidentiary value of sermon notes by lay auditors in contextualizing New England Puritan literature, see Neuman, *Jeremiah's Scribes*, ch. 2. For another work interpreting sermon literature in light of lay auditors' notes, see Stout, *The New England Soul*. For the ways in which New England Native laity selected elements of sermons by white Congregational missionaries that they found useful and combined them with elements of other belief systems in light of their own beliefs and interests, consider Linford D. Fisher, *The Indian Great Awakening: Religion and the Shaping of*

Native Cultures of Early America (Oxford: Oxford University Press, 2012), esp. 5–12; Mayhew, "Letter of Mayhew to Clarke," 17.

36. Mayhew, "Letter of Mayhew to Clarke," 16; James Henry Stark, *The Loyalists of Massachusetts and the Other Side of the Revolution* (Boston: James H. Stark, 1910), 405–409.

37. John Corrigan, *The Hidden Balance: Religion and the Social Theories of Charles Chauncy and Jonathan Mayhew* (Cambridge: Cambridge University Press, 1986), 120–122.

38. Akers, *Called unto Liberty*, 44–47.

39. Christopher Grasso, *A Speaking Aristocracy: Transforming Public Discourse in Eighteenth-Century Connecticut* (Chapel Hill: University of North Carolina Press, 1999), 260n.

40. Walmsley, *Thomas Hutchinson and the Origins of the American Revolution*, 65–68; John R. Galvin, *Three Men of Boston: Leadership and Conflict at the Start of the American Revolution* (Washington, DC: Brassey's, 1997 [1976]), 107.

41. Mullins, "'A Kind of War,'" 30–33; Walmsley, *Thomas Hutchinson and the Origins of the American Revolution*, 44–47. For the formation of the Boston Society for the Encouraging of Trade and Commerce, see John W. Tyler, *Smugglers and Patriots: Boston Merchants and the Advent of the American Revolution* (Boston: Northeastern University Press, 1986), 63, 285n17. For the characterization of Bernard's enforcement of the Navigation Acts as "customs racketeering," see Oliver M. Dickerson, *The Navigation Acts and the American Revolution* (Philadelphia: University of Pennsylvania Press, 1951); John J. Waters and John A. Schutz, "Patterns of Massachusetts Colonial Politics: The Writs of Assistance and the Rivalry between the Otis and Hutchinson Families," *William and Mary Quarterly*, 3d ser., 24 (1967): 558–561; M. H. Smith, *The Writs of Assistance Case* (Berkeley: University of California Press, 1978).

42. Galvin, *Three Men of Boston*, 106; Hutchinson, *History of Massachusetts-Bay*, 123–124; Tyler, *Smugglers and Patriots*, 61–62.

43. Edmund S. Morgan and Helen M. Morgan, *The Stamp Act Crisis: Prologue to Revolution* (Chapel Hill: University of North Carolina Press, 1995 [1953]), 127–128; Richard R. Beeman, *The Varieties of Political Experience in Eighteenth-Century America* (Philadelphia: University of Pennsylvania Press, 2004), 258; Walmsley, *Thomas Hutchinson and the Origins of the American Revolution*, 69; Gary B. Nash, *The Unknown American Revolution: The Unruly Birth of Democracy and the Struggle to Create America* (New York: Penguin Books, 2005), 49.

44. Morgan and Morgan, *Stamp Act Crisis*, 128–129; Archer, *As If an Enemy's Country*, 24–25. For Mayhew's pass on condemning the August 14 riot, see Knollenberg, "Thomas Hollis and Jonathan Mayhew," 175; see also Eliot, "Letters from Eliot to Hollis," 407.

45. *Boston Gazette, and Country Journal*, September 3, 1765; Walmsley, *Thomas Hutchinson and the Origins of the American Revolution*, 68; Nash, *Unknown American Revolution*, 45, 49. For another example of collaboration between Mackintosh and the Loyal Nine, see Archer, *As If an Enemy's Country*, 34–35.

46. Nash, *Unknown American Revolution*, 48–51; Alfred F. Young, *Liberty Tree:*

Ordinary People and the American Revolution (New York: New York University Press, 2006), 338–344.

47. Beeman, *Varieties of Political Experience*, 258; Walmsley, *Thomas Hutchinson and the Origins of the American Revolution*, 69–70.

48. Morgan and Morgan, *Stamp Act Crisis*, 198; Archer, *As If an Enemy's Country*, 40; John Adams, *Diary and Autobiography of John Adams*, vol. 1: *Diary*, 177–1770 (Cambridge, MA: Harvard University Press, 1961): 265; Henry Bass to Samuel P. Savage, December 19, 1765, *Proceedings of the Massachusetts Historical Society*, 44 (June 1911): 688–689; Beeman, *Varieties of Political Experience*, 251.

[2]

MOLLY PERRY

BURIED LIBERTIES AND HANGING EFFIGIES: IMPERIAL PERSUASION, INTIMIDATION, AND PERFORMANCE DURING THE STAMP ACT CRISIS

IN AUGUST 1765, A correspondent in Connecticut reported the rapid spread of a "noble patriotic fire" lighting up "in one place and another." The flames, which first "shown so conspicuous at Boston" in the riots recounted by Patrick Mullins in chapter 1, now "blaz'd here with all the vehemence and splendor of a comet." This "fire of liberty" appeared as an effigy display in the "most Publick Part of Town," where suspended "20 or 30 feet from the ground" hung "our reputable Stamp-Master in Effigy," who made "his public appearance . . . clad in a suit of white, trim'd with black." Mimicking the displays elsewhere, the gallows scene included a "Boot on one of the Shoulders" with a devil peering out at the crowd. "Exposed about an hour," the effigy display was dismantled to form a "procession glorious . . . thro' town" accompanied by loud cannon fire from the fort and a growing crowd shouting the "invectives, huzza's and disdainful music . . . of injured freedom." At the "height of a lofty hill," the body "was committed to the flames." In an attempt to intimidate the local customs official and broadcast shared grievances, the "principal part of the Inhabitants" followed their proxy stamp official's demise in the "patriotic fire" with "a few loyal and very constitutional healths" and toasts. The newspaper accounts reported with approval that "the most perfect decorum was observed in all their behaviour" and nearby towns acted "in much the same manner." As they celebrated the preservation of liberty at their mock funeral pyre, the gathered crowds participated in a series of vibrant, transatlantic rituals to influence imperial opinion and demand repeal of the Stamp Act.[1]

After months of petitioning and mounting an aggressive lobbying campaign, colonists demanding repeal of the Stamp Act pursued two strategies on the streets of colonial port towns. By hanging effigies, staging unruly parades, tearing down buildings, and threatening to destroy stamped cargoes, crowds aggressively targeted, intimidated, and forced the resignation of royal customs officials and the retreat of colonial governors. With the stamped paper removed from circulation, targeted violent actions effectively prevented local enforcement of the stamp duty after November 1, 1765.[2] At the same time, to achieve their ultimate goal of repeal, colonists turned across the Atlantic to solicit assistance from power brokers in England. Colonists recognized the importance of imperial public opinion and the necessity of persuasion in their protests. Appearances mattered to the anti-stamp cause. Through gestures of loyalty and symbols of shared political tradition, colonists opposed to the Stamp Act hoped to build a sympathetic transatlantic coalition. Cultural performances—particularly the appropriation of traditional effigy displays—played a central role in this dual strategy to secure repeal. This chapter closely examines street-level accounts of colonial protests to trace innovations and alterations in Anglo-American effigy displays from the fall of 1765 through the spring of 1766, revealing the fluid dynamics within the crowd, the centrality of violence to shifts in strategies of protest, and the contest in the street and across the British Empire over membership in the body politic.

On patriotic days throughout the calendar year, British subjects gathered in the streets forging transatlantic cultural bonds. English political history combined with traditions of rough music to create a widely accessible set of symbols, slogans, and public performances that resonated across the British Empire.[3] Toasting to the health of their monarchs, illuminating displays of honored patriots in their windows, parading through the streets with banners and drums, and constructing elaborate displays of devils and popes, individuals and communities laid claim to membership in the British body politic.[4] As celebrations, these public displays invited spectators and attracted audiences. In newspapers and pamphlets, the descriptions of these performances circulated the Atlantic basin emphasizing cohesion and common cause. At a time of imperial crisis and community disruption, these traditions of performance and display also created opportunities for subversion.

By adapting recognizable cultural rituals, anti-stamp activists hoped to cultivate a sense of wide public support throughout the British Empire. Through the street theater of effigy construction, exhibition, procession, and destruction, protesting colonists provided a political lesson to local and imperial audiences by demonstrating their grievances as disenfranchised British subjects. By engaging in traditional forms of English rough music—the exercise of extralegal community attack on an individual—communities violently displayed how the legislation threatened their core values. Repeated in port after port and recycled in paper after paper, effigy scenes communicated the degree of colonial resistance, provided a sense of a wide public crisis, and warned of imperial economic disruption.

During the Stamp Act Crisis, individuals in Boston first appreciated the possibilities that English effigy spectacles possessed as political street theater. As an extralegal tool applied by communities to publicly punish individuals, traditions of effigy hanging and rough music provided a mechanism to intimidate local officials connected with the Stamp Act and directly threaten any sympathetic "friends," while offering a public display that conveyed a clear political message. The effigy scene that greeted the awaking city of Boston on August 14, 1765, established the common pattern followed by towns stretching from Nova Scotia to St. Christopher. Early in the morning, "in the most public Part of Town," Boston residents and "peasants" visiting the city for the market day awoke to discover "the Effigy of a Gentleman sustaining a very unpopular Office, viz. that of the St[am]p-Master . . . hanging on a Tree." Calculated to convince Andrew Oliver to resign his post, the display also provided an imperial political lesson to spectators. Alongside the stamp master's corpse hung a symbol borrowed directly from contemporary street protests in London, "a Boot, wherein was concealed a young Imp of the D[evi]l." This play on Lord Bute's name provided a transatlantic critique of the minister's influence on the young king and his household. Pinned to Oliver's chest "was a Label, in Praise of Liberty, and denouncing Vengeance on the Subvertors of it." While the Council initially deemed the display simply a "Boyish Sport, that did not deserve the Notice of the Governor," the gallows quickly attracted the curiosity of individuals from throughout the larger Boston community.[5]

At the razor's edge of tradition and rebellion, dramatic scenes of hanging effigies attracted the attention of audiences both local and imperial. In Boston, the "Multitude of Spectators who continually assembled the Whole Day" for "the Diversion" did not observe a static tableau, but an active street theater designed to engage onlookers. On the busy market day, "not a Peasant was suffered to pass . . . 'till he had stop'd and got his Articles stamp'd by the Effigy." This didactic theater associated with the effigy display accomplished a critical goal of protest—transforming spectators into participants. The recruitment tool proved effective as the crowd swelled. At several times during the day, private individuals and the sheriff attempted to dismantle the display, only to conclude that it could not be accomplished "without imminent danger of their lives."[6] In printed reports and official correspondence, descriptions of the effigy recounted the scores of people gathered in support supplying a transatlantic audience with a distinct sense of unified public opinion against the Stamp Act in Boston.

The nature of the political theater shifted during the afternoon into evening, as Boston's effigy scene transformed into a mobile parade accompanied by a crowd intent on demanding and obtaining the resignation of the stamp master. As it "grew dark . . . the mob which had been gathering and growing all the Afternoon" proceeded "to the Town House bringing the Effigy with them." The assembly paused outside the Council chambers shouting "three Huzzas by way of defiance and passed on." The procession continued through the streets with their puppet to a building "lately Erected by Mr. Oliver," which they rapidly "pulled down to the ground." With the effigy intact, the crowd paraded past homes and businesses to Mr. Oliver's house to demand his resignation. In his official report to London, Oliver described the sheer terror he felt as the crowd's target. "Apprehensive" of "Danger from the Tumult," the stamp master and his family made "their Retreat across the Gardens" as the crowd violently "beheaded" his likeness, "broke all the windows," and burned "the Effigy together with the Timber and other Wood work of the House they had demolish'd." Members of the crowd then "proceeded to break open the Stables, Coach-Houses, &c . . . increasing the Bonfire" until "a Number of Spectators present" intervened to "dissuade going so far." While observers watched, the crowd, refocused, "set about pulling down a Range of Fence upwards of 15 Foot high" and then "went down the Cellars, and help'd themselves to the Liquor" and all "Silver Plate that the House afforded." The spectacle suspended, Governor Francis Bernard wrote, when the "mob . . . unwilling to lose their Frolick . . . were prevailed upon to disperse." Despite the late hour and the movement of many participants and spectators to their homes, some members of the crowd "assembled again and renew'd their Bonfire."[7]

The movement of the crowd through the city of Boston, their proxy attack on the stamp master's body, and the direct attack on his property signified to local observers the high price of "submission" to the Stamp Act. The spectacle informed imperial officials with a clear message that the act could not be enforced. The actions of the crowd provided the first sense that once unleashed this aggressive, boisterous style of English political action could quickly overwhelm the thin veneer of civic order in colonial towns. Engaging in politics on the street created opportunities for a wide spectrum of the community to participate, including women, itinerant sailors and dockside laborers, as well as free and enslaved African Americans.

The various directions and movements of the assembled crowd in Boston —both over the course of the day and through the streets of the city— suggest the fluidity of the entire spectacle. The surviving sources trace the comings and goings of individuals and groups from early in the morning to late at night, revealing various levels of engagement and participation. Driven by a common target and purpose, the events of the day allowed for a broad spectrum of colonial opinion and experiences on the street.[8] Though, by design, participation was encouraged, the lessons and message of that involvement varied significantly. Throughout the day there were multiple opportunities for individuals to join the anti-stamp theater, accompany the parade, observe the destruction, and witness the spectacle, all without requiring any oaths or sacrifice to the colonial cause. For many uncertain participants—caught up in the excitement of the moment and the coercive power of crowds—witnessing an effigy might prompt them to join with the assembly shouting vague slogans and huzzas. For others, simply observing the parade pass under their windows or down their streets constituted involvement in the street action. Amid a large assembly, these small gestures of sympathy and support provided a chance to protest relatively anonymously, with little fear of retribution. Such participation also proved a transitory moment, requiring no long-term commitment. An appreciation of this diversity of experience within the effigy crowds offers new perspectives on the experiences of colonial protest critically important for understanding the link between this imperial crisis and the coming of the American Revolution.

Highlighting the transatlantic focus of colonial protest, this chapter explores the elements and patterns of effigy spectacles from town to town. Colonists demanding repeal of the Stamp Act used a variety of tactics to convey their shared identity as Britons. As part of the dual strategy for securing repeal through local resistance and imperial persuasion, colonial protestors emphasized their shared history of constitutional struggle, attempted to collapse their geographic distance across the Atlantic, and hoped to diminish any demographic differences between the colonies and England. Throughout this process, colonists performed a variety of British cultural rituals to emphasize their commitment to empire. Often, for example, colonists combined the potentially seditious effigy display criticizing the king's chief ministers with a long set of loyal toasts "to the Best of Kings."[9] A close examination of the initial moments of protest reveals that long before signing lists or declaring absolute loyalties, colonists engaged in a variety of highly meaningful cultural rituals in order to influence—not abandon—their empire.

Following the "Transactions of the proceeding Night" in Boston, the effigy display and crowd action became "the general Topic of Conversation." Throughout the city, individuals discussed the origins of the display. The surviving record of this debate—primarily in newspapers and official reports—reveals the difficulty of precisely identifying the members of the assembly. Debate raged regarding the leaders, builders, members, and spectators of the "night's Frolick."[10] In his official report to London, Governor Bernard suggested the futility of prosecuting those responsible, for while "every one agree that this Riot has exceeded all others . . . both in Vehemence of Actions and Mischievousness of Intention," the question of responsibility and membership remained, for "never had any mob so many Abettors of Consequence as this. . . . It is said they were fifty Gentlemen, Actors in this scene distinguished with Trowsers and Jackets on besides . . . Numbers behind the Curtain." Lamenting the size and constitution of the crowd, Governor Bernard suggested the changing demographics of the group over the course of the spectacle, as it was reported that "disguised Gentlemen proceeded no farther than the Burning the Effigy, and then departed and had no hand in storming the House." Bernard concluded that "many Gentlemen who approved of hanging & burning the Effigy took pains . . . to prevent any farther mischiefs being done." Even the target of the effigy, Andrew Oliver, struggled to identify the responsible parties to Governor Bernard: "this Commotion intirely arose out of the Town of Boston" from general sense among "the Common Folk of the Town" who were determined "that a Man who offers a Stamped Paper to sell will be immediately killed; That all the Powers of Great Britain shall not Oblige them to submit to the Stamp Act." Considering the assembly at large, Bernard informed London that "upon Enquiry I find that such Persons living out of Boston, as were seen in the Crowd were thereby merely as spectators."[11] While contemporaries attempted to "penetrate the mob" to locate leaders and members, sources admitted that the comings and goings within the crowd prevented an accurate tally.

Historians interested in these early moments of imperial crisis have similarly attempted to identify the members of the mob. For decades, scholars of colonial protests and the Revolution adopted the central concern best expressed by the royal governors seeking to pinpoint the "movers of the people" and the "manipulators of the mob," locating the gentry leaders believed to be animating what was considered an irrational crowd.[12] Pressing against this interest in upper-class individuals and the formal organizations of protests, scholars followed the interpretive challenges posed by George Rudé and E. P. Thompson in an attempt to understand the rationality of crowd action.[13] Early American historians led by Alfred F. Young, Gary Nash, Dirk Hoerder, and Jesse Lemisch, among many others, refocused scholarly interest on these scenes of protest from the "bottom up."[14] In examining crowd participation, New Left historians located a new animus for the protests and new roles for lower-class individuals, but continued to emphasize the radicalism and absolute commitment of colonists. Due to the heavy hand of the looming revolution, historians often depict individual colonists during this early period as either ideological Patriots or Loyalists.

In scholarship, the Stamp Act Crisis serves as the breaking point for empire, a recruitment moment, as Pauline Maier describes, where a "joining" spirit among the "lower case 'sons' of liberty . . . who supported the American cause actively" reigned.[15] Despite interpretive differences, scholars of the American Revolution typically cast colonists as consistent protest participants motivated by either economic condition or ideological interest. Scholars like T. H. Breen have drawn a direct trajectory from these initial protests to American independence, emphasizing the active, committed participation of colonists in the process of building trust between colonial towns.[16] Scholars of the Revolution have only periodically questioned this portrayal of the road to revolution. Focusing on the wartime experience of individuals and communities, historians Ron Hoffman, Michael McDonnell, and John Shy trace the widespread disaffection of many individuals.[17] A close scrutiny of crowds across the British North American colonies reveals an earlier pattern of disaffection and limited commitment to imperial protests. Long before fighting ensued, the movements and actions of the crowds on the streets revealed the diverse lessons individuals and communities drew from the Stamp Act Crisis. Appreciating divisions within the crowd and acknowledging the often reluctant choice to protest by individuals and communities better captures the origins and nature of allegiance, loyalty, and disaffection during the subsequent movement for independence.

Crowd action surrounding effigies never demanded or articulated absolute ideological purity. Watching or participating in an effigy display rarely required more than raising a few "loyal toasts," shouting "huzzas," or echoing the vague sentiment of "Liberty! Property! And No Stamps!" Seldom were individuals on the street pressed to articulate complex political ideologies to justify their actions. References on the street to debates over constitutional representation that raged in pamphlets, for example, most often came in the form of humor, with hanging effigies often described as "virtually representing" detested ministers and imperial officials.[18] Participation in crowd action could serve as a training and a transformative experience, but it could also be a passing fancy, a mere "frolick."[19] For those watching a crowd or moving along its edges, agreeing aloud to "Liberty and No Stamps" necessitated little real commitment and no long-term promises. One could easily participate one moment and change one's opinion completely the next. As imperial policies altered, an individual often, as one contemporary described it, twisted his "face into many violent and frightful contortions" at the mention of English ministers but, in a few months' time, appeared transformed and "will not drink of the brook or fountain, but to the health of the King and his Minister."[20] Such transformations of behavior require a fuller treatment of precisely the ways in which ordinary colonists could and did participate in the street, the diversity of opinions about the meanings of protest, as well as the fluidity of identities and affiliations. Indeed, so vague were the commitments of individuals in Stamp Act crowds, that subsequent imperial protest strategies developed lists and associations to force colonists to take a clear, defined position. After the unruly riots of the Stamp Act Crisis, such lists also delineated precisely who would be included in this claim to the rights of Englishmen, excluding those deemed outside the body politic due to race, class, or gender.

A chief issue facing the study of crowd behavior and membership during the Stamp Act Crisis centers upon the surviving sources. Effigy displays and the dismantling of houses were attention-grabbing events. Around the British Empire, people demanded news and details about every hanging stamp man. The speed of information became critical to defending or advancing the imperial interpretation of the actions on the street. Officials in London demanded explanations from colonial and stamp officers. Businessmen, shipping interests, and ship captains requested information about the opening and closing of ports due to the unrest. News outlets solicited the latest report from every traveler and publication possible, often reprinting accounts verbatim in their newspapers. The control of information was vital to the course of the imperial crisis. Newspapers printed in the colonies overwhelmingly supported repeal of the Stamp Act, describing the spreading "patriotic fire" in accounts of each protest.[21] In relaying the sentiments of the American colonists and detailing recent events, Andrew Oliver simply attached in his letter copies of "this days Newspapers" for "I cannot give you a better account of the Temper & Behaviour of this & some of the Neighboring Colonies."[22]

The printed accounts provide an edited view of the participants and the events of the day. The other chief surviving source, the royal correspondence, reveals a different tension. Forced into a strange position as either spectators or targets, royal governors and stamp officials wrote accounts discrediting local resistance as riotous and violent. They spoke of a "contagion" spreading throughout the colonies from north to south.[23] At the same time, to defend their actions (or more often inaction), maintain their position, and make it possible for them to receive compensation for damaged or destroyed property, the official reports included lengthy descriptions of crowd action and the path of destruction. Written for opposing purposes with opposing viewpoints, both the printed sources and imperial correspondence present a common picture—the widespread, unanimous, boisterous disapproval of the Stamp Act in colonial port towns. The eagerness of both sets of primary accounts to lump together active participants with sideline spectators leaves scholars struggling to measure and gauge individual participation and decision making in these early moments of street protest. Although incomplete and often heavily edited, surviving accounts of effigy displays survive as one of the few relics of the oral culture of the street and hint at the diverse experiences of individuals during this moment of community disruption.

Throughout the British Empire, patriotic days and major military victories were commemorated publicly with parades and community gatherings. Yearly, colonial subjects participated in various celebrations on the street, declaring their loyalty to their monarch and celebrating the strength of the British Empire. Descriptions of the events in newspapers and correspondence recounted the excitement, the participatory feel, and the extreme pride these calendar days developed among participants and spectators. Two months prior to the first appearance of a hanging stamp master, colonial port towns celebrated the King's Birthday with fervor. In Charleston, South Carolina, the day included a morning parade of the local militia, followed by an "elegant dinner" for political notaries and clergy, a noontime discharge of cannon fire from the fort and vessels, and, in the evening, "illuminations and other demonstrations of joy . . . in a manner becoming . . . the loyal subjects of the best of kings."[24] In its yearly celebration, the town of Boston engaged in similar public displays of loyalty and patriotism, first parading and mustering all the militia and troops, who "performed their several Exercises in the Training-Field; after which the whole marched into King-street, where three Vollies were fired by each . . . followed by a Discharge of Field Pieces . . . the Guns at Castle William, and at the two Batteries in Town." After the display of British martial power, the "Company of Cadets provided a sumptuous Dinner at the Bunch of Grapes" for politicians and prominent gentlemen, which was followed by a gathering "at Faneuil-Hall, where his Majesty's and other loyal Healths were drank; and the whole conducted with great Decency and good Order."[25] The repetition and public ritual of the King's Birthday, in ports stretching from New London to Savannah, contained a pattern of celebration—the muster of the militia, the discharge of cannon, the sharing of oaths, and the honoring of the king's good health and imperial good fortune. These public gatherings served a recognizable integrative function in the British Empire, binding together scattered individuals by expressing both imperial knowledge and affiliation. Recounted in correspondence and reported in newspapers, these ritualized expressions of loyalty collapsed the geographic distance for colonists eager to view themselves as full members of the British Empire.

British subjects abroad expressed their close connection to their home islands on the streets through their ritual actions and ceremonial displays. Homes also served as sites of patriotic display. On traditional calendar days, families illuminated detailed paper figures of the royal family in windows visible to the processions and passers-by on the street. As well, families purchased and displayed prints, busts, and images commemorating great patriots and military victories. The consumer revolution included an expanding market for goods associated with the royal family, ranging from cloth marketed as the latest color spotted at Court to wax busts of the king and his children. In selecting, purchasing, and displaying products associated with the royal family in their colonial homes, individuals and families expressed a close connection with their monarch and asserted their identity as fellow Britons.

British colonists possessed an array of accessible rituals, material culture, and symbols to perform their partisan preferences and display themselves as Britons concerned with the latest political developments in England. The flourishing of newspapers cemented a broad public sense of close involvement in English political affairs. Colonists followed with particular fascination news from London about the cause of radical John Wilkes.[26] Colonial newspapers printed lengthy accounts of the public's response to the arrest and trials of Wilkes and his supporters. When crowds assembled in London, colonial newspapers provided reports from their correspondents and reprinted news from metropolitan papers. One account, printed in the *London Evening Post* and reprinted in several colonial newspapers, described the scene surrounding "Mr. Williams the bookseller" as he faced the pillory for reprinting the scandalous North Briton No. 45, in which, as it "turned out, he seemed rather to enjoy a triumph than undergo a punishment." Colonists learned that the guilty party, Mr. Williams arrived "at the appointed hour" for his punishment, only to find "thousands of spectators . . . many" of whom the newspaper reported "diverted themselves with a boot, a Scotch bonnet, and an axe all tied together on a rope fixed to ladders." The boot—that direct critique of the influence of Lord Bute—was set on fire "but not blazing with sufficient expedition," the paper reported; "the foot was cut off . . . and tossed among the people." As he passed his time on the pillory, the friends of Mr. Williams "who could get near him, filled their glasses and drank bumpers to the King George, Wilkes, Williams, and Liberty," periodically lifting a glass to his mouth. Upon learning of this event, partisan colonists discussed the proceedings and then echoed this exact toast, raising their glasses to participate in a show of delayed solidarity.[27]

The actions and symbols of the English Wilkes crowds became central in the anti-stamp displays. For colonial activists, the Stamp Act represented the most odious piece of legislation in an array of imperial reforms launched following the Seven Years' War. Many considered the cause of Wilkes and their own struggles for representative rule two sides of the same coin and, as such, attempted to unite their grievances both in written pamphlets and on the streets. Designed to communicate across the British Empire the dire threat to constitutional principles posed by the recent parliamentary legislation and reforms, colonial planners and participants employed widely understood, popular, and recognizable symbols to broadcast their grievances and solicit action. The constant presence of the boot, for example, at effigy displays and in political cartoons (see figure 8.1, where a boot floats in the upper right quadrant) provided a transatlantic criticism, tying together disparate protests in London and the American colonies.[28] The political symbols resonated with imperial audiences, and their use served as a handy method to build the perception of a widespread, transatlantic movement and the unity of public opinion, collapsing the separation between colonial grievances and metropolitan politics.

In the campaign for repeal, imperial public and private opinion mattered deeply to the colonial cause. Persuading powerful figures in England to act on their behalf required building a diverse coalition of supporters ranging from members of Parliament and ministers to city merchants and tradesmen. Colonial strategies of dissent shifted directly with the reception of street actions by English power brokers and publics. Colonists protesting the Stamp Act were eager to gauge English opinion and reaction to colonial effigy displays. Newspapers regularly published letters designed to provide a barometer of English sentiment. Colonial periodicals delighted in reporting news of a growing coalition: "[W]e hear that several Petitions have been presented to his Majesty" in support of our cause, including signatures from "a considerable Number of the principal Merchants of the City of London, all of which loudly complain."[29] Despite the best efforts of colonists to collapse the geographic distance between themselves and metropolitan politics, the newspapers regularly misinformed their readers with false information and rumor. The *Pennsylvania Gazette* mistakenly reported on April 25, 1765, for example, that the Stamp Act "has been greatly misrepresented in all our Papers. . . . The Bill having been most strenuously opposed . . . passed but by a small Majority, and contrary to the general Sense of the People in England."[30] Such rosy reports created a sense of widespread imperial approval of crowd actions, encouraging colonial optimism about the possibility of repeal.[31] Even following "repeated bad Accounts from America" of effigy displays and crowd disorder, anti-stamp colonists took heart from the reprinting of "A Letter from London," which stated, "I have the Pleasure to tell you, that it is generally believed that the new Ministry will repeal the Stamp-Act . . . for my own Part, I make no Doubt of it."[32] Such false or exaggerated information strengthened a sense among many colonists of their power and potential to influence the direction of imperial legislation and regulation.

Negative opinions of the anti-stamp action appeared only sporadically in colonial newspapers. Accounts warned that the actions and writings of some American colonists "will oblige the government here to think of steps that may check such haughty republican spirits," particularly since "the people of England . . . have long beheld the difference between the taxes they are . . . to pay and those paid in America."[33] As effigy protests effectively rendered enforcement of the stamp duty impossible, colonists learned slowly of the widespread disapproval of their actions but the effectiveness of the coalition-building strategy. An "Extract of a letter from a principal house in England to a gentleman in New-York" reported the economic effect of effigies: "[T]he present situation of the colonies is really alarming to every person who had large sums to come from them." The closing of ports due to the lack stamped paper or officials caused

English traders to "feel the force of the late act," as commerce is "stopped with you, and trade, the basis and foundation of England's wealth, is entirely shut up. We dread the consequence, and know not to what fatality we are destined."[34]

Alongside the increasing reports of negative English reaction to colonial street protests were lengthy descriptions of the riots and unrest in England and Ireland. In the months before the effigy displays in North American ports, colonists had read of London mobs, "breaking the Windows and making Riots at some Master Weavers, who are reported to have foreign Silks in their Custody." Before anti-stamp colonists' attacks on houses to locate stamped paper, London mobs "assembled in Bloomsbury-Square, and pulled down the Pales . . . after which another Mob assembled before the House of Mr. Mercer . . . the Windows of which they broked throughout."[35] Published days before the first wave of effigy displays in American ports, colonial newspapers printed descriptions of crowd gatherings by the weavers who assembled "by Beat of Drum, in Spitalfields . . . from whence they proceeded . . . to Westminster," where they "stopped the Carriages of the members, as they went to the House, praying them to take Pity on the poor Weavers." Since they were apparently unmoved by the "Decorous" gathering, "a Message was delivered them from the Lords, signifying that they could not proceed to the Reconsideration of their Grievances, 'till next Session." That night, unsatisfied with the parliamentary response, "the Mob were so unruly, they tore up the very Pavement to supply them with Stones to pelt the Guards."[36]

The news accounts of the Spitalfield weavers provided for colonists not only an example of public crowd action, but also insights on how the king and British politicians would interpret such assemblies. In London, the first sign of the mob quickly drew together the "the First Troop of Horse-Guards . . . a Party of Horse-Grenadiers, and three Companies of the Foot-Guards, all under Arms" to "prevent any Tumult."[37] The king issued a proclamation "for the suppressing of Riots, Tumults, and unlawful Assemblies" in direct response to the "tumultuous and riotous Mob."[38] When rumor spread that the weavers would march again, "proper precautions were taken to prevent their joining and marching in bodies, by placing a strong guard . . . to prevent any riots or obstructions to the Members or Peers."[39] Fearful of metropolitan response, many anti-stamp advocates hoped to draw a clear distinction between colonial crowd action and the English mobbing spirit. Some colonists advocating repeal feared association with the Spitalfield weavers, preferring to describe their gatherings as comprising people of many classes and trades or directly contrasting the constitutional claims of colonial actions with the weaver's economic demands. For others, the dual riots and assemblies in London and Boston provided evidence of a common, "Great Discontent" that "prevails, as well in England and America."[40] Writing as "Humphrey Ploughjogger" in the *Boston Gazette* October 14, 1765, John Adams directly linked the causes and disorders, preferring that "the Spittlefield [*sic*] weavers should pull down all the houses in old England, and knock the brains out of all the wicked men there, than this country should lose their liberty."[41] Concerned for positive British opinion, from August 1765 to May 1766 colonists soliciting repeal redoubled their efforts to contain the violence, shifted strategies to defend the legitimacy of the crowd actions, and emphasized the symbolic, peaceful nature of the public displays.

Attuned to their transatlantic audience, colonists expressing hatred of the Stamp Act constructed elaborate public displays to simultaneously educate their communities, render the legislation inert, communicate their shared British identity, and persuade Parliament to repeal the legislation. To convey their message at home and abroad, supporters recognized the necessary steps to justify street actions, describing in detail failed attempts to work through traditional channels of recourse.[42] Historians tend to consider the Stamp Act protests an explosion, but colonial advocates of repeal painted a portrait of the long months of petitioning and campaigning that passed before the effigies appeared. Anti-stamp colonists believed that if they demonstrated that they had exhausted all other methods of redress, English traditions of rough music and political protest justified their extralegal actions in the street as the only recourse available to disenfranchised subjects.[43]

In constructing and reporting the effigy displays, both advocates and critics described the detailed messages communicated by each spectacle and the complexity of construction. Displays suspended "20 and 30 feet from the ground" required skill and craftsmanship, as did quickly dismantling them to parade through town. The precise builders are impossible to unmask, since surviving sources provide only sporadic references to the involvement of particular trades or tradesmen; they might merely mention, for example, the use of ships' nails and cordage for the gallows or the clothing worn by the hanging corpse. While unwilling or unable to reveal the identity of those who constructed the displays, reports detailed the symbols and written messages explaining the nature, purpose, and legitimacy of a gallows scene. Effigy displays encouraged repetition between towns to emphasize shared views. In New London, the distributor of stamps hung with the typical accompaniment of "a boot on one of the shoulders, and the devil . . . looking out of the same," and "we hear from Norwich" the effigy was "manifested . . . in the same manner as the above."[44] The effigy display provided ample room for both simple and elaborate political messages—ranging from "No Stamps!" to the lengthy statement affixed to the display in Charleston, which expressed "the sense of a people, unshaken in their loyalty, but tenacious of their liberty," who believed strongly "that all internal duties impressed upon them without the consent of their immediate or even virtual representatives was grievous, oppressive, and unconstitutional; and that . . . admiralty courts in America, tended to subvert one of their most darling legal rights and privileges, that of trial by jury."[45] Through effigy spectacles, supporters hoped to communicate with Britons around the Atlantic basin.

Detailed who's who guides accompanied many of the accounts, describing the precise targets and rationale of the display. The *Connecticut Courant* reported both the figures and their crimes: "Mr. G[ren]v[i]lle dressed in scarlet Robes, with a Boot at his Shoulder, out of which appear'd the Devil, presenting him the Stamp Act," hung beside "Lord C[l]y[d]e, and Gen M[u]rr[a]y," both "dressed in laced Cloathes and Hats," each wearing a label that described his crime, "the First for being one of the principal Authors of the Stamp-Act, the Second for having endeavored to enforce it . . . and the Third for having executed the first Stamp'd instrument that has appeared in this Place."[46] Clarity of message was critical for the repeal efforts. The display in New Brunswick included "Papers denoting his horrid crime . . . affized to his breast, and from his mouth hung labels expressing such words and sentiments as may well be supposed to come from the lips of such an abandoned miscreant." For casual observers or royal officials, the message was straightforward: "[M]ay such be the fate of every vile traitor . . . may they live despised! Die Unpitied!" The detailed messages conveyed "to the neighboring colonies, that neither the dirty insinuation of pimps and panders, nor the frowns of power, have been as yet, able to extinguish the spirit of liberty in the province of New-Jersey," nor the spread of the "patriotic fire" elsewhere.[47]

Meant to hang before the largest possible audience, effigies appeared primarily on days when the maximum number of people gathered in the streets of colonial towns. Colonists advocating repeal recognized the opportunity provided by market, court, and election days, when individuals from nearby towns and counties visited the larger ports. In Newport, Rhode Island, constructors of the effigy display maximized the visual impact through both timing and location, choosing their display to coincide with "a Town Meeting for the Choice of Representatives" when "Effigies were carried through Main Street with Halters around their necks . . . to a Gallows previously erected near the Court House, where they were hung up, at the very Instant the people were choosing their Representatives."[48] Fearful that advance public notice of effigy displays would invite measures by royal officials and militias to prevent public protest, descriptions of effigies routinely describe the "surprise" and "Sudden appearance" of the gallows scene. These colonial flash mobs calculatingly utilized days when colonists gathered for other reasons as an opportunity to educate, recruit, and intimidate. This proved an effective way to gather a crowd with limited need for advance warning or coordination. Whether their attendance was intentional or casual, bringing together the largest possible audience locally enabled advocates of repeal to broadcast imperially a false sense of the unity of colonial public opinion.

Within weeks, this pattern of appropriating public days for protest had become so clear that Lieutenant Governor Francis Fauquier wrote with apprehension that he hoped "we shall weather the Storm which seems ready to burst" during the upcoming general court days in Virginia.[49] Fauquier wrote to London that he hoped Williamsburg would "remain Quiet" as the town filled with "Jurors and Witnesses from the Back Country" and even "wish[ed] the Winds" would detain the arrival of the stamp distributor "'till the Tryals of the Criminals at the General Court were over. And the Town rid of that class of people who attend."[50] From August to November, reports of effigies described an increasingly bolder information campaign, ranging from widespread "hints" that "the effigy of some certain person were preparing to be exhibited on Tuesday" to public notices given "by about a Dozen Persons . . . ten days ago . . . that they were then preparing three Effigies."[51] Once colonists recognized the pattern of inaction by governors, militias, and royal armed forces, the effigy displays and parades became more openly publicized.

Protesting colonists quickly appropriated traditional days of patriotic celebration to demand repeal. As a traditional day of effigy display, Pope's Day provided an ideal opportunity for public gatherings and political messaging in towns stretching from Boston to Basseterre on the island of St. Christopher, where "on the fifth of November, the Inhabitants had a grand Entertainment . . . when the Effigies of several Persons were hung up and burnt."[52] For spectators and participants, effigy displays provided an entertainment reminiscent of the yearly grand processions. Planners adapted traditions of effigy construction, as well as the accompanying elements of celebratory days to excite and attract a crowd. Visual cues throughout the town peaked curiosity and recruited spectators to witness and join anti-stamp crowds. In several port towns, including Philadelphia, protest spread to the harbor as "all the vessels . . . hoisted colours half mast high" in "sincere mourning of the approaching loss of LIBERTY."[53] In Boston, parents complained that the "hussa's of the mobs, the rattleing of drums, the clamour of the soldiers . . . and the continual hubbub" lured all their children away from daily chores and activities, lamenting that "[a]s for James, wee cannot keep him from amongst the hurly burly."[54] The spectacle of effigies enticed colonial residents to witness the actions.

The loud sounds of protest touched each part of town. Echoing the traditional sounds of communal gatherings—ranging from the beating of drums signaling a crowd in Philadelphia to bells tolling the death knell for liberty in Annapolis—effigy spectacles attracted audiences and encouraged participation.[55] Crowds often signaled success with loud, celebratory music. In Charleston, following the public resignation of the stamp officials, "the air rang with the musick of bells, drums, hautboys, violins, huzza's, firing of cannon &c &c." Summoned, the growing crowd followed "the flag . . . being carried before them, the music continuing" to "Mr. Dillon's tavern" to "take some refreshment there."[56] Joyous music served as an indicator that the crisis was over, a fact that could be celebrated by the entire community regardless of political opinion, creating a fresh opportunity for a new, diverse, and even larger gathering.

Repurposing patriotic days often required serious alterations in traditional crowd membership. In Boston, the yearly saturnalia and effigy parades of Pope's Day regularly featured free and enslaved African Americans on the street and Bostonians in blackface. In prior years, Pope's Day had devolved into annual, organized street brawls where "the servants and Negroes would disguise themselves" and "armed with clubs . . . engage each other with great violence." News reports of Pope's Day, November 5, 1765, described a surprising break with this tradition of disorder. On that otherwise notoriously violent public day, the whites of Boston peacefully drew together under the banner of "lovely unity." The carefully choreographed spectacle passed without incident: two sets of "pageantry representing the pope" now included characters to protest the Stamp Act, "effigies signifying tyranny, oppression, slavery." The elaborate displays were carried, per tradition, from the city's north and south neighborhoods, and upon reaching one another the participants greeted each other with "three huzzas . . . in a very ceremonial manner" before "proceeding to the tree of liberty." A display of both British patriotism and protest, the peaceful street theater of Pope's Day impressed the newspaper reporter. Searching for an explanation for the transformation, the author noted, "[T]o the honour of those concerned," even as "the spectators filled the streets; not a club was seen . . . nor was any Negro allowed to approach near the stage."[57] Control of the local audience and spectators—in print, if not in truth—enabled this anti-stamp advocate to broadcast a clear message across the empire of the restrained nature of colonial dissent and emphasize the legitimacy of the crowd.

On the ground, a gang of "100 or 150 men trained as regular as a military corps" followed the commands of shoemaker Ebenezer Mackintosh. Governor Francis Bernard described these patrols intimidating royal forces and policing the spectacle with cudgels. Their effectiveness at segregating traditional effigy displays reveals invisible networks of crowd communication that clearly broadcast warnings of the violence awaiting anyone attempting to cross the color line and approach the stage.[58] For Boston's blacks, absence served as an intelligent strategy to avoid a dangerous white crowd. By actively excluding black participants from this traditional day of power reversals, colonial whites delineated precisely who they believed could claim the rights to British liberty.

Controlling the appearance in crowds of free and enslaved blacks—as well as Indians, itinerant sailors, and women—advocates and planners attempted to sweep away the central demographic differences between colonies and metropole. Their efforts to manipulate the members of the crowd were directly countered by reports that described blacks in Charleston joining in the shouts of "Liberty!"[59] London officials also learned that "some Negroes" played a pivotal role in St. Christopher, rescuing the royal stamp distributor from "certain death" by an enraged mob.[60] As colonists and royal officials solicited imperial support for their constitutional cause, written descriptions of street crowds regularly emphasized or entirely erased African Americans and itinerant sailors from the scenes of protest, revealing a racial and class discourse closely tied to political debates. The constitutional legitimacy of crowd action was directly tied to the demographic constitution of the mob.

On the street, colonists costumed themselves in "sailors habits" and wore soot and blackface, evoking a particular set of racist, bigoted images that resonated imperially and derived from cultural productions, including the theater. Describing their protests to an imperial audience, colonial authors and royal officials both reflected and informed a rising tide of anti-black racism in England, where a growing number of people of color and a popular culture saturated with "grotesque racial imagery" predisposed readers to associate blackness with violence.[61] This association of crime and disorderly behavior made blacks as political icons and caricatures particularly useful scapegoats when a community preferred not to accept responsibility—or punishment—for its extralegal actions.

No one paid more attention to the emerging patterns of effigy displays than those most likely to find their bodies swinging from the gallows, their businesses and homes attacked, and their lives threatened. Effigy displays were fundamentally violent. In the English tradition of rough music, the hanging straw body served as a proxy to inform the target of his abhorrence to the community and his future extralegal punishment.[62] Individuals connected—or rumored to be connected—to the stamped paper recognized the effigy as a signal of more severe attacks later that night and in the following days. As rumors and news spread quickly of the violent events in Boston from August 15 to 26, stamp distributors, royal officials, and their associates in a variety of port cities, "well knowing the Dispositions of the People towards all King's Officers," feared for their lives "from an inflamed Mulltitude."[63] Many sought shelter and "quitted town" for country estates or fled to the protection of nearby military and naval instillations. Zachary Hood, the appointed stamp master for Maryland, left Annapolis with such dispatch "hurried on by his fear" that he "rode his Horse to death, and hardly gave himself time to breath till he got under the protection of the cannon of Fort-George, in New York."[64]

Anti-stamp activists hoped to render the legislation impossible to enforce throughout the colonies in British North America. In newspapers and private correspondence, anti-stamp advocates lauded the effectiveness of effigy displays in securing the resignation of local stamp officials.[65] The perceptions and fears of violence attending the effigy spectacles were so great that from August to November 1765 a number of officials publicly announced their resignations before the crowd could hang their likenesses. Explaining his rationale for resigning to a London correspondent, New York distributor James McEvers predicted the crowd's actions, "as I have a Large Store of Goods and Seldom Less than Twenty thousand Pounds Currency in it with which the Populace would make sad Havock."[66] Prior to the public hanging, planners solicited officials, inquiring if stamp distributors, like Augustus Johnston, "would resign the Office." If the target refused, the "Gentlemen . . . Informed me," the question would be asked again "the next day, and that the Mob were determined to oblige me to resign." When he again refused, the stamp distributor was warned: "[T]hey did not think it would be safe for me . . . and advised me to leave . . . and secure myself privately at some distance." One of the rare stamp distributors determined to hold his post, Johnston learned the next morning that although his effigy spectacle "had been the publick Conversation for many days," the "Authority in the Town . . . would not do their Duty." Like many stamp officials, Johnston left town hours before his likeness was hung and burned "amidst the Acclamations of great Numbers of People . . . with all the Marks of Infamy that the most inveterate Malice could invent."[67]

Determined to follow the success of other towns, anti-stamp colonists pursued their targets until repeal was secured, often over multiple evenings and with increasingly violent threats. Believing the display to be a single-day event, Johnston returned home, only to discover that the mob had grown and intensified, for as "I was setting with my Family . . . in hopes that we should have no more Disturbance" a "Messenger came to my House in great Haste & informed me that the Mob had again Collected" that following night at eight o'clock. As the crowd dismantled houses nearby, Johnston retreated aboard the HMS *Cygnet*, recognizing that if "I was seen by the Mob they would oblige me to resign, or deprive me of my Life." The next morning, realizing that "not only myself and Family" but also "my friends" faced the crowd's wrath, Johnston finally resigned—"I signed a paper purporting, that I would not accept the Office unless the Inhabitants of the Town consented thereto." The crowd then "compelled" him further to pen a letter to the Lords of the Treasury, which "I complied with for the same reasons which induced me to resign." Thus securing the resignation, the gathering celebrated their preservation of liberty, broadcasting widely their success and "good order" in newspapers and correspondence.[68]

At times, anti-stamp colonists dispensed with the displays of proxy violence entirely. While most attacks targeted property and the straw-filled likeness of the stamp master, the exceptional moment of imperial crisis and community disruption could quickly escalate into bodily harm. The crowd that gathered on the "Island of New-Providence" provided one of the most bone-chilling attacks of the imperial crisis. With the distributor "flatly refusing" to resign his commission, the crowd "told him . . . . they would bury him alive." When he refused again, the assembly prepared a coffin, "forced him into it, fastened on the Cover, and lowered the living Lump to the Bottom of a Grave dug for that purpose and slowly threw after it about two Bushels of Dirt." As he lay contemplating his death by mob, the stamp distributor "then consented to resign his odious Employment, and the People . . . drew him up, heard him re-deliver his Resignation in a more articulate Manner, gave him his LIBERTY, and heartily congratulated him on his Restoration to the fresh air."[69] Tales of this ritual violence, public shaming, and forced renunciations filled official reports to London, communicating the clear message that the stamp duty could not be enforced, but also creating a lasting impression of disorderly mob rule throughout the American colonies.

By mid-November 1765, the dramatic, violent events in Newport, New York, and Boston had provided terrifying examples for stamp officials facing colonial demands. When Nova Scotia's stamp distributor discovered a note slipped under his door demanding that he "follow the Example of Sundry of the Stamp Men in Other Colonies," he clearly understood what the mob envisioned when they threatened, "Your Ruin is designed if you don't Resign that damnable Office."[70] While the attacks on persons and property had become "notorious" throughout the American colonies, many stamp officials arrived directly from British ports to quickly discover the "sense of the people" for themselves. As his ship pulled into the outer harbor in Boston, New Hampshire's stamp distributor learned with "great Surprise" that "the whole Continent is in a State of Confusion and Disorder." The coastal pilot warned George Meserve that his safety on land could not be guaranteed until he resigned his commission and relinquished the stamped paper. Detained on his ship for two days, the stamp distributor publicly declared his resignation and received a warm welcome in Boston, complete with an entertainment at the Exchange tavern.[71] While effective locally, rising levels of violence appeared rebellious and chaotic, calling into question the legitimacy of crowd actions.

By November 1765, the violent attacks of the previous three months prompted both supporters and critics of the street protests to wonder aloud "what lengths the People who have made such a beginning may go to render the Act of parliament ineffectual."[72] Anti-stamp colonists received with pleasure the exaggerated news that by October 28 "we are informed there is not one of the Person appointed, from New Hampshire to Georgia, that will execute" the Stamp Act. The resignation of the stamp officials, however, was only half of the process of preventing enforcement. The stamped paper became the next target of effigy display.[73] Through violent threats—including displays of hanging, burning paper—the stamps quickly transformed into "a Commodity no Body knows what to do with, and are more . . . . dangerous" to handle "than . . . Pestilence."[74] Governors across the colonies reported a growing sense

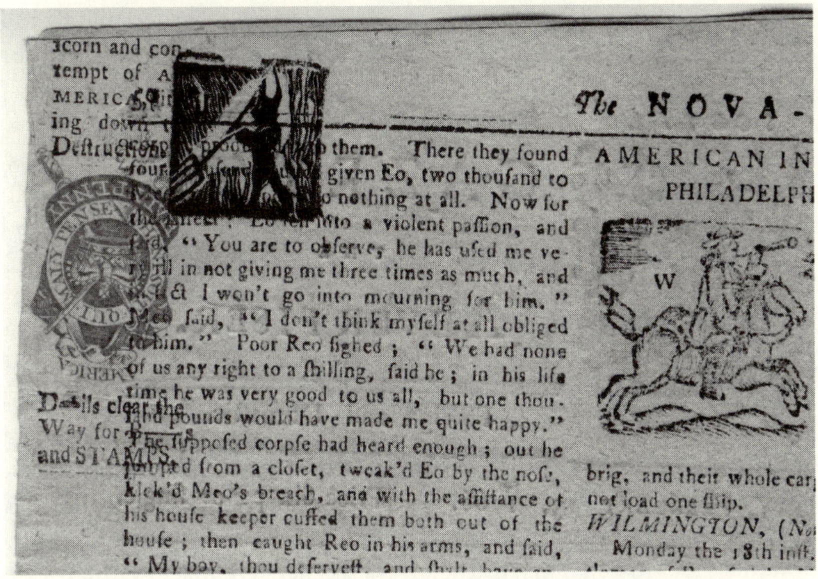
scorn and con-
tempt of A-
MERICA, pitch-
ing down to
Destruction.

Devils clear the
Way for B—s
and STAMPS.

them. There they found ... given Eo, two thousand to ... nothing at all. Now for ... into a violent passion, and ... "You are to observe, he has used me very ill in not giving me three times as much, and ... I won't go into mourning for him." Meo said, "I don't think myself at all obliged to him." Poor Reo sighed; "We had none of us any right to a shilling, said he; in his life time he was very good to us all, but one thousand pounds would have made me quite happy." The supposed corpse had heard enough; out he jumped from a closet, tweak'd Eo by the nose, kick'd Meo's breech, and with the assistance of his house keeper cuffed them both out of the house; then caught Reo in his arms, and said, "My boy, thou deservest, and shalt have ...

The NOVA-
AMERICAN IN
PHILADELPH

brig, and their whole car
not load one ship.
WILMINGTON, (No
Monday the 18th inst.

Figure 2.1. In addition to hanging stamped papers from the rafters of taverns and burning them, colonists affixed counter-stamps to them. The counter-stamp on this Halifax newspaper, reportedly designed by Isaiah Thomas as an apprentice printer in Nova Scotia, features a woodcut devil stabbing the royal stamp with his pitchfork. Above the royal stamp is the legend "[Behold me, the] scorn and contempt of AMERICA pitching down to Destruction." Below the royal stamp is the warning "Devils clear the Way for B—s and STAMPS." Courtesy of the American Antiquarian Society.

"that if the Stamp paper was to arrive here & be landed" no power could "preserve it from being burnt."[75]

With the local resignation of stamp distributors, communities turned increasingly outward, gauging the commitment of other towns to the anti-stamp cause. The arrival of stamps from fellow British colonies became moments for ritual, public shaming. In Philadelphia, a crowd assembled at the rumored arrival of a mass of stamped paper from Halifax, only to discover "the ream proved to be only a half a sheet, with eighteen pence worth of oppression." Surrendered by the owner, "the half sheet was . . . suspended and burnt amidst the acclamations of a great number of gentlemen." The "stamped news-paper from Halifax" received the same public treatment, first "hung up in the coffee-house" beside "labels, on one side, Liberty, Property, and no Stamps . . . On the other side, Liberty triumphant and Oppression in chains," and that night, "the paper was set on fire, accompanied with loud huzzas" (figure 2.1).[76] The indignities and "insults" suffered by the stamped paper paled in comparison with the violence perpetrated against its distributors and holders, signaling a shift toward symbolic displays by January 1766.

Throughout the Stamp Act Crisis, participants in street effigies and demonstrations demanded their rights as fellow Britons. Laboring to build an imperial coalition to secure repeal, the crowds at ritual effigies universally articulated a shared British identity. Individual members of these crowds became a central focus in the debate over the legitimacy of colonial political arguments. Eager to criticize effigy spectacles as disorderly mob rule, opponents portrayed colonial streets as sites of mixing and the leveling of diverse individuals. Royal and stamp officials emphasized the violent activities of a motley crew of "saucy boys, negroes and molattoes, Irish teagues and outlandish jack tarrs" run amok. The accounts described a dangerous cooperation across classes, outlining the quick descent into an uncontrollable mobocracy. Tales of colonial difference resonated with English audiences, who viewed the colonies as mixing places, distinct from and increasingly repugnant to the home isles. In all, opponents of the protests portrayed the colonial street as a dangerous site of interaction, inclusion, and unrest, a place where orderly gatherings quickly devolved into criminal mobs involving the "lowest sorts."[77]

As reports of negative English reaction to colonial effigies circulated, anti-stamp colonists became increasingly concerned about the presence and activities of wide swaths of the colonial population. Attuned to imperial perceptions and opinion, this rapidly evolving debate over the legitimacy of colonial crowds led to shifts in protest strategies and attempts to control and limit membership in these "constitutional assemblies." In each public gathering, advocates emphasized the "good order," "chearfulness," and "peace" maintained throughout, often glossing over or erasing violent realities. With the stamp officials in retreat and the stamped paper removed from circulation, published descriptions of street actions reveal a growing determination to broadcast a revised imperial political message about precisely who deserved equal rights as British subjects.

The first hanging effigy in Boston on August 15 provided a new, aggressive model of colonial protest, and the events surrounding Pope's Day that November signaled a change in strategy. A new model emerged for a "constitutional" protest that emphasized genteel participation and limited crowd involvement.[78] Whereas the spectacle surrounding Andrew

Oliver's effigy used theater to draw participants into the action, encouraged crowd participation, and lasted from the early morning late into the night, the rise of "grand Entertainments" such as the "Unity Feast" provided an opportunity to stage a parade followed by a private event, all ending by early evening. In Boston, the November 5 parade drew clear lines between participant and spectator, even using force to segregate the crowd and broadcast the message of limited dissent.

Eager to divorce themselves from the unruly actions of August 26, participants and planners in the November 5 parade emphasized the "good Conduct" of the day. To celebrate, organizers threw a "very grand Supper" days later, moving the spectacle from the street into the tavern. Inside, the "conductors" ordered and sorted those invited—"having discriminated the Company into several Classes, they took their Rooms and Seats respectively"—with "some of the principal Merchants in Town, and other Gentlemen" dining together separate from the remainder who "join[ed] together with Heart and Hand." Channeling the energy of the streets inside limited the unintended and unwelcome local audiences—including African Americans, Native Americans, unruly youths, and itinerant sailors—who had become so closely associated imperially with the violent, disorderly Boston mob. Denying their place at the table established from the very early moments of imperial crisis a contest that would be continually fought on the streets over the contours of the body politic. At the same time, the anti-stamp activists communicated across the British Empire the involvement of the economic interests of the city most connected to imperial trade, suggesting a new course to influence and persuade imperial power brokers. This would inaugurate a strategy of economic protest involving the interested, propertied members of town, exclude the itinerant and marginal members of the community, and ultimately evolve into non-importation associations.

The contest waged on the street and page over the participation of individuals in colonial effigy displays and parades raises a central question in crowd studies: What were the experience and degree of social mixing and interaction on the street? Whereas past historians use these sources to emphasize the camaraderie and common cause among members of the crowd, the surviving sources point to the wide diversity of engagement and experiences within the assembly.[79] Early effigy displays and parades may have provided spaces of mixing and interaction, but they increasingly became restricted events that upheld existing social hierarchies. That both opponents and advocates of the effigy displays often counted spectators and bystanders as members of crowd action, actively segregated and denied participation to others, and manipulated their texts to further their position imperially suggests the difficulty of precisely knowing the nature of crowd participation in the Stamp Act Crisis. The sheer variety of experiences within the Stamp Act crowds indicates that individuals understood this exceptional period of imperial crisis and community disruption in a variety of ways, but largely as a passing moment. Few individuals in the crowd formed lasting political affiliations, and those who participated or watched took away a variety of lessons. The celebrations on the street after the repeal of the Stamp Act expressed the communal conviction that, in their protests and demands for repeal, the colonists had effectively persuaded a large enough imperial coalition to influence their empire, renewing their faith and security as proud British subjects.

Notes

1. *South-Carolina Gazette*, September 28, 1765; London, British Library, Stowe MSS 265 f. 62–63.

2. From England, the stamped paper was sent to major regional ports, such as Boston, Newport, and Charleston. There, customs and stamp officials were instructed to distribute the papers to smaller towns in the region. The protests in major port towns often led royal officials to fear the destruction of the stamped paper and prompted the storage of the paper in safe places, including forts and naval vessels. This effectively prevented the distribution of papers regionally, leaving many communities in the difficult position of having to choose how to act once the Stamp Act when into effect on November 1, 1765. For a list of the ports see "Account of the Ships by which the Stamps were transmitted to America and the Times of Putting them on Board," Stowe MSS 265 f. 205–206.

3. "Rough music" is the general English term for the variety of ritual punishments that communities used to attack violators of the "moral economy." This extralegal popular justice provided a way for communities to publicly shame individuals deemed aberrant or obnoxious. Offenses included the violation of sexual mores (including rape, wife beating, husband nagging), but could also include economic issues such as price gouging leading to food rioting. The practices have a number of names, including "skimmington," "riding the stang," "tar-and-feathering," and, in France, "charivari." For the purposes of this chapter, I focus primarily on the tradition of effigy creation, display, parade, and destruction. See Alfred F. Young, *Liberty Tree: Ordinary People and the American Revolution* (New York: New York University Press, 2006), 42–43, 150; Steven J. Stewart, "Skimmington in the Middle and New England Colonies," in *Riot and Revelry in Early America*, ed. William Pencak, Matthew Dennis, and Simon P. Newman (University Park: Pennsylvania State University Press, 2002), 64; Bryan Palmer, "Discordant Music: Charivari and White Capping in North America," *Labor / Le Traveilleur* 1 (September 1978), 5–62. For a transnational perspective see the work begun by Natalie Zemon Davis, "The Reasons of Misrule: Youth Groups and Chari-

vari in Sixteenth-Century France," *Past and Present* 50 (February 1971), 41–75, and E. P. Thompson's work, which builds upon her study, ch. 8 of *Customs in Common* (New York: New Press, 1991).

4. My research and interpretation build upon past studies of the aggressive, engaged disputes over the body politic described in the work of Linda Colley, Nicholas Rogers, and Kathleen Wilson, who demonstrate the variety of ways in which British identity was forged through public debate. See Linda Colley, *Britons: Forging the Nation: 1707–1837* (New Haven, CT: Yale University Press, 1992); Nicholas Rogers, *Crowds, Culture, and Politics in Georgian Britain* (New York: Oxford University Press, 1998); and Kathleen Wilson, *The Sense of the People: Politics, Culture and Imperialism in England, 1715–1785* (New York: Cambridge University Press, 1995).

5. *Boston Evening Post*, September 2, 1765; Governor Francis Bernard to Earl of Halifax, August 22, 1765, Bernard Papers, IV, 144–148, Harvard College Library. The events in Boston are derived from the accounts of Governor Francis Bernard and Stamp Master Andrew Oliver, in Stowe MSS 265 f. 15–22, 54–56; National Archives, formerly Public Record Office, Kew, London Treasury 1/ 439 f. 18, 24.

6. *Boston Gazette*, August 19, 1765; *Boston Evening-Post*, August 19, 1765.

7. Stowe MSS 265 f. 15–22, 54–56; *Boston-Gazette and Country Journal*, August 19, 1765, suppl.; *Connecticut Courant*, August 26, 1765; *Boston Gazette*, August 19, 1765, suppl.; Dairy of John Rowe, August 14, 1765, Massachusetts Historical Society, *Proceedings*, 2d ser., 10 (1895), 61; Governor Bernard to Earl of Halifax, August 15, 16, 1765, Bernard Papers, IV, 137–144; Edmund S. Morgan and Helen M. Morgan, *The Stamp Act Crisis: Prologue to Revolution* (Chapel Hill: University of North Carolina Press for the Institute of Early American History and Culture, Williamsburg, VA, 1962), 128–130.

8. Much scholarly debate has centered on the rationality and irrationality of the mob, drawing upon the research of sociologist Gustave le Bon and the response by George Rudé. Little attention has been paid to spectators—to those on the margins of the crowd or those watching from above, throwing open their windows and witnessing these spectacles. Recent work on theater audiences suggests some way to consider divisions and clashing agendas of street assemblies.

9. *South Carolina Gazette*, June 8, 1765; *Pennsylvania Gazette*, June 20. 1765.

10. Governor Francis Bernard to the Lords Commissioners for Trade and Plantations, August 16, 1765, Stowe MSS 265 f. 18–20.

11. Ibid., f. 15–22, 54–56; T 1/ 439 f. 18, 24; *Boston Evening Post*, September 2, 1765; Governor Francis Bernard to Earl of Halifax, August 22, 1765, Bernard Papers, IV, 144–148.

12. Even in their excellent work, *The Stamp Act Crisis*, Edmund and Helen Morgan fall victim to the desire to determine who was "behind the curtain" and led the crowd; for example, they question who hired John Webber in Newport rather than consider his own motivations for action. For an excellent overview of consensus and conflict schools of crowd studies, see Thomas P. Slaughter, "Crowds in Eighteenth-Century America: Reflections and New Directions," *Pennsylvania Magazine of History and Biography* 115.1 (1991), 3–34; Lieutenant Governor Colden to the Secretary of State, November 5, 1765, Stowe MSS 264 f. 126–129.

13. George Rudé, *The Crowd in History: A Study of Popular Disturbances in France and England, 1730–1848* (London: Serif, 1964); E. P. Thompson, *The Making of the English Working Class* (New York: Vintage Books, 1966).

14. In addition to the works written or edited by Alfred F. Young, see Gary Nash, *Urban Crucible: The Northern Seaports and the Origins of the American Revolution* (Cambridge, MA: Harvard University Press, 1979); Dirk Hoerder, "Boston Leaders and Boston Crowds, 1765–1776," in *The American Revolution: Explorations in the History of American Radicalism*, ed. Alfred F. Young (DeKalb: Northern Illinois University Press, 1976), 235–236, 240; and Jesse Lemisch, "Jack Tar in the Streets: Merchant Seamen in the Politics of Revolutionary America," *William and Mary Quarterly* 25 (1968), 371–407.

15. Pauline Maier, *From Resistance to Revolution: Colonial Radicals and the Development of American Opposition to Britain, 1765–1776* (New York: W. W. Norton, 1991).

16. See T. H. Breen, *The Marketplace of Revolution: How Consumer Politics Shaped American Independence* (Oxford: Oxford University Press, 2004).

17. See Ronald Hoffman, "The 'Disaffected' in the Revolutionary South," in *The American Revolution*, ed. Young, 274–316; Michael A. McDonnell, *The Politics of War: Race, Class, and Conflict in Revolutionary Virginia* (Chapel Hill: University of North Carolina Press, 2007); John Shy, *A People Numerous and Armed: Reflections on the Military Struggle for American Independence* (Ann Arbor: University of Michigan Press, 1990).

18. "Extract of a Letter from Lebanon in Connecticut," *South Carolina Gazette*, September 28, 1765.

19. Stowe MSS 265 f. 15–22.

20. *Boston Gazette*, August 19, 1765; *Boston Gazette*, September 16, 1765.

21. *South Carolina Gazette*, September 21, 1765, 3; Carol Knight, *The American Colonial Press and the Townshend Crisis, 1766–770: A Study in Political Imagery* (Lewiston, NY: Edwin Mellen Press, 1990), 22, 24, 27, 29, 32, 46–49.

22. Andrew Oliver to Thomas Whately, September 2, 1765, Stowe MSS 265 f. 60.

23. Lieutenant Governor William Bull Jr. to Lords Commissioners for Trade and Plantations, November 3, 1765, Stowe MSS 264 f. 60.

24. *South Carolina Gazette*, June 8, 1765.

25. *Pennsylvania Gazette*, June 20, 1765.

26. See Pauline Maier, "John Wilkes and American Disillusionment with Britain," *William and Mary Quarterly* 20.3 (1963), 373–395.

27. *London Evening Post*, February 14, 1765; *Gazetteer and New Daily Advertiser* (London), February 15, 1765; *South Carolina Gazette*, April 13, 1765.

28. The reproduction of Wilkes symbols in colonial effigies and repetition in new locales demonstrate that colonists placed significant weight on communicating clearly over geographic space a common sentiment, indicating their membership in a wider movement to influence the course of empire. Colonists expanded upon this theme, painting the sole of the effigy's boot green, a reference to Minister Grenville. *South Carolina Gazette*, October 5, 1765.

29. *Pennsylvania Gazette* October 31, 1765.

30. *Pennsylvania Gazette* May 2, 1765.

31. As early as October 31, 1765, it was "generally reported the stamp act . . . would be repealed by the new ministry." *South Carolina and American General Gazette*, October 31, 1765.

32. *Connecticut Courant*, October 14, 1765.

33. *South Carolina Gazette*, July 20, 1765.

34. *South Carolina Gazetteer and Country Journal*, December 17, 1765. News of the uncertainty caused by the closing of mainland American ports (due in large part to the lack of stamped paper clearances) radiated from across the British Empire, particularly in the West Indies, where islands in the Leeward chain and Barbados began more aggressively lobbying for relief in Parliament.

35. *Pennsylvania Gazette,* July 25, 1765.

36. *Pennsylvania Gazette*, August 1, 1765; *South Carolina Gazette*, August 3, 1765.

37. *Pennsylvania Gazette*, August 1, 1765.

38. Ibid.; *Pennsylvania Gazette*, August 8, 1765.

39. *Pennsylvania Gazette*, August 8, 1765.

40. Many, in fact, recognized that street action in colonial towns could be more easily orchestrated, for there existed few military forces or resources to oppose crowd actions. *Connecticut Courant*, December 31, 1765.

41. *Boston Gazette*, October 14, 1765.

42. Newspapers reported that "the agents for the colonies . . . all of them having instructions to suggest the rights and privileges of the colonies," were requested "to learn if Petitions disputing that power" would find receptive audiences in Parliament and Whitehall. *Pennsylvania Gazette*, May 16, 1765; *South Carolina Gazette*, October 31, 1765.

43. *South-Carolina and American General Gazette*, July 24, 1765; George Saxby to the Commissioners of his Majesty's Stamp Duties, Stowe MS 265 f. 287–289.

44. *South Carolina Gazette*, September 21, 1765.

45. Ibid.

46. *Connecticut Courant*, December 31, 1765.

47. *South Carolina Gazetteer and Country Journal*, December 17, 1765.

48. Augustus Johnston to Commissioners of His Majesty's Stamps, August 31, 1765, T 1/439.

49. For an excellent look into court days, see A. G. Roeber, "Authority, Law, and Custom: The Rituals of Court Day in Tidewater, Virginia, 1720 to 1750," *William and Mary Quarterly* 37.1 (1980), 29–52.

50. Unfortunately for Governor Fauquier his hopes would be disappointed. George Mercer arrived on October 30, 1765, and was immediately requested to resign. Governor Fauquier had to intervene, "taking him by the arm" away from the crowd "safely through the awed assembly, to the accompaniment of angry murmurs" to the Governor's mansion. At some point in the night, Colonel Mercer resigned his commission. Fauquier would eventually join the ranks of a number of governors who opened the port to trade without stamps, as he grew concerned for the annual export of tobacco. Fauquier to Lords of Trade and Plantations, October 2 and November 3, 1765 Stowe MSS 265 f. 189b; Morgan and Morgan, *Stamp Act Crisis*, 161–162.

51. *South Carolina Gazette*, October 5, 1765; Augustus Johnson to Commissioners of His Majesty's Stamps, T 1/439 f. 9.1

52. *Connecticut Courant*, December 31, 1765.

53. *Connecticut Courant*, October 28, 1765.

54. "In the midst of this disorder and confusion" elicited by the excitement of the street, "[t]hers no getting them kept to their sett times of schooling, eating, going to be, rising in the morning." James Gordon to William Martin, September 1, 1765, Massachusetts Historical Society, *Proceedings* 2.13 (1900), 393; Morgan and Morgan, *The Stamp Act Crisis*, 134.

55. *South Carolina Gazette*, October 5, 1765.

56. *South Carolina Gazette*, October 31, 1765.

57. *Pennsylvania Gazette*, November 21, 1765. See Alfred F. Young, *Revolutionary Founders: Rebels, Radicals, and Reformers in the Making of the Nation* (New York: Vintage Books, 2012), 18–23; Nash, *Unknown American Revolution*, 18.

58. Bernard to Pownall, November 26, 1765, Sparks MSS, Letterbooks, V:1–23.

59. In Charleston, South Carolina, protesters in the anti-stamp procession quickly recognized the subversive possibilities for slave spectators at this moment of community disruption. As white crowds paraded through the streets shouting, "Liberty and No Stamp Tax!" a group of slaves joined with their own rough music, shouting "Liberty!" With the *South Carolina Gazette* closed indefinitely, a number of slaves took advantage of the suspension of runaway advertisements as an opportunity to claim their own liberty. See Sylvia R. Frey, *Water from the Rock: Black Resistance in a Revolutionary Age* (Princeton, NJ: Princeton University Press, 1991), 9, 51; Peter H. Wood, *Black Majority: Negroes in Colonial South Carolina from 1670 through the Stono Rebellion* (New York: Alfred A. Knopf, 1975), 69–70; Philip D. Morgan, "Black Society in the Lowcountry, 1760–1810," in *Slavery and Freedom in the Age of the American Revolution*, ed. Ira Berlin and Ronald Hoffman (Charlottesville: University Press of Virginia for the United States Capitol Historical Society, 1983), 93;. Nash, *Unknown American Revolution*, 61.

60. *London Chronicle*, January 28, 1766; Tucketts to Thomas, December 5, 1765; *Halifax Gazette*, December 26, 1765; Council Minutes of St. Kitts, November 5, 1765, CO 241/9; Andrew Jackson O'Shaughnessy, *An Empire Divided: The American Revolution and the British Caribbean* (Philadelphia: University of Pennsylvania Press, 2000), 90–91.

61. There have been a series of excellent studies on the black presence in Britain, describing it as both broader and more important than previously considered. Estimates of the number of blacks in 1770s in London range from 3,000 to 15,000, depending on the source (typically based on descriptions either by a West India planter or by London newspapers). Catherine Molineaux, *Faces of Perfect Ebony: Encountering Atlantic Slavery in Imperial Britain* (Cambridge, MA: Harvard University Press, 2012), 8, 14; Kenneth L. Little, *Negroes in Britain: A Study of Racial Relations in English Society* (London: K. Paul, Trench, Trubner, 1948); David Brion Davis, *The Problem of Slavery in the Age of Revolution, 1770–1823* (New York, Oxford University Press, 1999); F. O. Shyllon, *Black Slaves in Britain* (London: Oxford University Press for the Institute of Race Relations, 1974); Dilip Hiro, *Black British, White Brit-*

ish (New York: Monthly Review Press, 1973); Winthrop Jordan, *White over Black: American Attitudes Toward the Negro, 1550–1812* (Chapel Hill: University of North Carolina Press, 1968); James Walvin, *The Black Presence: A Documentary History of the Negro in England, 1550–1860* (New York: Schocken Books, 1972); James Walvin, *Black and White: The Negro and English Society, 1555–1945* (London: Penguin Press, 1973); Norma Myers, *Reconstructing the Black Past: Blacks in Britain, c. 1780–1830* (London: Frank Cass, 1996).

62. Stewart, "Skimmington in the Middle and New England Colonies"; Palmer, "Discordant Music"; Thompson, *Customs in Common.*

63. Robinson to Earl of Halifax, August 28, 1765, Stowe MSS 264 f. 179–195.

64. Criticizing Hood's retreat, the newspaper reported, "[H]e remains hid from the resentment of his countrymen, but not from the terrors on his conscience." *Connecticut Courant*, October 14, 1765; *South Carolina Gazette*, October 5, 1765; Zachariah Hoot to Benjamin Franklin, September 23, 1765; Zachariah Hood to Commissioners of Stamps, November 10, 1765, T 422; James Gordon to William Martin, September 10, 1765, Massachusetts Historical Society, *Proceedings* 2.13 (1900), 393; Morgan and Morgan, *Stamp Act Crisis*, 160.

65. Hoping to build an intra-colonial movement, "Accounts from Boston . . . *encouraged*" colonists elsewhere to follow "the behaviour of the Mob there" to ensure "the Success they met with, in obliging Mr. Oliver to resign." Johnston to His Majestys Commissioners of Stamps, August 31, 1765, T 1/439.

66. If the Stamp Act could be enforced, McEvers recommended, based on "the Present Disposition of People here . . . a Stranger would be more Agreable than a Native" and "First month or Six Weeks of Service in the Office would be the most Dangerous and Disagreeable part of it." McEvers to Barlow Trecothick, August 26, 1765, T 1/439 f. 21.

67. *Newport Mercury*, September 2, 1765; Augustus Johnston to Commissioners of Stamps, August 3, 1765, T 1/439; Morgan and Morgan, *Stamp Act Crisis*, 199–200.

68. Augustus Johnston to Commissioners of Stamps, August 31, 1765, T 1/439; *Newport Mercury*, September 2, 1765.

69. *Pennsylvania Gazette*, October 31, 1765. Threats of violence accompanied nearly every hanging effigy, and in the few towns where the stamped paper was used and distributed, it was reported that the distributor "is a prisoner in his own house, and is guarded by a party of soldiers night and day, lest he should fall a victim to the justly enraged people, who threaten his life, and have conveyed letters to him, desiring him to prepare for another world, for he should soon quit this one." *Connecticut Courant*, December 31, 1765.

70. Letter attached to packet of Hinchelwood, stamp distributor, Nova Scotia, November 1, 1765, Stowe MSS 264 f. 69–70.

71. See Meserve to the Commissioners of His Majesty's Stamps, September 30, 1765, Stowe MSS 265 f. 207; *South Carolina Gazette*, October 5, 1765; *Massachusetts Gazette and Boston News-Letter*, September 12, 1765; Morgan and Morgan, *Stamp Act Crisis*, 160–161.

72. Sharp to Halifax, September 5, 1765, Stowe MSS 264 f. 230.

73. Colden to Lords Commissioners for Trade and Plantations, December 6, 1765,

Stowe MSS 264 f. 10–12; *South Carolina Gazetteer and Country Journal*, December 17, 1765.

74. *Connecticut Courant*, October 28, 1765.

75. Sharp to Halifax, September 5, 1765, Stowe MSS 264 f. 230.

76. *Connecticut Courant*, December 31, 1765.

77. Lemisch, "Jack Tar in the Streets," 399. In many reports, opponents described a "leveling spirit" when "Abettors of Consequence" rubbed elbows and attacked houses, as in Pennsylvania when the son of the chief justice was spotted "at the head of the Mob, animating and encouraging the lower Class." Targets of mob violence often described this common mixing of classes, such as when Henry Laurens looked closely at the assembly attacking his home, attempting to penetrate their costumes of "Soot, Sailors Habits, slouch hats &c" to determine their identities. Despite their appearance as common sailors, he recognized and began calling the names of his nine gentry acquaintances in the pack. Henry Laurens to Joseph Brown, October 28, 1765, Laurens Letter Book, Historical Society of Pennsylvania; Hughes to Commissioners of His Majesty's Stamps, October 12, 1765, Stowe MSS 264 f. 121.

78. Violence continued to be a tool in the arsenal, although eschewed in these protests. Rough music traditions were often revived in subsequent protest moments, particularly with the growth of direct attacks, including tar and feathering. Concerned for imperial reception of colonial actions, advocates of repeal of the Stamp Act continually altered the activities accompanying the effigy spectacles. Food and drink, for example, played a prominent, evolving role alongside the hanging displays. Planners in Newport, Rhode Island, learned quickly that offering a "Free picnic" with "strong drink in plenty with Cheshire cheese" effectively recruited a crowd, but quickly devolved into "intemperance" and "riot," which led to bad publicity in Britain for their cause. Following several publicized instances of wide-scale property destruction and looting of cellars, reports of colonial effigy displays include descriptions of "grand Entertainments," hosted in the early evening after the morning of effigy display and destruction. Whereas the open display hung before the entire port community, the formal dinners with guest lists channeled the energy and activities in the streets by limiting the involvement of those deemed unruly and outside the polite body politic.

79. New Left scholarship brought us important insights into restoring the crowd to a place beyond simply the mob. The work of Alfred F. Young in particular demonstrates the creative role played by sailors, by highlighting references to the nautical items used in displays around the Liberty Trees. However, in trying to restore lower classes to a revolutionary narrative centered in political pamphlets and republican debate, New Left scholars often represented actions on the streets as a class or protoclass struggle. Rediker and Linebaugh use examples like my case studies here to demonstrate that blacks and sailors worked as a common collective, presaging class struggle. In their accounts of the mobs containing sailors and slaves, they tend to describe a radical interracial moment rather than a multiethnic event. From my research, I believe these crowd scenes were often profoundly exclusionary and far less about demonstrating common economic position than about claiming and clamoring for a common British identity, while denying the same to fellow subjects.

[II]

THE POETICS OF TAXATION

[3]

GILBERT L. GIGLIOTTI

"DARING TO TRY THE KING'S PATIENCE?": (FUTILE?) RESISTANCE VERSUS INSATIABILITY IN *FABULA NEOTERICA*

IN THE 27 MAY 1765 supplement of the *Boston Gazette* appeared an anonymous, twenty-four-line, neo-Latin poem in dactylic hexameter, *Fabula Neoterica vel Dialogus inter Leonem et Murem*, "A Modern Fable or A Dialogue between a Lion and a Mouse."[1] The beast fable, printed just below an item comparing the Stamp Tax, as it would be imposed in the colonies on 1 November, with the comparable duty already enacted in Britain,[2] offers a curious take on the current state of the royal–colonial relationship—one that suggests that, while accepting the Stamp Act may only encourage more taxation, colonial resistance might offer no better an outcome. As we shall see, by allusively presenting a king too greedy for his own good and a colony too quick to react, the neo-Latin poem invites further discussion between Britain and its New World subjects in the months leading up to the enforcement date. Rejecting the simple dichotomy of acceptance or resistance, a binary perpetuated by many scholars but troubled by Molly Perry's account of transient and shifting allegiances in the preceding chapter, the poem problematizes so facile a characterization of the crisis and reminds all concerned of their duties—political, ethical, even familial—to one another.

Here is the original poem, with my own translation following:

Fabula Neoterica vel Dialogus inter Leonem et Murem

L. *Ecce Leo lucis habitans impastus opacis*
(Rex passim qui dictus erat rabidus nemorumque)
Notas percurrit quaerendo pabula sylvas—
Forte via inspiciens Murem timidum atque minutum,
Sic loquitur tonitru—quo visne animal minimum tu

Hic obstare viam? Vel hic tentare furorem
Quare audes? Subito cui tam respondit atroci

M. *Mus trepidans—Rex mi, me nunc contendere tecum*
Vim natura parens non dat mihi pectore forti;
Parce tuum obsequio necnon compescito et iram;
Amplis his sylvis majora Animalia non sunt
Esuriem potiusque tuam satiare reperta?

L. *Quid tibi—Tu effrons, si parvis mea viscera multis*
(Scilicet ut quondam dapibusque epulabar opimis)
Esse repleta velim? Poterisne opponere fatum?
Scis, nemoris regione mei quodcunque movebit,
Arbitrio ut summo Regis submitteret idem?
Nostris in manibus vitae mortisque potestas—

M. *Omnibus, O Princeps, famulis conceditur arvi*
Dignus honos Genio nati sine Murmure juris—
Hinc ibi prosternam, si vis me elidere plantis
Primaevam in cinerem, vacuis volitare per Auras—
Mure vorato, mox uno morsuque Leonis
Vis fuit atque famis posthac multo magis ardens

FINIS

A Modern Fable or A Dialogue between the Lion and the Mouse

L. Behold a hungry Lion, inhabiting a shady grove
(a King of the Forest dubbed—here and there—"mad"),
rushing through familiar haunts hunting food.
Spying in his path, by chance, a Mouse timid and tiny,
he thunders: "Why, squirt, block my way?
Why dare try my ire?" Hurriedly to the dreadful one,

M. the trembling Mouse replies: "My King, Mother Nature
granted me not a brave heart's strength to contest you.
Spare one submissive, and keep your wrath under wraps.
Are there not, in this spacious wood, bigger beasts
better to satisfy your hunger?"

L. "What's it to you—you presumptuous little . . . ,
if I fill my belly with countless small creatures?
(For I on occasion enjoy splendid feasts indeed.)

Can you stop such a fate? You know, no,
whoever stirs here defers to the King's command?
In my hands, the power of life and death—"

M. "By all the servants of this land, O Ruler, is conceded
sans complaint, the honor due the Spirit of Law.
I throw myself face down at your feet, and if you wish
to crush me into the dust or hurl me through the air—"

The Mouse was eaten, in one bite, for the Lion had the muscle,
but, from then on, he burned with an even greater hunger.

THE END

While there can be little doubt that the poem comments on the current political crisis (as both the fable's positioning below an article on the Stamp Act and the long tradition of royal lions in beast fables and political cartoons attest; see figure 8.2), what so intrigues the reader about the poem is the dissatisfaction of both characters at the end. The mouse has been eaten, but the lion is hungrier than ever. The significance of this surprisingly dissatisfying ending is tied to the interpretative enterprise central to the poem's neo-Latin form (i.e., the poet's invitation to the audience to enter into a conversation with the long Latin literary tradition) that promotes neither a simple call to repeal the tax nor its timid acceptance but rather demonstrates the need for further debate and a genuine *dialogus*, a dialogue, that will demand more of the king and his colonies. The poem, in short, requires its readers to unpack a series of allusions to texts by such familiar *auctores* as Virgil, Cicero, and Ovid and models—in its unpacking of their often-contradictory voices—the means by which the current debate might be conducted.

The genre of the beast fable dates back most famously to the sixth-century BCE fabulist Aesop, although, due to the limited number of post-classical readers in the West skilled enough to read him in his original Greek, most knew the Aesopic fables through his fifth-century CE Latin versifier Avianus.[3] Most readers, however, would have been quite familiar with the hungry beasts and their prey that inhabit the fables, a staple in school curricula.[4] And, as David Shields has argued, "the fable enjoyed intense vogue as a vehicle of political discourse in British America during the eighteenth century,"[5] in part because "the more general speaking of a fable lent it the moral authority of philosophy" so the "rebukes a fable delivered could possess greater moral weight than the strident particularities of an allegory."[6]

There is, for example, the hungry lion in Avianus's fable XVIII, *De quattuor iuvencis et leone*, "Concerning the Four Oxen and the Lion," who manages, with *pravis . . . verbis* (11), "with crooked words," to separate and kill all four of the oxen, despite their oaths of mutual protection. Or there is another lion in XXVI, *De leone et capella*, "Concerning the Lion and the Goat," who tries unsuccessfully to convince a goat that better food and greener pastures await, if she would only

. . . praeruptis ardua saxis
Linque, nec hirsutis pascua quaere iugis;[7]

leave steep mountains with the ragged rocks
and not seek food on the tangled mountain ridge

The goat, however, while acknowledging *vera* (9), the "true things" the lion says, wisely stays on the mountainside due to *maiora pericula* (9), "the greater dangers" the lion presents.

There is also the lion in XXIV, *De venatore et leone*, "Concerning the Hunter and the Lion," who argues with his friend, the hunter, as to whether humans or lions are the braver species. When shown a painting of a man killing a lion, the lion responds that, if his kind could also paint, not only would the lion be depicted as victorious, but

Tunc hominem adspiceres oppressum murmure magno[8]

Then you would see the man overcome by but a roar

In each case, the lion is depicted as strong and smart, and, if not always successful or even ethical, the king of the beasts either outfoxes or is outmaneuvered by his prey. In short, somebody always wins (although the goat may not be descending the mountain anytime soon).

Similarly, in other fables, smaller objects of prey are not necessarily outmatched. Like the goat who steers clear of the lion above, the mouse in XXXI, *De mure et bove*, "Concerning the Mouse and the Bull," knows his own strengths and weaknesses, as well as those of his enemies. In this fable, *mus . . . parvus . . . / ausus* (1–2), "the small mouse having dared" to wound the bull *ab exiguo . . . dente* (2), "with his small tooth," runs back into its hole. The bull, not knowing exactly what just hurt him, begins to bellow and threaten indiscriminately (5–6). The mouse finally comes out to address the bull, *indignantem . . . fatigans* (7), who is "now tiring of his anger":

Non quia magna tibi tribuerunt membra parentes,
Viribus effectum constituere tuis.[9]

> Although your parents bestowed upon you great limbs,
> they did not also grant you efficiency in that strength.

The mouse, in the end, teaches the bull the lesson that bigger isn't always better, that strength isn't always the best weapon.

In these examples, the reader can see the origins of the *Fabula Neoterica*, the rapacious predator and loquacious prey, but in these verses on the Stamp Act, unlike each of the preceding examples, neither of the interlocutors gains a true victory in the end. In this rare example of a colonial American *fabula*, the hungry lion, upon spying "by chance" (4) the mouse in his path, roars "like thunder" (5) about how the mouse *audes* (7), "can dare," to block his path and try his temper. The trembling mouse wonders if there are not, in fact, other bigger (11) animals deeper in the forest who might better satisfy his hunger (12). The lion, not taking kindly to advice from a rodent, asks rhetorically whether the mouse would be able to prevent his fate (15) if the lion really wants to eat him. Having already admitted how ill-equipped nature (9) has made him, the mouse can only throw himself on the mercy of his king. At that moment, despite complete acceptance of the lion's supremacy, the helpless mouse is eaten in one bite (23), and, despite the meal, at poem's end the royal British lion is "burning with an even great hunger" (24).

What makes this fable so intriguing is *not* the death of a mouse that emblematizes colonial weakness.[10] As P. Gila Reinstein has noted, the fable essentially (and despite its reputation) has never been a feel-good genre. It is rather a pragmatic one. Fables, she writes,

> recognize the world is a dangerous place, full of exploiters, bullies, and false friends. . . . The world is what it is: the enemies, the people in power, are tyrannical lions, tricky foxes, vindictive snakes; the victims, the little people, are vain crows, foolish donkeys, self-important rabbits, and ill-advised lambs. No one is perfect—neither oppressor nor oppressed—and no one can change who he is. The best you can do, according to the fables, is to stand up for yourself, selfishly, if need be, since you can expect no one else to stand up for you; expect to be attacked and have the sense to lie low when threatened; and, if you are lucky, take your revenge when you get the chance.[11]

Thus, in the fables above, the four oxen make the mistake of believing the lies sown by the lion, break their wise pact of allegiance, friendship, and protection, and are slaughtered as a result. The goat, on the other hand, recognizes why the lion is suggesting she graze in the meadow and wisely declines the invitation. The mouse, after biting the bull, knows it has to run for cover. The dangers all face are very real and, if not handled correctly, are deadly indeed. Thus the hallmark of the Aesopic genre, its pragmatism, offers outcomes that, while imperfect, make difficult situations survivable; fables teach how to live another day.

In *Fabula Neoterica*, however, what surprises is the lack of self-knowledge and survival skills, as it were, of the two characters. While the mouse correctly concludes that he could not fight the lion, he does not (like the mouse or goat in the earlier fables) recognize and rely on his own gifts—his small size, quickness, elusiveness, and brains—and instead defines himself only in direct comparison with the lion. Indeed, the poem emphasizes this disparity, by paralleling *vis* (24), the "strength," that is the lion's alone at poem's end, with the earlier *vim*, which "Mother Nature" had not bestowed upon the mouse (9). In addition, it is the mouse who (self-destructively, as it turns out) introduces the idea of the lion's eating him.

The lion, meanwhile, lets the mouse, whom he has spotted only "by chance," set the agenda and distract him from his hunt for food. After all, could the tiny mouse really be blocking the lion's path (6)? Would a hungry lion, even one that is rumored to be *rabidus* (2), "mad," ever seriously consider eating a single mouse? Does the king of the jungle need to assert to so small a creature that "the power of life and death" is in his royal hands (18)? Neither party here is, in Reinstein's word, "perfect," but more important neither is true to his nature or, apparently, adept enough to survive. The colonial mouse should have been smart enough, once spotted, to dart silently to safety, and the royal lion need not have stooped to stop at all. Instead the mouse's sycophancy leads to his unsatisfying, and decidedly unproductive, death. For not only has nothing been solved, the situation has deteriorated: the hungry lion is hungry still, only now *multo magis* (24), "even more so."

Before proceeding, we should note David Shields's caveats about the interpretation of the genre of the political fable. For while Aesopic literature is identified with the "*sensus communis*" and readers can see "how popular opinion might be enlisted against the high-handed activities of the powerful," we would be mistaken, he argues "to see the fable as a form of *Tendenzdichtung* necessarily serving the revolutionary aspirations of the people."[12] Not every tyrannical lion, in short, is a king to be overthrown.

Indeed, it also must be remembered that colonial objection to the Stamp Act was not universal. For example, while the legislation would have a far greater impact on the British West Indies than the thirteen mainland colonies, the islands, in general, accepted the tax and "conspicuously failed to join the pamphlet campaign against Britain."[13] As Andrew O'Shaughnessy has shown, St. Kitts and Nevis protested and even rioted, but "the largest and most populous islands—Barbados and Jamaica—complied with the Stamp Act," and, "unlike the majority of distributors on the mainland, their stamp officials never resigned."[14] Thus, while in hindsight the *Fabula Neoterica*'s position may seem to resist, or contradict, the familiar revolutionary historical narrative, its potentially palliative outlook was not unfamiliar at the time.

For the obvious colonial response, even to apparent imperial overreach on taxation and other policies, was not revolution. According to Brendan McConville, what drove the colonies was as much "affection for and faith in imagined kings and constitutions" as "Country thought or natural-rights ideology."[15] Eric Nelson offers another alternative to our fixation, in hindsight, on revolution. He argues that some patriots had no quarrel at all with the king, but only with Parliament. They saw George III as a potential ally against parliamentary overreach and looked for a solution to the current crisis in the re-establishment of the royal–colonial relationship that existed before the Glorious Revolution.[16] Given the many, often contradictory views that were being voiced simultaneously, therefore, it makes sense that this neo-Latin poem emphasizes the frustration the parties must have felt at the heart of the conflict. History knows the actions, of king and colonies, that would follow the Stamp Act Crisis, but the neo-Latin fabulist was primarily considering pragmatic ways to avoid the mutual destruction depicted in his poem and survive. The solution is far from obvious; the issue needs further discussion.

To explore fully the poet's position here, we also must recognize that the *Fabula Neoterica* is part not merely of the beast fable tradition but also of the neo-Latin tradition. The poet, after all, could just as easily have written the poem in English, which certainly would have engaged a wider readership. By composing it in Latin, the poet engages his audience not only through generic conventions but also, through quotations and allusions, in a conversation with the great authors of classical antiquity. For this, at its core, is the artistic project of neo-Latin poetry, a project that began with Petrarch and the humanists, who sought to rescue the Latin language from what they deemed the barbarity of its medieval state. They sought to restore Latin to the height of its former beauty: the Golden Age of Virgil, Horace, Ovid, and Cicero. And this restoration project encouraged not only imitation but a heightened awareness of quotation and allusion, the force of which relied heavily on the conscious juxtaposition of the new and original contexts.

This *ars poetica* has led scholars to criticize the exclusivity of neo-Latin verse, in general, and American neo-Latin poetry, in particular. Variously labeled a "coterie language,"[17] *vers de société*,[18] or merely another example of *poésie precieuse*,[19] neo-Latin versifying, according to these critics, from its inception has exemplified "a literature which arises in small groups of cultivated people and which aims at producing an elegant, intellectual and aesthetic pleasure, without endangering the civilized atmosphere essential to the group."[20] Such a literary group, in turn, is a "polite society in which the blessings of culture and civilization can be enjoyed without intrusion of the most troublesome problems of the age."[21] Neo-Latin poetry cultivated an intellectual coterie not only to exclude those outside the group but also to foster an ethos of inclusivity among the elite and forestall forms of expressions that might threaten the social hierarchy.

On the one hand, these poems were written by the educated primarily for their peers (since it was through the curricula at every level that these neo-Latin writers and their readers immersed themselves in classical texts). As William J. Ziobro has noted about their familiarity with many texts:

> The incoming college student was called upon to reread many of the Latin authors whom he had previously encountered in grammar school. Among the Latin authors most commonly read in the first year of college were Virgil, Cicero (orations), Caesar, Livy, and Sallust. During the second and third years of college, the Latin authors most frequently read were Cicero (philosophical essays), Horace, Juvenal, Ovid, Quintilian, Terence, and Tacitus. Finally, the fourth year was often considered a review year, designed to prepare the student for the final, public examinations. Once again, many of these same classical authors were reread.[22]

The better readers know the sources, the richer and more meaningful their neo-Latin reading experience will be, and the author of *Fabula Neoterica*, like other colonial neo-Latin writers, composed the poem in the expectation that it would be read by elites familiar with the classical canon and capable of recognizing the poem's relation to the ancient precedents.

On the other hand, the neo-Latin verse of Anglo-American poets hardly avoided Mourgues's "troublesome problems of the age" and addressed the economic and political concerns shared by the masses. From mourning the death of a Puritan patriarch (and expecting the worst—both spiritually and politically—because of it) or drumming up support for the troops during the French and Indian War to criticizing British policy or voicing Tory sentiments on the eve of the Revolution, Anglo-American neo-Latinists, like the poet of *Fabula Neoterica*, did not hesitate to confront the issues of the day in periodicals such as the *Boston Gazette*.[23] As Charles E. Clark has argued, colonial newspapers "contained more than reports of public events. In comfortable juxtaposition with the 'intelligence' from Europe and the record of local legislative acts, ship arrivals, remarkable occurrences, and street gossip, there resided the essays, the poetry, and the learned letters that linked the newspaper world of ordinary affairs with that of formal learning."[24] It is within this juxtaposition of the political and the aesthetic that our newspaper poet quietly quotes Virgil, Horace, Ovid, and Cicero in Latin, expecting at least some of his readers to recognize and appreciate the myriad, and often conflicting, political implications of these carefully chosen allusions—not to mention the skill displayed in the Latin verse.[25]

And the poetics of this Latin verse are well executed. The poet's command of the various aspects of dactylic hexameter—from the variety of effects produced by the only two possible metrical feet (the dactyl, — ˘ ˘, and the spondee, — —) to his use of elision (the joining of a word ending in a vowel, diphthong, or *m* with the next word when it begins with a vowel, diphthong, or *h*)—is quite deft. The threatening feel of the lion's search for food, for example, is accentuated by the heavily spondaic third line: the reader can feel the king of the jungle's paws pounding the ground.[26] The poet highlights the lion's dismissive attitude and inherent disbelief in the *Quare audes*, "How do you dare . . . ?" of line 7, with the elision—the "light, hurried half-pronunciation"[27]—of the final syllable of *Quare* and the first syllable of *audes*. That dismissiveness carries over to the lion's next line (13), with its opening aposiopesis followed immediately by the elision of . . . *Tu effrons*. . . . Similarly, the mouse's fear is underscored by a pair of elisions in line 10 (. . . *tuum obsequio* . . . and . . . *compescito et* . . .), as well as the stuttering "*re*" in the penultimate foot of line 12 (. . . *sati/are re/perta*). The onomatopoetic elision of . . . *me elidere* . . . , . . . "to crush me" (21), meanwhile, makes concrete the deadly threat the mouse faces. That our poet, over the course of years of schooling, had internalized the nuances of Latin metrics is clear, but the more significant achievement demonstrated by the poem is its use of specific allusions to Virgil, Horace, Ovid, and Cicero to call for more productive discussion, and less harmful posturing, over the Stamp Act.

In the very first line, the poem invokes Virgil's *Aeneid*, the first-century BCE epic about the mythic origins of the Roman Empire. Through a "golden line" (a hexametric line, and favorite of the Roman poet, in which a verb, at the verse's center, separates two adjectives from the two nouns they modify),[28] the poet makes a pair of allusions in *leo . . . impastus* and *lucis . . . opacis*. Together these allusions offer conflicting commentary on the present tension between Britain and the colonies, including monarchical greed, eternal friendship, a burgeoning national future, and the weight of filial duty.

The first allusion, the "hungry lion," recalls the familiar simile in book IX of Nisus as a hungry lion, when the Trojan slaughters the unsuspecting Rutulians in their camp:

> ***impastus*** *ceu plena* ***leo*** *per ovilia turbans*
> *(suadet enim vesana fames) manditque trahitque*
> *molle pecus mutumque metu, fremit ore cruento.*[29]

> As **a hungry lion**, raging through the full sheepfolds
> (for mad hunger prompts), chews and drags the
> flock soft and silent from fear, he rages with bloody mouth.

The raid by Nisus and his younger companion Euryalus is, of course, famed both for the iconic friendship it celebrates and for its tragic ending, and therefore any allusion to it can but elicit a mixed response of awe and sadness. For Nisus, the lion, is awe-inspiring; his enemies, like sheep, are dumb with fear, and he kills them quickly and easily. At the same time, however, he and Euryalus have made a sneak attack upon a sleeping enemy, so even the respect for the lion's strength must be tempered somewhat. Sheep may be a natural prey for lions, but they are far from worthy opponents—even a flock of them. Nor is it insignificant that Virgil's comparison of Nisus to a lion driven by *vesana fames* (340), an "insane hunger," is recalled by the *Rex . . . rabidus* (2), the "mad" king in the 1765 poem, although the king's madness is only a rumor spoken *passim* (2), "here and there." Our poet thus posits a royal lion that mixes legitimate authority with an avarice that borders on insanity, a combination that can lead to the abuse of his vulnerable subjects.

Furthermore, the narrative tide of Virgil's epic will turn quickly against the two Trojan friends. It will be only some 130 lines until Virgil and his readers mourn their premature deaths in one of his most pathetic of the poem's "pathetic half-lines":[30]

> *Quin ipsa arrectis (visu miserabile) in hastis*
> *Praefigunt capita et multo clamore sequuntur*
> *Euryali et Nisi.*[31]

But (miserable to be seen) on raised spears,
Followed by a great shout, they fasten the very heads of
Euryalus and Nisus.

The reader of Virgil has an emotional stake in Nisus and Euryalus, and their demise is a powerful loss indeed. And astute colonial readers could link this unhappy loss of the leonine Nisus to the unwelcome result of resisting imperial authority and royal decrees. Even amid the political troubles of 1765, separating from the king was hardly viewed as a good option. For, "ironically, from our perspective, it was the monarch on whom the colonials pinned their hopes of evading a rupture they never desired."[32] Our *leo . . . impastus*, therefore, must not be too easily dismissed as simply another royal oppressor.

Further enriching (complicating?) the reader's interpretation of the poem is the second Virgilian allusion in the very first line. "*Lucis . . . opacis*" appears in *Aeneid*, book VI, when Aeneas, having been led to the Underworld by the prophetess Sibyl, dutifully seeks the shade of his father, Anchises. Musaeus's spirit responds to the question of where the shade of the Trojan patriarch dwells:

nulli certa domus; ***lucis*** *habitamus* ***opacis****,*
riparumque toros et prata recentia rivis
incolimus. sed vos, si fert ita corde voluntas,
hoc superate iugum, et facili iam tramite sistam.[33]

There is a specific home for no one; we dwell **in the shady groves**
and we reside on the couches of the banks and grass fresh
with streams, but, if your will stirs your heart thus,
pass over this ridge and I will set you on an easy path.

The location of our fable, it seems, is Elysium, the abode of the blessed:

. . . locos laetos et amoena virecta
fortunatorum nemorum sedesque beatas.[34]

. . . the happy places, the pleasant greens,
and the blessed seats of the groves of the fortunate.

Such paradisiacal imagery linking America to the mythical antediluvian Golden Age or the Garden of Eden had been used consistently in a wide variety of texts by European settlers to describe the abundance of the New World landscape,[35] but what kind of blessed grove has madly hungry lions roaming through it? The poet's insertion of an unbalanced lion into this paradise signals an end of innocence—or, perhaps, a new beginning.

For most of *Aeneid* VI, of course, is Anchises' foretelling the fate of Aeneas's descendants, that is, the history and glory that will be Rome's. This ancient patriotic celebration, in turn, would easily suggest to *Gazette* readers what, by 1765, had already become a popular American theme: the Rising Glory of America. The premise, which posits and commends America as the next socio-cultural capitol in the Western progression of history (*translatio studii*),[36] dates back at least to Bishop George Berkeley's 1725 "On the Prospect of Planting Arts and Learning in America" and had been a persistent topic in American periodicals since the 3 July 1729 publication of the anonymous "Let Philadelphia's generous Sons excuse" in the *American Weekly Mercury*.[37] By recalling Anchises' celebration of future Roman glory, the poet seems to propose that America has outgrown its colonial status and is now on the verge of a new chapter in its progression from western outpost to cultural center.

Then again, it must be remembered that from the epic's publication upon Virgil's death, its hero had been celebrated as a symbol of *pietas*, his duty to the gods, to his country, and to his family. The image of Aeneas devotedly leaving his burning city at the order of Jupiter himself, with his lame father on his back, carrying the *penates*, or household gods, of Troy while leading his young son by the hand,[38] was the subject of countless works of art and indeed had become iconic. Aeneas is ever the obedient believer, citizen, and son who never fails to fulfill his duties—even when they conflict with his own desires and preferences.[39] Any reference to the epic story of Aeneas, especially to his relationship with his father, consequently cannot but carry, in part, the message of duty. This filial aspect of the Virgilian allusion might be read as what McConville has termed a "rhetorical flight . . . by the beleaguered colonists . . . demand[ing] that the imperial father of their imagination restrain a tyrannical Parliament."[40] The greed is not the king's but the Parliament's, and so the colonists' loyalty to the king need not be obviated. The very first line of *Fabula Neoterica*, therefore, sends decidedly mixed signals: everything from imperial rapacity, eternal friendship, and potentially devastating loss, to American destiny and colonial duty.

A neo-Latin poet's full exercise of allusion or direct quotation relies on the audience's recognition of the original context of the words, which, given (as already noted) the familiarity college-educated readers of the *Gazette* had with the classical Latin canon, is not hard to imagine. Even as innocuous a phrase as *mihi pectore* (9), when occurring in the same position in the line as its hexametric models, consequently can recall two oft-studied canonical works, Ovid's *Metamorphoses* and Horace's *Sermones*, better known as the *Satires*. In a similarly complex way, these allusions address the appropriate relationship between a king and his subjects, a relationship that involves a shared understanding without slavish obedience.

The first occurrence of the phrase comes from Ovid's massive 8 CE epic and compendium of myth. The passage leads up to the famous scene of Hercules' death and transformation on the enormous pyre he had built and set ablaze himself. As they watch, Ovid writes, the gods fear for Hercules, *pro vindice terrae* (241), "for the champion of the Earth," and, having recognized the fear his fellow gods have for his son, "Saturnian Jupiter" addresses them:

> *. . . nostra est timor iste voluptas,*
> *O superi, totoque libens* ***mihi pectore*** *grator,*
> *quod memoris populi dicor rectorque paterque*
> *et mea progenies vestro quoque tuta favore est.*[41]

> Your fear is my delight,
> O Gods, and, glad, I congratulate **myself with** my whole **heart**,
> that I am called both ruler and father of a mindful people,
> and that my progeny also is guarded by your favor.

Here the reader is shown a king whose relationship with his subjects is as it should be: he is mindful of and pleased by his subjects, who are respectful and attentive in return. They share the same concerns.

But if the Ovidian use of the phrase offers the model of a good "ruler and father," the identical phrase in the identical metrical location in its line in a Horatian satire from 30 BCE gives the reader a very different view of a master and his disciple. For the hexametric dialogue in Horace's *Sermones* II.iv offers the image of Catius, a blindly loyal student of a ludicrous philosophy, who recounts, chapter and verse, its version of Platonism based entirely on food. By conversation's end, Horace can only pretend that whatever else he might need to hear of this "philosophy" must come from the "teacher" himself:

> *Docte Cati, per amicitiam divosque rogatus*
> *ducere me auditum, perges quocumque, memento.*
> *Nam quamvis memori referas* ***mihi pectore*** *cuncta,*
> *nam tamen interpres tantundem iuveris . . .*[42]

> Learned Catius, requested by our friendship and the gods,
> remember to lead me to the one you've heard, whenever you go again.

> For, although you repeat all things **to me with a** remindful **heart**,
> yet, as an interpreter, you can please me only so much . . .

The context of this allusion suggests that one can be too deferential, too trusting, and, while the life of the gullible Catius may not be in the same danger the obsequious mouse's was, his wholeheartedly uncritical rehearsal of his master's ideas bodes ill for his future.[43] Once again, the same phrase evokes conflicting interpretations, of both good leaders and mindless followers and the duties—constitutional, philosophical, and social—that each has to the other.

And, since overthrowing the monarchy was not the obvious solution, even as "the number of conflicts within British American society escalated" during the eighteenth century, such musing about a better, if different, royal–colonial relationship made sense. For, as McConville argues, some in the colonies began "to imagine the empire and the monarchy remade in an old new way. The things of God and the things of man would be put back together in the person of the king."[44] Both the lion and mouse, therefore, would need to rethink how they interact with each other. Since the mouse can be neither a satisfactory meal for nor a powerful enough rival to the lion, a new relationship must be forged. Eric Nelson's argument, in *The Royalist Revolution*, that colonists favored a reassertion of the royal prerogative toward imperial administration (without parliamentary oversight) is one possibility. The mouse and lion aren't natural enemies at all; the lion is, or should become once again, the mouse's protector.[45]

The final borrowing in the 1765 poem, the prosaic *multo magis* (24), "much more," draws on Cicero, another classical literary staple and a stylistic touchstone for neo-Latin writers,[46] to underscore again this complex relationship of king and colonists. The Roman orator/statesman/philosopher was read repeatedly in schools—especially his four orations *against* the political revolutionary Catiline and his philosophical treatise *De officiis* (*On Duties*).[47] Since the adverbial phrase has no ancient poetic precedent and Cicero's use of it in his extensive literary corpus is quite limited, its *three* appearances in the oft-read *De officiis* are noteworthy—and, in the 1765 poem, allusively powerful since, as we shall see, they touch upon questions already raised by the other allusions, such as Aeneas's filial duty and the proper royal relationship of Jupiter to his subjects.

De officiis is a philosophical work written in late 44 BCE in the wake of Julius Caesar's assassination and the author's post–civil war return to public life. A "work of *practical* ethics," *De officiis* has "an important place in the history of *political* thought" due to its "emphasis on social and political morality."[48] Its significance also stems from its condemnation of "citizens who abstain from political activity."[49] Ironically Cicero himself would be assassinated by the end of 43 BCE. The work examines the meaning of and relationship between the four virtues needed to govern, that is, to ensure that the bonds between citizens should be unharmed: wisdom, justice, greatness of spirit (courage), and seemliness (decorum).

Here are the three instances of the phrase in their original contexts:

> *Reliquis autem tribus virtutibus necessitates propositae sunt ad eas res parandas tuendasque, quibus actio vitae continetur, ut et societas hominum coniunctioque servetur et animi excellentia magnitudoque cum in augendis opibus utilitatibusque et sibi et suis comparandis, tum* ***multo magis*** *in his ipsis despiciendis eluceat.*[50]

> As for the other three virtues [justice, greatness of spirit, and seemliness], their aim is necessities: they are to procure and to conserve whatever is required for the activities of life, in order both to preserve the fellowship and bonding between men, and to allow excellence and greatness of spirit to shine out—both in increasing influence and in acquiring benefits for oneself and those dear to one, and also, and **much more**, in disdaining the very same things.

and

> *Atque hoc* ***multo magis*** *efficit ipsa naturae ratio, quae est lex divina et humana; cui parere qui velit (omnes autem parebunt, qui secundum naturam volent vivere), numquam committet, ut alienum appetat et id, quod alteri detraxerit, sibi adsumat. Etenim* ***multo magis*** *est secundam naturam excelsitas animi et magnitudo itemque comitas, iustitia, liberalitas quam voluptas, quam vita, quam divitiae; quae quidem contemnere et pro nihilo ducere comparantem cum utilitate communi magni animi et excelsi est.*[51]

> Nature's reason itself, which is divine and human law, achieves this object [i.e., that the bonds between citizens should be unharmed] to **a far greater extent.** Whoever is willing to obey it (everyone will obey it who wants to live in accordance with nature) will never act so as to seek what is another's, nor appropriate himself something that he has taken from someone else. For loftiness and greatness of spirit, and indeed friendliness, justice, and liberality, are **far more** in accordance with nature than pleasure, than life, than riches. Indeed to disdain these, when comparing them with the common benefit, and value them as nothing, is the mark of a great and lofty spirit.[52]

Both passages stress the importance of all citizens in a state working toward the greater good and de-emphasizing the acquisition of personal influence, wealth, and other material benefits, especially at someone else's expense. The truly reasonable person, one who follows natural law, would never take what was not his; indeed, the reasonable person disdains anything but what is necessary for himself, even as he might find himself pursuing gain in support of his family. Social ties and the just treatment of all trump riches and even life itself. Cicero's political message to the reader is clear: truly good government demands rational, that is, selfless, individuals.

Throughout the *De officiis*, it must be acknowledged, Cicero criticizes monarchs and monarchies as individuals and systems that too often focus exclusively on personal gain (in power, wealth, and prestige) at the expense of the governed. He even quotes the Roman poet Ennius's celebrated line:

> *Nulla sancta societas nec fides regni est*[53]
>
> To kingship belongs neither sacred fellowship nor faith

Time and again, Cicero refers to the murdered Caesar as the archetypal, acquisitive tyrant, so a reader might be tempted to argue that any allusions our poet makes to the *De officiis* must be read as decidedly revolutionary. The problem with this interpretation is, as stated earlier, that neither character in the dialogue seems interested in acting on behalf of the common good: neither the colonial mouse nor the royal lion.

But is the lion demanding something to which he is not entitled, is he "seeking what is another's"? As haughtily as *Rex mi* may act, the mouse certainly never suggests his not having the right to do as he pleases. In fact, he asserts the *agreement of all* on their duties to *Genio nati . . . juris* (20), "the Spirit of Law":

> By all the servants of this land, O Ruler, is conceded
> sans complaint, the honor due the Spirit of Law.
> I throw myself face down at your feet, and if you wish
> to crush me into the dust or hurl me through the air—

The poet could be suggesting that this loyal subject is questioning the justice of the Stamp Act (not the right of Lord Grenville and Parliament to levy the tax or of the king to enforce it, only its basic fairness to the colonies), but, given the mouse's unseemly alacrity in offering up any other animal in his place, he can hardly be said to display much concern for the body politic. Alternatively, this Ciceronian allusion could be deployed to argue that, in fact, those who protest the tax are withholding what is rightfully the king's and are themselves fomenting disunity and threatening the bonds of the citizenry. Colonial Governor Thomas Hutchinson, after all, employs the *De officiis* in his defense of British policies in his 1765 *History of Massachusetts*.[54] In short, if Cicero's treatise offers practical guidance to right behavior, neither member of this forest state acts bravely or decorously (much less wisely or justly), and, as a result, the bonds of the state are being weakened before our eyes.

Left unanswered by the poet, of course, is how to strengthen those bonds once again, but a call for more discussion seems clear. For true dialogue on these important issues is a rare thing, as James Madison noted in his commonplace book: "The King's and the People's rights never agree better than by not being spoken of."[55] And the lack of communication in the poem leads to both a colony devoured and an unsatisfied monarch.

Not surprisingly, given that newspaper publishers were the ones who would be bearing the brunt of the new tax, few statements of support for the Stamp Act were published in colonial newspapers during 1765,[56] and it would be a stretch indeed to argue that *Fabula Neoterica* favors the tax. Equally problematic (even granting that the *Boston Gazette* was "filled with fiery political matter" written by "a constellation of Boston revolutionary leaders, including Samuel Adams, John Adams, James Otis, Josiah Quincy Jr., and Joseph Warren")[57] is any argument of its unambiguously promulgating resistance.

Instead, the interpretative and purposely inconclusive dynamic at play is inextricably tied to, and demonstrative of, the poem's neo-Latin composition with its tangled web of classical allusion. The poem's construction, as we have seen, directs the reader back to a complex collection of sources in which to discover meaning. Those texts may—and in some cases do—contradict one another on specific questions or raise different issues altogether, but the very act of unpacking those texts argues for, while modeling the art of, further discussion, more dialogue. The tax does not take effect for another five months, the poems seems to say, so perhaps what plays out in the poem does not have to become reality: England need not grow more agitated, and the colonies need not end as a woefully insufficient meal for the king. And, perhaps, in this New World Elysium, wisdom, justice, courage, and seemliness can still reign supreme.

Notes

The author would like to thank Taylor Dempsey, his undergraduate Latin independent study student in Fall 2013, for her research assistance in this project.

1. "*Fabula Neoterica vel Dialogus inter Leonem et Murem*," *Boston Gazette*, suppl., 27 May 1765. The printed title reads *Neotreica*, clearly a typographical error.

2. The item notes that the Stamp Act is "nearly agreeable to that of the Mother Country, save the following additional clause . . . That all Sums of Money granted and imposed by the Act as Rates or Duties . . . shall be deemed and taken to be Sterling Money of Great Britain, and that such Monies shall and may be received and taken according to the Proportion and Value of 5ʃ. 6d. the Ounce in Silver; and that all said Forfeitures and Penalties which shall be incurred in the said Colonies and Plantations shall and may be prosecuted, sued for, and recovered, with full Costs of Suit, in any Court of Record." Ibid.

3. Aesop was versified into Latin first by Phaedrus in the first century CE, but his influence is indebted to the later Latin writer, since Avianus is the first to allude to Phaedrus's work. Michael Grant, *Greek and Latin Authors, 800 B.C.–A.D. 1000* (New York: H. W. Wilson, 1980), 319. Both Latin translations were read in the colonies. William J. Ziobro, "Classical Education in Colonial America," in *Classical Antiquity and the Politics of America*, ed. Michael Meckler (Waco, TX: Baylor University Press, 2006), 20.

4. Ziobro, "Classical Education in Colonial America," 22.

5. David S. Shields, *Oracles of Empire: Poetry, Politics, and Commerce in British America, 1690–1750* (Chicago: University of Chicago Press, 1990), 148.

6. Ibid., 151.

7. XXVI.3–4.

8. XXIV.15.

9. XXXI.9–10.

10. Despite the primacy of his being beaten at the beginning of line 23, the grammar of the final lines subordinates the mouse's death to the lion's increased appetite. For *Mure vorato*, literally "the mouse having been eaten," is an ablative absolute, a Latin grammatical construction by which a writer "indicates the circumstances under which the main action takes place . . . but assigns [those circumstances] a secondary role." Joseph P. Solodow, *Latin Alive: The Survival of Latin in English and the Romance Languages* (New York: Cambridge University Press, 2010), 98.

11. P. Gila Reinstein, "Aesop and Grimm: Contrast in Ethical Codes and Contemporary Values," *Children's Literature in Education* 14 (1983): 47–48.

12. Shields, *Oracles of Empire*, 148, 152.

13. Andrew Jackson O'Shaughnessy, *An Empire Divided: The American Revolution and the British Caribbean* (Philadelphia: University of Pennsylvania Press, 2000), 81.

14. Ibid., 92.

15. Brendan McConville, *The King's Three Faces: The Rise and Fall of Royal America, 1688–1776* (Chapel Hill: University of North Carolina Press, 2006), 9.

16. Eric Nelson, *The Royalist Revolution: Monarchy and the American Founding* (Cambridge, MA: Belknap Press, 2014), 13.

17. Alan Joel Wiesenthal, "The Latin Poetry of English Augustans" (PhD diss., University of Virginia, 1979), 24.

18. J. A. Leo LeMay, *Men of Letters in Colonial Maryland* (Knoxville: University of Tennessee Press, 1972), 294.

19. Harold Segel, *The Baroque Poem* (New York: E. P. Dutton, 1974), 103; Leonard Forster, *The Poet's Tongues: Multilingualism in Literature* (Cambridge: Cambridge University Press, 1970), 47.

20. Forster, *The Poet's Tongues*, 47–48.

21. Odette de Mourgues, *Metaphysical, Baroque, and Precieux Poetry* (Oxford: Clarendon Press, 1953),115.

22. Ziobro, "Classical Education in Colonial America," 25–26.

23. Cf. the range of American publications that published neo-Latin verse in Leo Kaiser, "Census of American Latin Verse, 1625–1825," *Proceedings of the American Antiquarian Society* 91 (1982): 197–299.

24. Charles E. Clark, "The Newspapers of Provincial America," in *Three Hundred Years of the American Newspaper*, ed. John B. Hench (Worcester, MA: American Antiquarian Society, 1991), 388.

25. The deep and abiding classical knowledge of the formally educated in the American colonies in the eighteenth century is beyond debate. To recognize this, one need only peruse a few pages of studies, such as Ziobro, "Classical Education in Colonial America," 13–28, or Richard M. Gummere, *The American Colonial Mind and the Classical Tradition* (Cambridge, MA: Harvard University Press, 1963).

26. Five of the line's six feet are spondees, and only the traditionally dactylic fifth foot is a dactyl.

27. Clyde Pharr, *Vergil's Aeneid, Books I–VI* (Boston: D. C. Heath, 1930), 74.

28. L. P. Wilkinson, *Golden Latin Artistry* (Norman: University of Oklahoma Press, 1985), 215.

29. *Aeneid* IX.339–341.

30. "Perhaps this is the reason of the mediæval opinion about Virgil, as of a prophet or a magician; his single words and phrases, his pathetic half lines, giving utterance, as the voice of Nature herself, to that pain and weariness, yet hope of better things, which is the experience of her children in every time." John Henry Cardinal Newman, *An Essay in Aid of the Grammar of Assent* (London: Longmans, Green, 1930), 78–79.

31. *Aeneid* IX.465–467.

32. McConville, *The King's Three Faces*, 249.

33. *Aeneid* VI.673–676.

34. *Aeneid* VI.638–639.

35. Zachary M. Hutchins, *Inventing Eden: Primitivism, Millennialism and the Making of New England* (New York: Oxford University Press, 2014), 21–30; Michael Householder, "Eden's Translations: Women and Temptation in Early America," *Huntington Library Quarterly* 70 (2007): 11–12; Martin Snyder, "The Hero in the Garden: Classical Contributions to the Early Images of America," in *Classical Traditions in Early America*, ed. John Eadie (Ann Arbor: Center for the Coordination of Ancient and Modern Studies, 1976), 140–148.

36. This Eurocentric version of history traced civilization's path from Greece to Rome to Renaissance Italy to Western Europe to England to . . . America.

37. J. A. Leo Lemay, *A Calendar of American Poetry in the Colonial Newspapers and Magazines and in the Major English Magazines Through 1765* (Worcester, MA: American Antiquarian Society, 1972), 23.

38. *Aeneid* II.705–711.

39. As Virgil makes clear time and again: from Aeneas's preferring to die defending Troy (III.298ff.) or to stay and build a city with Dido (IV.333ff.).

40. McConville, *The King's Three Faces*, 247.

41. *Metamorphoses* IX.241–246.

42. *Sermones* II.iv.88–91.

43. Our neo-Latin poet, it should be noted, meets the challenge that neo-Latin writers often gave themselves: to use the identical phrase, in the same metrical position, but with at least a slightly different grammatical construction. Thus, instead of Ovid's dative (*mihi*) with an intransitive verb (*grator*) and an ablative of means (*pectore*) modified by *totoque* earlier in the line, or Horace's indirect object of *referas* (*mihi*) with an ablative of means (*pectore*) modified by *memori* in the line, our poet's *mihi pectore* combines the indirect object of *dat* with an ablative of specification modified by *forti*, the final word of the line.

44. McConville, *The King's Three Faces*, 191.

45. Nelson, *The Royalist Revolution*, 33.

46. Cicero's writings hold a special place in the history of neo-Latin literature as the battleground of the humanists' fight over the very definition of correct Latin, including vocabulary, syntax, meter, and genre. See Joann Dellaneva, ed., *Ciceronian Controversies* (Cambridge: I Tatti Renaissance Library, 2007).

47. Richard M. Gummere mentions references to Cicero throughout his *American Colonial Mind and the Classical Tradition*, including references to *De officiis* that span John Cotton's 1635 *Keyes to the Kingdom* to Governor Thomas Hutchinson's 1765 *History of Massachusetts* (111).

48. Cicero, *On Duties*, ed. M. T. Griffin and E. M. Atkins (Cambridge, MA: Harvard University Press, 2001), xxiii.

49. Anthony Everitt, *Cicero: The Life and Times of Rome's Greatest Politician* (New York: Random House, 2003), 258.

50. *De officiis* I.17.

51. Ibid., III.23–24.

52. The translations are by E. M. Atkins in Cicero, *On Duties*, ed. Griffin and Atkins.

53. *De officiis* I.25.

54. Gummere, *The American Colonial Mind*, 111.

55. As quoted in McConville, *The King's Three Faces*, 245.

56. David A. Copeland, *Debating the Issues in Colonial Newspapers* (Westport, CT: Greenwood Press, 2000), 202.

57. Jeffrey L. Pasley, *The Tyranny of Printers: Newspaper Politics in the Early American Republic* (Charlottesville: University of Virginia Press, 2001), 38.

[4]

CAROLINE WIGGINTON

LETTERS FROM A WOMAN IN PENNSYLVANIA, OR ELIZABETH GRAEME FERGUSSON DREAMS OF JOHN DICKINSON

TO READ THE HISTORIOGRAPHY of the Stamp Act Crisis is to learn it was a contest between men. Prime Minister George Grenville orchestrated its passage; Virginian orator Patrick Henry heatedly counseled legislative resolutions in protest; in American cities the Sons of Liberty rioted; and British statesman William Pitt offered rousing but double-edged words in support of its repeal.[1] We know, of course, that women felt the impact of its passage and the subsequent unrest, yet their scarcity in its accounts suggests that they were mere bystanders. They neither guided the political theory that underpinned the colonial response nor marched in the streets, smashing windows and hanging effigies; they neither attempted to protect stamped paper nor called shirking imperial agents to account in a mark of parliamentary compliance.

Yet it is precisely in women's absence from this narrative that others have found their participation. Indeed, historian Mary Beth Norton, importantly recovering women's revolutionary era presence, identifies the 1760s as the decade in which American women emerged from their "devot[ion] exclusively to private affairs." As she tells it, that emergence was largely at the instigation of "male political leaders [who] had to focus on the realm of the household" and who, out of necessity, needed women's support if their economic boycotts were to work.[2] Thus women's activism manifested first as a refusal to consume British goods.[3] And if sometimes women said no, they must have also said yes. They did so by purchasing boycotted goods, by marrying with stamped paper, by preparing their husbands for rioting, and by cleaning up its mess. They did so by assenting to resistance, heeding the call to envision an altered colonial relationship. And they did so by composing poetry: it was a medium in which they wrote about the contours and limits of their actions and assent, and communicated their visions.[4] Just as neo-Latin verse, as shown in the preceding chapter, might disrupt the binary of accept–resist, women's vernacular poetry could further pry open the dialogue surrounding the Stamp Act Crisis and present an opportunity to assent to activism without advocating revolution and violence. It is to poetry that we can turn to recover how the Stamp Act Crisis inspired women's intellectual activism and how that activism built upon a literary history. Poetry is something women did, and it reflects both how refusal could be a kind of political action and how they conceived of their concurrence and presence.

This essay examines one moment where Elizabeth Graeme Fergusson, a woman largely self-educated under the guidance of her mother, used poetry to moderate the activist fervor of the Stamp Act Crisis and its aftermath. It argues that her poem "The Dream" assents to and organizes resistance through a turn to poetry, a genre that performatively circulates and reinforces heterosocial and intimate affiliations. Turning away from Britain and from other colonies alike, she orders resistance around intra-colonial relations, rural labor, and self-sufficiency. Rather than a contest between men, she refigures the Stamp Act Crisis as a concern among neighbors, a moment to capitalize upon local bounty and labor, thereby imagining an inclusive if idealistic future. She arranges a space for all Pennsylvanians, including women, in a well-ordered colony. For Fergusson, women and their labor had always been part of the project of prosperity, their assent necessary, their refusal disastrous. The poem demands that we see women as always woven into the Stamp Act Crisis and its reverberations.

For those familiar with Fergusson, it should come as no surprise that she responded to the crisis by producing an ambitiously long manuscript poem. According to her biographers, Elizabeth Graeme Fergusson (1737–1801) was the "most learned woman in America."[5] The daughter of Dr. Thomas Graeme and Ann Diggs Graeme, she grew up in a world of privilege, education, and travel. Her family split its time between Philadelphia and their home, Graeme Park, twenty miles outside the city. During the Stamp Act Crisis, Fergusson traveled in Europe, distant from the unrest experienced in Philadelphia and other colonial urban centers. She returned to find she had dodged the turmoil, an outsider to its spent passion. She also returned to find that her sickly mother had died in her absence. Within months, she mourned her beloved elder sister as well and became a foster mother to her orphaned niece and nephew. In her grief, she retreated to Graeme Park and embarked upon a prolific poetic period. As acts of self-consolation, she paraphrased the psalms, translated François Fénelon's *Les Aventures de Télémaque* (*The Adventures of Telemachus*) into English verse, and composed a number of other works. For her, poetry responds to relational crises. It restores order in the face of domestic and communal rupture.

Fergusson also regularized her mother's informal literary gatherings, thereby establishing what some have identified as America's first literary salon. The salon included a number of luminaries and artists, some regular attendees and some occasional, including visitors to Philadelphia. Numbered among the coterie were Dr. Benjamin Rush, Reverend Jacob Duché and his wife Elizabeth, Dr. John and Mary Morgan, harpsichordist Francis Hopkinson and his wife Ann, poet Annis Boudinot Stockton and members of her family, musician James Bremnar, sculptor Patience Wright, and landscape painter Betsy Pyle.[6] Heterosociability characterized these gatherings, as did variety in political, religious, and artistic sentiments as well as interlocking familial and evolving affective relations. Elizabeth Duché, Mary Morgan, and Francis Hopkinson were siblings; Stockton was to become Rush's mother-in-law; Fergusson, still an unwed Elizabeth Graeme during the height of the salon, was to marry one its visitors—Scotsman Henry Hugh Fergusson—in 1772.[7] Thus the salon leveraged literary pursuits and conversation to collect and organize what was otherwise a disperse jumble of potential intimates. Its belletristic productions create what David Shields terms a "sensus communis": "a form of communal identity brought into being by speech acts or writing."[8]

The salon likely read a version of Fergusson's "The Dream," composed in 1768 and retranscribed in 1790 into her bound manuscript collection, *Poemata Juvenilia*. The poem recounts a reverie in which "haughty" Albion arrives in Pennsylvania and "claim[s] Dominion" over recalcitrant New World subjects.[9] In response, long-dead founder William Penn appears upon a "lucid Cloud" and reminisces carving a colony from the wilderness wherein "Manly Liberty and virt[u]ous Peace" would reign, threatened only by faction.[10] He then hands a scroll to Fergusson. Rather than read it herself, she consigns it to a "youth[ful]" John Dickinson, the author, she purposefully footnotes, of *Letters from a Farmer in Pennsylvania*.[11] On behalf of Penn and Fergusson, Dickinson faces a gathered crowd and reads aloud the scroll: thirty-three manuscript pages of rhymed georgic couplets that detail rural Pennsylvanian bounty and self-sufficiency. The scroll's message seeks to release the local colonists from a subservient and divisive pursuit of British commodities. At the conclusion of his delivery, a "buzing murmur of Applause," gradually increasing in volume, spreads through the "Neighboring Ground" and causes Fergusson to awaken to the violence of an approaching storm.[12]

Through the peculiar inclusion of Dickinson as herald, Fergusson explicitly links her poem to the political debate that raged in the Stamp Act Crisis's aftermath. Dickinson, a Delaware Valley lawyer and statesman who rose to prominence during the crisis, shaped much of that debate. His influence swelled through his popular serial essays, *Letters from a Farmer in Pennsylvania* (1767–68).[13] *Letters* fanned the flames of opposition by proclaiming that the Stamp Act's repeal in fact exacerbated threats to colonial liberty as its legislative successors—the Declaratory, New York Restraining, and Townshend Acts—dangerously and illegally asserted parliamentary authority over the colonies, despite the continued lack of colonial representation. *Letters* offers instructions for how to justify and order their resistance. Scholars incorporate such publications as Dickinson's *Letters* into a narrative that underscores how they foment revolution and incite nationhood. Like Pauline Maier, they see the Stamp Act and its aftermath as a move from "ad hoc violence to an ordered opposition."[14] But what if John Dickinson's *Letters* was in fact the gift of a Philadelphia *salonnière*? Suppose that rather than prose, his admonitions were originally enclosed in a scroll that materialized from the clouds and transformed into verse?

Fergusson's "The Dream" alleges precisely such counterfactuals. She responds to the homosocial fervor of the Stamp Act Crisis and its aftermath by moderating its masculine exclusivity through the invocation of poetic form. Her verse assents to Dickinson's pacific activism of boycotting and home industry, but corrects his proto-nationalist fraternity. Her manuscript letter-as-scroll replaces his printed *Letters*, a collection that neither addresses women nor includes their voice. She retroactively swaps his authorship of *Letters* with a vision in which he is her chosen agent. As a result, the printed *Letters* now appears to be a mistranslation, a delivery gone astray from the more suitable measured meter and rhymed manuscript couplets of "The Dream." In verse, he at last dispenses the proper message, thereby serving the belletristic production and sensus communis of the heterosocial salon rather than a homosocial agenda of American brotherhood.

John Dickinson Orders a Resistance

In naming John Dickinson in "The Dream," Fergusson designates as her herald an intimate rather than an abstract figure of the crisis. As the

Graeme family's lawyer and friend, John Dickinson occasioned Fergusson's salon, where politics were a subject of conversation and verse.[15] When his *Letters* began its serial appearance, it was discussed widely, undoubtedly at the Saturday evening meetings of the salon and at the Sunday dinner parties hosted by her father. Thomas Graeme presented Fergusson with the book version of *Letters* soon after its compilation and publication, advising her to "atend to [its] arguments."[16] Part of what *Letters* did was to advance the ordering of resistance that had begun during the Stamp Act Crisis, presenting a sequence of recommended actions alongside their justification. Dickinson's recommendations sought to oppose complacency on the one hand and disjointed and counterproductive violence on the other. *Letters*' weekly serial appearance as periodical essays in the *Pennsylvania Chronicle and Universal Advertiser* effectively structured a case against Parliament's actions and connected the Stamp Act, even in its repeal, to subsequent legislation and future colonial ties with England. Here, I wish to linger on the public homosocial American vision of resistance that the printed *Letters* provides in order to more fully foreground how Fergusson's "The Dream" counters through a return to manuscript poetry and its vision of peaceful rural labor and natural rhythms.

Letters structures the case by delineating the core of Dickinson's argument and call to action in the first three letters and then elaborating upon and defending those positions in the remainder. In the first letter, he wonderingly remarks, "I have observed, that little notice has been taken of an act of parliament, as injurious in its principle to the liberties of these colonies, as the *Stamp Act* was: I mean the act for suspending the legislation of *New York*."[17] Defying those who would claim that the New York Restraining Act—which suspended that colony's assembly until it supplied the British troops quartered there—was none of their concern, he declares, "[T]he cause of *one* is the cause of *all*."[18] He reasons: "If the parliament may lawfully deprive *New York* of any of *her* rights, it may deprive any, or all the other colonies of *their* rights; and nothing can possibly so much encourage such attempts, as a mutual inattention to the interests of each other. *To divide, and thus to destroy*, is the first political maxim in attacking those, who are powerful by their union. He certainly is not a wise man, who folds his arms, and reposes himself at home, viewing, with unconcern, the flames that have invaded his neighbor's house, without using any endeavors to extinguish them."[19]

Having all but shouted "fire" to his fellow colonists, his second letter fans the flames by carefully enumerating how the Townshend Acts, ostensibly passed to regulate trade, were in fact taxes.[20] His blistering essay concludes by identifying the real "question" as being "whether the parliament can legally take money out of our pockets, without our consent. If they can, our boasted liberty is but *Vox et praeterea nihil*[,] A sound and nothing else."[21] The third letter culminates what seems a loose introduction to the themes and reasoning of the entire set by articulating "the meaning of these letters": "The meaning of them is, to convince the people of these colonies that they are at this moment exposed to the most imminent dangers; and to persuade them immediately, vigorously, and unanimously, to exert themselves in the most firm, but most peaceable manner, for obtaining relief."[22] Having enjoined his "dear countrymen" in the previous letter to "ROUSE" themselves, Dickinson now channels that passion away from "turbulence and tumult" and towards "actions of prudence, justice, modesty, bravery, humanity and magnanimity."[23] As with the "ancient *Spartans*" who "marched up to scenes of havoc, and horror, with the sound of flutes, to the tunes of which their steps kept pace," Dickinson's *Letters* sets a cadence by which his fellow colonists may regularize their resistance.[24] He instructs them first to try petitioning and then, if those "applications . . . prove ineffectual," turn to boycotts and home industry: "[L]et us try, if our ingenuity, industry, and frugality, will not give weight to our remonstrances. Let us all be united with one spirit, in one cause. Let us invent—let us work—let us save—let us, continually, keep up our claim, and incessantly repeat our complaints."[25] His repetition—let us, let us, let us, let us, let us—syntactically performs the unification, a drumbeat calling his male readers to action. Adherence to his rhythm will avert the excessive punishment that an "appeal . . . made to the sword" would invite from the "mother country," and will ease reconciliation once "she returns to her 'old good humor, and her old good nature.'"[26] He distinguishes between prudent and disorderly resistance. The latter is akin to self-destruction: "But if once *we* are separated from our mother country, what new form of government shall we adopt, or where shall we find another *Britain* to supply our loss? Torn from the body, to which we are united by religion, liberty, laws, affections, relation, language and commerce, we must bleed at every vein."[27]

Having counterbalanced his crescendo of outrage with a crafted call to ordered action, Dickinson extends a past of successful Stamp Act protests into a united future of orderly activism. The remaining letters in turn present and refute counterarguments, reiterate and linger on points already made, and refine further the interrelationship between the Stamp

Act and subsequent parliamentary legislation, but these first letters have set the stage. Formally, by invoking the epistolary form—in each saluting his audience as "My dear Countrymen," signing as "A Farmer," and employing the first and second person—he makes the abstract questions of political philosophy, imperial authority, and political resistance into something that is relational, that emerges within and between "Countrymen," a word that suggests both male citizens and shared dependence upon the land. His use of the letter as his form and a periodical as his publication venue democratizes his audience. His letters could be and were reprinted widely (Carl Kaestle notes that their "frequent reprinting and sustained praise . . . demonstrated a popularity surpassing that of any previous political tract in America").[28] They could be shared, read aloud, collected, and their familiar prose addresses all countrymen, whether learned or common. That he, "A Farmer," is learned—making references to law and history, concluding each letter with a Latin phrase—adds to his authority without estranging him.[29]

Dickinson's vision of orderly resistance, like the histories of the Stamp Act, presents a decidedly homosocial vision. This is a man speaking to men about how to negotiate their bondedness with each other in terms of their shared mother, whose arbitrary discipline demands a turning to each other even as they maintain nominal attachment to her. They are united as country*men*, their transatlantic tie to Britain something of an umbilical cord. If they heave against it violently, they will sever their connection to her and each other, "bleed[ing] at every vein" in a gruesome and fatal birth. If, however, they discipline themselves to Dickinson's cadence, they can stretch their cord so that it no longer constrains their liberty. Instead, they shall be like "ancient *Spartans*," keeping "pace" together.[30] Their resistance shall be glorious and heroic. Thus, woman obtains only as metaphor, the gender of the mother country and, at points, the individual colonies. In this way, *Letters* anticipates what Dana Nelson terms the "national manhood" of the early American republic.[31] Women as wives, mothers, daughters, neighbors, and fellow citizens who will share in the boycott, and, crucially, the labor of home industry, are absent. Shared feeling among white male citizens downplays difference and enables democracy (here, joint action and colonial self-determination). It is the tightening of this bond that Fergusson's "The Dream" resists. Her verse restrains the inter-colonial feeling of countrymen and turns instead to the Pennsylvania rural neighborhood where the quotidian labors of men and women alike produce self-sufficient harmony.

The Lady "Evanishes"

When her father presented Dickinson's collected *Letters* to Fergusson and desired she "atend" to its "arguments," she was unlikely to have been a novice to its contents. Yet here was a bound and complete version, one that further cemented the argumentative arc via which Dickinson organized ongoing resistance and mapped a line of union that held woman distant. Inspired by his words but resistant to the homosocial vision that went contrary to the salon's heterosociability, Fergusson began her own intercession into political philosophy. Rather than epistles for print, she penned a 700-line manuscript poem, one composed of heroic couplets and irregular stanzas. In turning to the couplet, Fergusson opted for a celebrated and traditional mode of "serious political and philosophical discourse"; as J. Paul Hunter reminds us, "couplets were the standard of both effectiveness and beauty for a very long time. . . . Not only were intricate couplet poems read, discussed, praised, and depended upon to elucidate historical and current intellectual issues, but they were regarded as the standard of verbal pleasure."[32] Poetry in couplets is ubiquitous in the eighteenth-century archive, and its 200-year reign roughly enfolds British colonization of North America. Thus we might think of couplets as coextensive with imagining the British Empire, the poetic rhyme and meter via which colonial–metropole relations and encounters had always been versified. Unlike Dickinson's prose periodical *Letters*, which appeals to a populist fraternity of American countrymen, Fergusson's "The Dream" presents continuity with a tradition of measured, philosophical verse that circulates among familiars.

The titular dream transpires as Fergusson's poetic persona wanders with "heedless Steps" alongside the Delaware River. When she is overtaken by "Morpheus" and falls unexpectedly asleep,

> The Mind unfetterd fled her native Home,
> And unimprisoned did unbounded Roam;
> Burst every Barrier of her waking Care,
> And launc[h]'d unbodied thro' the yielding Air.[33]

When recalling Fergusson's salon performances, Benjamin Rush effusively observes, "Upon these occasions her body seemed to *evanish*, and she appeared to be all mind."[34] Poetry allows Fergusson to evanish, or exist as dream. But the dream is not simple fancy. Couplets structure her in intellectualism, and it is no surprise when Fergusson's "unbodied" mind falters in her unfettered flight and tumbles back to earth "thro' the yielding Air," still unbodied and still bound. The opening couplets enact first the freedom of the mind and then the fettering of its uncontrolled liberty, a combination that Edward Cahill claims to be characteristic of eighteenth-century aesthetic and political understandings of liberty: the mind may roam but not too far, maintaining its position between "servility" and "extravagance."[35] Thus her mind tumbles from its unbodied flight into an aesthetic terrain optimal for exploring political philosophy.

That terrain materializes as a "spacious Vale" next to the ocean. Upon Fergusson's landing, the Atlantic parts like the Red Sea, and she observes Albion on the opposite coast, "glow[ing]" with "haughty warmth."[36] As the "Guardian of England," Albion angrily "command[s]" obedience.[37] Albion and Fergusson face each other across the parted waters of the Atlantic, in this moment making visible that women have always been present in the crisis. The waves surge in response to Albion's fury, yet William Penn, founder of Pennsylvania, descends calmly upon a "lucid cloud."[38] He admonishes Albion that great "Power" is still subject to "Laws, / And God, and Reason certain Limits draws."[39] He recounts a history of prosperous colonial founding, the reward of peace and toil, but nevertheless always tenuous and since troubled by faction and envy. He reassures, however, that "Some Patriotic merit yet remains, / With ardent Zeal on Pennsylvanias Plains."[40] Lamenting the destructive "fire" that "passion" ignites, he cries, "Sad fate of Language! that 'tis not confind, / To shew the feelings of the honest Mind."[41] He promises that time will tell "Who hates pious Virtue or pure Virtue Loves."[42]

Through Penn, the poem presents a philosophy of literature that eschews passion in favor of virtue and measured emotion. Penn is Albion's affective foil, the deliverer of Israelites in Egyptian slavery to her Pharaoh, a celestial being who opposes her fury with history and reason. Whereas her speech is short, an "indignant" twelve lines appearing on a single manuscript page that testify to the explosive emotions that propel her sentiments, his is a steady march of twenty-six couplets spanning four pages, a thoughtful exposition on an enduring if changeable relationship. It is language's "Sad fate" that it can be manipulative as well as sincere, thoughtless as well as careful. The couplet leashes unbound language to show virtue and honesty, just as the opening couplets brought Fergusson's soaring mind to ground.

Penn's comparative prudence lingers after his departure. At the conclusion of his speech, Penn and his cloud "vanish," but, as with Fergusson's evanishment into "all mind," Penn becomes all writing. In farewell, he "thr[ows]" upon her "Bosom" a "fair long written Scroll" and instructs her to "show [his] Children what is written here / May Pennsylvania hold my precepts dear."[43] The ocean transforms into a "plain" upon which Fergusson sees a "busy Multitude," the Pennsylvanians to whom she is to bestow Penn's epistle, a scene that deepens the verse's suggestive biblical parallels with the story of Moses, here recollecting his descent from Mount Sinai with the Ten Commandments on stone tablets. Rather than be the Moses to Penn's Old Testament God, Fergusson "resign[s]" the "scroll" to "One youth Conspicuous [who] towerd above the rest."[44] A note at the bottom of the page in Fergusson's hand reveals that this youth is "Mr John Dickinson a gentlemen who wrote a Series of Letters Calld the Farmers Letters which were almost universaly admird For explaining the Rights of Taxation and the Constitution of Pennsylvania."[45] It is he who "straight unwind[s]" the scroll's "Characters" and "read[s] their meaning to the listning Crowd."[46]

This moment of transfer is a peculiar one. Having poetically displaced first Albion and then Penn, why doesn't Fergusson read the scroll herself? And why John Dickinson? Fergusson's alternative title to "The Dream" is "The Philosophical Farmer," and it suggests that this moment of transfer, in which Dickinson appears and accepts with "modest Diffidence" the task of reading Penn's message aloud, is in fact the inflection point of the poem, the moment in which Fergusson's hand briefly manifests as she passes on the scroll. Her formlessness resolves into a "Bosom" and one feels the presence of her unmentioned hand, the part of her body that performs the scroll's "resign[ation]." There is something gestural, then, about Fergusson's brief and partial manifestation as body, just as there is something gestural about the implication of this moment: that "Philosophical Farmer" is a role Dickinson has been assigned, a commission for which Fergusson first selected him because he "towerd above the rest," only subsequently observing that "Freedom had inspird his Breast."[47] Indeed, the poem itself does not name Dickinson, leaving that task to a footnote. It is his inscription in heroic couplets that transforms him into a figure of note for more than his stature.

There is also something tongue in cheek about this moment. Recall that Fergusson numbered Dickinson among the ranks of her salon. If she read it aloud to her literary circle—perhaps while nodding significantly in Dickinson's direction, were he present, brandishing his bound *Letters* aloft in his absence—this moment would amuse. If shared with a correspondent, perhaps lips would twitch or eyebrows rise in appreciation.[48] The moment recalls for Fergusson and her coterie that whatever Dickinson's public popularity, he is also part of a literary and intellectual salon that, more so than Dickinson's "countrymen," reflects the heterosociability of the colonies. His and other men's visibility as the philosophers of the political crisis has been a happenstance of physicality: height, sex. Such happenstance does not guarantee the merit of their words. Indeed, as the first book of Samuel tells it, Saul was chosen king of the Israelites in part because of his height, and he was not a good king.[49] This moment in "The Dream," therefore, amuses even as it bites. It suggests that Dickinson, like Saul, may be a poor leader unless he submits to Penn and Fergusson and delivers the poetic message faithfully. He must not exceed his charge.

Dickinson's submission to moderation is signaled poetically and intellectually, mediated by crafted couplets that reflect Penn's warning to control one's passion. The poem presents a critique of Dickinson's form, the printed epistle, as one that rejects heterosociability and belletrism, a populist and masculine rather than dignified mode. Dickinson's message may be good, but his form is not. Thus Fergusson is like the couplet, the conduit via which the message gets transferred. She refigures the presence of women within the political debates of the 1760s. It may seem a contest between men, but women give form to the philosophy, their refusals and assents, as in their boycotting and consumption of goods, their home manufactures, a quotidian if "evanished" transfer point in an ordered political activism.

The Philosophical Poet

The bulk of "The Dream" is a transcription of the scroll spanning some 500 lines. It is ostensibly read aloud by Dickinson, though he and his towering body are never noted again. Only quotation marks running down the left margin remind that these lines are his oration. Instead, Fergusson's own philosophy of ordered resistance, cast as Penn's remedy for faction, captivates the audience. Hers, unlike that of Dickinson's *Letters*, does not center on a colonial union of countrymen who petition and boycott. Rather, it evinces little concern with other colonies and foregrounds a valorization of Pennsylvanian bounty and shared labor. Detailing the natural ingenuity and commodities of the colony, its dream is rooted in the region's rural capacity and scenes of domestic production.

The scroll proffers its bitterest message first, that Pennsylvanians "must rich <u>Commerce</u> for a time resign," and with it "Britons wealth."[50] But in recompense Pennsylvania's "fertile plenty" will offer blissful harmony and a release from the fetters of faction and dependency. The scroll then turns to the "methods" for the achievement of its vision, offering

Nature as the maternal replacement for Albion, the proper "Parent" for a well-ordered populace:

> "Keep simple Nature in your steady Eye
> "Observe her movements, her Directions spy;
> "Tho' the great Parent of a numerous Race
> "She smiles benignly on that favord Place;
> "Where she is Courted, honord, and reverd;
> "Her precepts valu'd; and her Laws are heard:
> "There will she rise in Majesty Divine
> "As Gods Chief Agent most Illustrious Shine.
> "Not Rough and Rugged as the savage kind,
> "Whom Rules cant fetter, nor soft Manners bind;
> "Not deaf to social and endearing Life,
> "Not bold, Contentious, full of angry Strife;
> "Not chargd with vengeance and malicious guile
> "Unconscious of the sympathetic Smile
> "Where Bosoms feel not for a Brothers Grief
> "Nor Souls fly speedy to a Friends relief;
> "Not such the Manners that I wish to Reign
> "In Brutal Roughness on my favord Plain."[51]

Order follows from "steady" "Observ[ation]" of the natural world. Nature "favor[s]" those who adopt the "precepts" and "Laws" that they discover through such observation. Nature provides the rhythm. This rhythm recollects that of Dickinson's spartan cadence, and Fergusson too presents a drumbeat through repetition: "Not Rough and Rugged," "Not deaf," "Not bold, Contentious, full of angry Strife," "Not chargd with vengeance and malicious guile," "Not such the Manners." Hers is slower, less martial, retaining time within her cadence for the "social and endearing Life" even as its lingering upon the negative—Not, Not, Not, Not, Not—reminds that women's participation in colonial resistance most often manifested as refusal.

In the next stanza, the scroll further refines Fergusson's ordered vision by casting it as a "happy Medium" and then presenting the other extreme which Pennsylvania should avoid:

> "A happy Medium be my Sons your guide
> "From rustic rudeness, and a splendid pride:
> "As you would flee the Savage Indians roads,
> "Trod by the Nations of your green Abodes;

"To shun the softning Lure of British Wealth,
"The fair subverter of your Countrys Health:
"Too nice, too elegant, for your new Soil;
"A sweetend poison; a distructive smile.
"Live Independant of her gewgaw Charms
"In shunning them you shun a train of Harms:
"Turn then from Commerce your too blinded Eyes,
"And learn your Countrys own produce to prize.[52]

The happy medium is between the "Brutal Roughness" of the preceding stanza and the "softning Lure" of British luxury. She casts this balance as specific to Pennsylvania, "your new Soil." British goods are a "sweetend poison," undermining the "Countrys Health." Her scathing "gewgaw Charms" subtly aligns the two poles, suggesting that Pennsylvanians are like "Savage Indians" if they trade their "Independan[cy]" for such worthless trinkets.[53] It is through cultivating Pennsylvania's own "produce" that they shall achieve commercial liberty. The stanza concludes with a return to natural rhythms:

"Nor think the Subject mean that points the Way
"How Toil industrious pleasure shall convey;
"Labor and Rest shall just Alternates know,
"Sweet is the Rest, which does from Labor flow;
"And sweet that Labor too, supreamly Blest!
"Which Strength recovers by the Balm of Rest:
"Shew by your Actions, not in wordy War,
"That Patriotic Liberty is dear;
"Dear to your Souls as Ophirs purest Gold,[54]
"And for no price, be sacred Freedom Sold.[55]

"Toil" has its own "pleasure[s]," generating a "Sweet" "Alternat[ion]" between "Labor and Rest." Labor produces the twin blessings of production and pleasure. The coy allusion to the "supream[]" blessing that follows labor evokes that other labor, childbirth. It becomes clear in this moment that the "social and endearing life" necessitates women as co-laborers, producing goods and children. In these stanzas, Fergusson dreams of a recipe for balance, a "happy Medium": labor and rest, softness and strength, bounty and moderation, rusticity and luxury, liberty and reverence. She rejects the "wordy War" of political philosophy in prose for the poetic and quotidian balance that emerges from natural observation and attentiveness to the rhythms of rural life and its seasons. The form of the poem itself reflects such balance with strict adherence to rhyme and meter, but with irregular stanza lengths—here eighteen and twenty-two lines respectively, elsewhere of many other lengths—that match the demands of rural production and its diurnal and seasonal shifts rather than those of a soldier's matched march, which admits no false step.

Fergusson's philosophy turns in part on a conflated domesticity that merges colonial distance and liberty with household production. Addressing women specifically, the scroll advises them to engage in labor like spinning the wool sheared from their family "Flocks" and washing "Linnen": "This Task my Daughters Be immediate thine / In Life Domestic ye were born to Shine."[56] As she moves to a more abstract meditation upon the connection between industry and religious virtue, it becomes unclear if she still speaks to women. Yet the connection between luxury and vice continues as British "Manufactures," "Taxes, and "Trade" "each good invade / And strike at Liberty, that lovely Maid!"[57] Indeed, "gay Fashions Law" promulgates "Envy" among "Neighbor[s]."[58] The remedy is to eschew "foreign Pleasures" and "foreign Joys."[59] As Kate Haulman explains, the end of the Seven Years' War marked the beginning of efforts to tie women's fashion to virtue and republicanism: "Attempting to discipline female and feminized appetites, and with them women's spending power, the new model of femininity encouraged Anglo-American women—of the young, unmarried, and urban variety in particular—to renounce fashion's artifice, shun the gaze, and become modest, frugal, and productive 'country' wives."[60] Yet here, the public–private ideological divide has shifted to a foreign–domestic one, wherein Pennsylvanian women are conjoined with men, participants and producers whose "country" labor preserves liberty and makes good neighbors. Speaking specifically to men, Fergusson further advocates "Rural" industry.[61] She ties their present occupation with classic and natural models, especially those of Virgil, the bee, the spider, and the beaver. Poetry, sovereignty, heroism, and natural order are confluent. The scroll provides the moral: "Thus all Creation is a living Page, / Which should th'Eye of Reasons Sons engage."[62] Such moments contrast with Dickinson, who, in case petitioning should fail, calls for boycott and home industry as part of his ordered resistance, yet neglects to seek women's assent to such a plan. In his *Letters*, the women who would provide the labor of resistance are marginal. Here, women are essential participants. Fergusson makes clear that men, too, can choose women as their partners and agents, just as Penn has done with Fergusson and God has done with Nature.

In its turn to nature for a model of labor and rural life, the scroll

Figure 4.1. This William Buck engraving of a 1755 portrait of Graeme Park portrays the idealized heterosocial labor poetically depicted, by Fergusson, as a solution to the economic difficulties posed by the Stamp Act. Buck's engraving was published in S. F. Hotchkin, *The York Road, Old and New* (Philadelphia, 1892).

builds upon its rhymed couplet form and invokes the georgic mode (see figure 4.1). In the eighteenth-century georgic, farming and poetry complement each other; agricultural labor constrains natural bounty in the service of human need and a poem constrains language in the service of an intellectual and imaginative vision.[63] Georgic constraint has a political tenor: farming is "a cultural and civilizing activity, a means of building up the state and ensuring its peaceful prosperity."[64] The labor of husbandry mirrors the labor of state building, just as agricultural production supports political stability. Fergusson implicitly signals her assent to that constraint by offering a "Digression" on Virgil and the "deathless fame" he so deservedly earned.[65] John Dryden's 1697 translation of Virgil's *Georgics*—the translation that "established the georgic as a popular mode and genre"[66]—uses rhymed couplets, and Fergusson's "The Dream" follows his lead. Dryden's translation also emphasizes that the state-building agricultural labor celebrated by the georgic occurs after a conflict, often a revolution but also perhaps rioting and violence à la the

Stamp Act Crisis. According to Karen O'Brien, "Dryden transformed Virgil's country world into a principled political retreat, an alternative realm from which to imagine and predict the restoration of a legitimate British monarchy and empire."[67] O'Brien's subject is the *imperial* georgic of the eighteenth century, adding the adjective to highlight the century's use of the georgic to associate the colonies' rural production to metropolitan rule and trade. "It was georgic, more than any other literary mode or genre," she explains, "which assumed the burden of securing the aesthetic and moral links between country, city, and empire."[68] Fergusson's georgic, however, restores not the colonial mercantile relation with Britain, but Penn's founding moment of self-sufficient and virtuous settler colonization.[69] Philadelphia, not London, partners with Pennsylvanian farmland, growing like a "fragrant Flower" fertilized by the colony's "honest Harvest."[70] The georgic invocation of the scroll serves a Pennsylvanian poetic vision of self-sufficiency and virtue rather than a British imperial vision.

Fergusson cements the connection between poetry, independency, and prosperity when she imagines the domestic scene—as both household and Pennsylvanian—as one in which "every Sex and age" of the family labors and reads. The rhythm of domesticity is the "gentle rural themes" of James Thomson's *The Four Seasons*, the "smooth numbers" of Virgil. She suggests it is these georgic rhythms that in part mark Pennsylvanians as Virgil's rightful heirs. "[M]odern Ital[ians]" are now "Dead to each manly and each honest joy / Loose Loves, loose Sonnets all their Hours empl[oy]."[71] Fergusson's heroic couplets, not "loose Sonnets," set a virtuous pace; they are the measure of Pennsylvanian harmony. Within such poetic and industrious domestic order, there is room for still other literature:

"Milton, and Lock, and Addison are read,
"Each Page where Virtues lovely Form is spread:
"The Tale, the Poem, and the Fable may
"If managd right all useful Truths convey:
"To one one [*sic*] bright point may different Roads converge
"And Vice, and folly in their Pictures Scourge;
"Raise up meek Merit, crush the Foot of Pride
"That seeks Mild Virtue in her Cell to hide;
"Draw forth the Honest to the Public Sight
"And place their goodness in a Beam of Light;
"When such the motives of th'Authors Plan
"Do not too rigidly his conduct scan;

"When Truth and Virtue Animates and Warms
"He may like Proteus move in various Forms.[72]

The works of John Milton, John Locke, and Joseph Addison receive a modest endorsement, the same as their less prestigious cousins, the "Tale, the Poem, and the Fable."[73] Their worth lies solely in their "convey[ance]" of "useful Truths." These truths must pertain to "Mild Virtue," and bring "her" to "Public Sight." In using "her," Fergusson makes virtue a woman, and a commendable author cannot abandon her to her "Cell." He must transmit—as Dickinson has done with Penn's and Fergusson's scroll—her message. "[M]anagd right[ly]," the page manifests that heterosocial source of virtue and form, bringing Pennsylvanians as readers, laborers, and listeners to a "bright point" of "converge[nce]." Literature given proper form, then, is the technology of union. Page and Fergusson resemble each other, the one transferring truth, the other a philosophical scroll.

Fergusson's "The Dream" seems to sanction somewhat Dickinson's *Letters* and to attribute his best ideas—an eschewal of violence and luxury, a turn to home industry—to Penn and Fergusson. Yet it also corrects both *Letters*' prescriptive fraternal activism and American jingoism. She presents a formal response that molds communal restoration to poetic craft and thereby invests her philosophy with a belletristic traditionalism that retains heterosociability. Hers is the antidote to conflict with England and a consuming colonial union. Instead, she turns inward and inland, coupling city and backcountry into a virtuous and self-sufficient colony. She imagines a neighborhood wherein Pennsylvanians complement each other and that turns away from a more capacious American nationalism, unconcerned with the state of other colonies. She absolves her contemporary Pennsylvania from any real difference: the Paxton brothers and others who resented Philadelphian dominance of colonial politics, women who were barred from politics, bound servants and enslaved Africans. In many ways, she admits their presence only to craft a poem that subsumes their own rhythms and meters to hers.

The Storm of Revolution

By transcribing the poem into *Poemata Juvenilia* in 1790, a manuscript collection of her past writings, Fergusson suggests through the volume's title that her dream emerged from callow naïveté. It is a juvenile poem, the production of an unmarried woman, then about thirty, at the end of a long girlhood. She adds an introductory note with the transcription:

> This little peice was wrote in October 1768: At a time when Th'Americans thought themselves unkindly treated by the English; upon which the Colonies were Endeavoring to turn their thoughts on the produce of their own Country; and trying to retrench the use of those Comoditys Which are imported from Britain: as they thought Both their Libertys, and Propertys unjustly Struck at by the Taxes and Dutys which the Mother Country levied on the American Colonys.
>
> How little did I think when I was writting this Rural Peice that I should have my Husband and Nephew exild in Consequence of the Independancy.

Fergusson's naive optimism resembles the easy hurt of "Th'Americans" who *think* themselves "unkindly treated," "unjustly Struck." "How little" did they anticipate the "Consequence[s]" of revolutionary violence and schism.

For Fergusson, those consequences were indeed dire. She had married a young and handsome Scotsman, Henry Hugh Fergusson, in 1772, and though much of her sympathy lay with American interests, he aligned himself forcefully and publicly with the British during the Revolution.[74] By then, her father had died, and she possessed Graeme Park in fee simple. When Henry refused to turn himself in to answer the charge of treason, instead deserting Fergusson and America for Europe, the Pennsylvanian authorities began the process of confiscating Graeme Park, charging her rent to remain on her family's property and inventorying and selling its effects. Fergusson retained only a few possessions, some of which she purchased at auction. It did not help that her own reputation was in tatters, after twice delivering messages that were deemed Loyalist and traitorous. The first, a 1777 letter that she carried to General George Washington on behalf of Jacob Duché, urging him to surrender to the British in light of what seemed to be their sure victory, was publicized by Washington himself. The second, in which she transmitted the offer of a British bribe to Pennsylvanian leaders, was, according to her version, a mere conversation rather than a transmission. No matter the sentiments underlying her actions, such events undermined her petitions to retain her estate, necessitating a long battle and the support of old friends, including those from the salon, to resecure the estate. By 1790, when she transcribed "The Dream" into *Poemata Juvenilia*, she was a deserted wife whose prosperity and prestige lay largely in the past.

One wonders if the poem's end reflects this wartime trauma, new lines added during its 1790 transcription in order to foreshadow her vision's failure. In its closing moments, Fergusson's awakening belies the optimism of the preceding 350 couplets: "In one short Hour the placid Scene was fled / And gloom and Darkness oer all Nature spread."[75] These words suggest that the scroll has been delivered in vain, its philosophical advice shall be speedily neglected. Or perhaps the scroll has sped along the storm, its georgic turn to Pennsylvanian self-sufficiency rather than imperial submission less measured than she suspected. The effort to maintain women's voice in a heterosocial Pennsylvania, even out of the public eye, has failed, and the diversity of conversation and opinion so esteemed by the salon has deteriorated into rank factionalism wherein avid men have the authority to shatter women's lives and misconstrue their message. America "thought" its liberty was at stake, but it was its men who impinged on heterosociability and a rural life of measured labor and intellectualism in its defense.

Fergusson disrupts a history of the Stamp Act Crisis that leaves women on the margins. She suggests that Dickinson's efforts towards a continuity of ordered resistance requires the assent and imagination of women, a return to a fully domestic scene. Yet she also remains hidden, declining to read the scroll herself and unable, in 1790 at least, to sanction her vision. Dickinson's *Letters* was not the georgic model of Fergusson's verse, and the storm of divisive faction overtook Pennsylvania. The poem calls to mind the ways that women were written out of the historical narrative, towered over by youthful and avid patriots.

Notes

The author wishes to thank Erin Drew, Abram Van Engen, Wendy Roberts, Greta LaFleur, Angela Calcaterra, Kacy Tillman, Travis Foster, as well as the editor of this volume for their thoughtful feedback and invaluable advice during the writing of this essay. Research support was provided by an American Council of Learned Societies New Faculty Fellowship and a short-term McNeil fellowship from the Historical Society of Pennsylvania.

1. The classic account of the crisis is Edmund Morgan and Helen M. Morgan, *The Stamp Act Crisis: Prologue to Revolution*, rev. ed. (New York: Collier, 1963). For more on Grenville and the Act's passage, see ch. V, 75–98. For more on Henry and his anti–Stamp Act oratory and resolutions, see 121–31. For more on the Sons of Liberty, see ch. XI, 231–62, though much of Part II, "Road to Revolution," concerns them. For more on Pitt and the repeal, see ch. XV, 327–52.

2. Mary Beth Norton, *Liberty's Daughters: The Revolutionary Experience of American Women, 1750–1800* (Ithaca, NY: Cornell University Press, 1996), 156.

3. Ibid., 155. For other important historiographies of women in the revolutionary and early national periods, see Nancy F. Cott, *The Bonds of Womanhood: "Woman's Sphere" in New England, 1780–1835*, 2d ed. (New Haven, CT: Yale University Press, 1997); Mary Kelley, *Learning to Stand and Speak: Women, Education, and Public*

Life in America's Republic (Chapel Hill: University of North Carolina Press, 2008); Linda K. Kerber, *Women of the Republic: Intellect and Ideology in Revolutionary America*, pbk. ed. (Chapel Hill: University of North Carolina Press, 1980); Mary Beth Norton, *Founding Mothers and Fathers: Gendered Power and the Forming of American Society* (New York: Vintage, 2011); and Rosemarie Zagarri, *Revolutionary Backlash: Women and Politics in the Early American Republic* (Philadelphia: University of Pennsylvania Press, 2007). Barbara Clark Smith details women's participation in revolutionary era food riots: "Women conducted nearly one-third of the riots. Here, then, were possibilities for political action that resistance and revolution opened for women, not as republican wives or mothers but as social and economic actors within household, neighborhood, and marketplace." See Smith, "Food Rioters and the American Revolution," *William and Mary Quarterly*, 3d ser., 51.1 (1994): 5.

4. Though this essay focuses on Fergusson, it is worth mentioning Hannah Griffitts's poem "The female Patriots" (1768), as it acknowledges the odd potential simultaneity of absence and presence in women's revolutionary era activism. In the poem, Griffitts, an eighteenth-century Quaker poet who lived in the Philadelphia area and who knew Fergusson, summons her fellow women to boycott: "Let the Daughters of Liberty, nobly arise, / And tho' we've no Voice, but a negative here / The use of the Taxables, let us forbear:—." See Milcah Martha Moore, *Milcah Martha Moore's Book: A Commonplace Book from Revolutionary America*, ed. Catherine La Courreye Blecki and Karin A. Wulf (University Park: Pennsylvania State University Press, 1997), 172. Here, absence from the marketplace functions as political presence. Moreover, Griffitts's "negative" "Voice" becomes a present and active one through the drafting and publication of a poem. It circulated in manuscript form (it is found in Milcah Martha Moore's commonplace book) and was published in the *Pennsylvania Chronicle*.

5. Anne Hollingsworth Wharton bestows this panegyrical title upon Fergusson. See Wharton, *Salons Colonial and Republican* (Philadelphia: J. B. Lippincott, 1900), 13. Fergusson's more recent biographer, Anne M. Ousterhout, lifts the phrase for her book's title. See Ousterhout, *The Most Learned Woman in America: A Life of Elizabeth Graeme Fergusson* (University Park: Pennsylvania State University Press, 2004).

6. For more about the salon's participants, see Susan Stabile's introduction to Ousterhout, *Most Learned Woman*, 2–3; and Ousterhout, *Most Learned Woman*, 122. All Fergusson's biographers discuss the salon. See Benjamin Rush, "An Account of the Life and Character of Mrs. Elizabeth Ferguson," *Port Folio* (1809): 523; Wharton, *Salons*; Stabile, Introduction, 6–15; and Ousterhout, *Most Learned Woman*, 122–23. Rush's florid description is oft quoted: "These evenings were, properly speaking, of the attic kind. The genius of Miss Graeme evolved the heat and light that animated them. One while she instructed by the stores of knowledge contained in the historians, philosophers, and poets of ancient and modern nations, which she called forth at her pleasure; and again she charmed by a profusion of original ideas, collected by her vivid and widely expanded imagination, and combined with exquisite taste and judgment into an endless variety of elegant and delightful forms. Upon these occasions her body seemed to evanish, and she appeared to be all mind."

7. In later years, the Revolution exacerbated what were at this time less stark political divisions. For example, Duché came to "openly disapprove[]" of independence,

writing a letter to General George Washington that embroiled him and Fergusson in a Loyalist scandal; Francis Hopkinson was an eventual signer of the Declaration who found Duché's actions outrageous. See Ousterhout, *Most Learned Woman*, 122.

8. David S. Shields, *Civil Tongues and Polite Letters in British America* (Chapel Hill: University of North Carolina Press, 1997), xviii; see 120–40 for his discussion of Fergusson's salon.

9. Elizabeth Graeme Fergusson, *Poemata Juvenilia*, n.d., [4], vol. 2 of *Papers, 1752–1799*, ms. 13298.Q., Library Company of Philadelphia, Pennsylvania. In order to emphasize the distinction between Dickinson's printed *Letters* and Fergusson's manuscript "The Dream," I have not modernized Fergusson's original punctuation, spelling, or capitalization except when necessary for clarity's sake. Fergusson's "The Dream" is found in an unpaginated section of the volume and is marked as entry no. 82. The poem itself runs to almost fifty pages and is approximately 700 lines long. To aid with reference, I have included bracketed numbers to indicate which page of the poem's section a citation might be found were the pages to be numbered consecutively starting with the beginning of the poem proper. While the poem was inscribed in 1790, it was written in 1768 at Graeme Park, according to Fergusson's note. She adds: "How little did I think when I was writting this Rural Piece that I should have my Husband and Nephew exild in Consequence of the Independancy." For more on this, see later in the chapter. Note that Fergusson transcribed a revised and expanded version of the poem in 1793. Though here I focus on the transcription that appears faithful to the pre-Revolution original, the later version is fascinating in terms of the insight it provides into Fergusson's sentiments regarding the Revolution's aftermath. She also includes some backstory about the poem's original composition and her experience of the Stamp Act Crisis while in England. As she tells it, she learned of the act's passage when a friend, the prominent London physician Samuel Fothergill, came to her residence and declared, "[Y]ou were yesterday made a Slave of." See Elizabeth Graeme Fergusson, *Lania to a Friend*, vol. 1 of *Papers, 1752–1799*, ms. 13298.Q., Library Company of Philadelphia, Pennsylvania, 40.

10. Ibid., [6–7].

11. Ibid., [10].

12. Ibid., [45].

13. Dickinson's 1764 public opposition to Joseph Galloway and Benjamin Franklin's petition for a royal government was perhaps his first notable entrée into Pennsylvania politics. See David L. Jacobson, "John Dickinson's Fight Against Royal Government, 1764," *William and Mary Quarterly*, 3d ser., 19.1 (1962): 64. He was also the draftsman of the Resolutions of the Stamp Act Congress.

14. Pauline Maier, *From Resistance to Revolution: Colonial Radicals and the Development of American Opposition to Britain, 1765–1776* (New York: Vintage, 1974), 53.

15. Ousterhout, *Most Learned Woman*, 122.

16. As quoted in ibid., 133.

17. John Dickinson, *Letters from a Farmer in Pennsylvania in Empire and Nation*, ed. Forrest McDonald (Englewood Cliffs, NJ: Prentice-Hall, 1962): 4. Unless noted otherwise, emphases are original to the text.

18. Ibid., 6.

19. Ibid.

20. Dickinson helps crystallize colonists' vague sentiment that Britain could regulate trade but that revenue generation was the sole province of the colonial assemblies, since their representatives composed the assemblies and they had no parliamentary representation. "No taxation without representation."

21. Dickinson, *Letters*, 15.

22. Ibid., 17.

23. Ibid., 14, 17.

24. Ibid., 17.

25. Ibid., 20.

26. Ibid., 18–19. Dickinson notes that these are the sentiments of Lord Clarendon.

27. Ibid., 19.

28. Carl F. Kaestle, "The Public Reaction to John Dickinson's *Farmer's Letters*," *Proceedings of the American Antiquarian Society* 78 (1968): 323.

29. Kaestle in part attributes Dickinson's "Farmer" pseudonym to the *Letters*' unprecedented popularity: "The idea of a farmer . . . appealed to an almost universal American conviction about the good life of the soil. What better atmosphere for clear-headed political theorizing than the uncorrupted, unhurried farm estate?" Ibid., 334.

30. Speaking of the long nineteenth century, Caroline Winterer explains that while many Greek examples could be deployed in both support and critique of American democracy, "Sparta was partially immune from these negative assessments, for its disciplined soldier-farmers seemed to be suitable exemplars for America's young agrarian republicans. " See Winterer, *The Culture of Classicism: Ancient Greece and Rome in American Intellectual Life 1780–1910* (Baltimore: Johns Hopkins University Press, 2002), 20. Dickinson may be taking his image of Spartans marching to flutesong from Plutarch's *Lycurgus*.

31. This phrase is the main title of Nelson's 1998 book. See Dana Nelson, *National Manhood: Capitalist Citizenship and the Imagined Fraternity of White Men* (Durham, NC: Duke University Press, 1998). For other discussions of fraternal feeling and democracy, see Peter Coviello, *Intimacy in America: Dreams of Affiliation in Antebellum Literature* (Minneapolis: University of Minnesota Press, 2005); Caleb Crain, *American Sympathy: Men, Friendship, and Literature in the New Nation* (New Haven, CT: Yale University Press, 2001), and Richard Godbeer, *The Overflowing of Friendship: Love between Men and the Creation of the American Republic* (Baltimore: Johns Hopkins University Press, 2009).

32. J. Paul Hunter, "Sleeping Beauties: Are Historical Aesthetics Worth Recovering?" *Eighteenth-Century Studies* 34.1 (2000): 2–3.

33. Fergusson, *Poemata Juvenilia*, [3].

34. Rush, "Account," 523; emphasis mine.

35. Edward Cahill, "Liberty of the Imagination in Revolutionary America," in *American Literature's Aesthetic Dimensions*, ed. Cindy Weinstein and Christopher Looby (New York: Columbia University Press, 2012), 41.

36. Fergusson, *Poemata Juvenilia*, [4].

37. Ibid., [5–6]. It is unclear as to why Fergusson chose Albion over the typical

Britannia. Perhaps this is due to Albion's more traditional association with the island of Great Britain itself and the geographic confrontation that Fergusson establishes at the beginning of the poem. Otherwise, Albion and Dickinson's Britannia seem similar figures. Interestingly, in her pre-poem review of the contents, she uses "Britannia," not "Albion."

38. Ibid., [6].

39. Ibid.

40. Ibid., [8].

41. Ibid., [9].

42. Ibid.

43. Ibid., [9–10]. Though Fergusson does not refer to Penn's Quakerism, the Society of Friends did include women in its governance and saw them as equally justified in giving voice to prophecies and religious instruction.

44. Ibid., [10].

45. Ibid. A few more words conclude Fergusson's footnote, but their meaning is unclear: "its Charter ?" The last line, which begins with "of Pennsylvania," may be in another hand.

46. Ibid.

47. Ibid.

48. In her 1793 transcription, Fergusson recalls that she shared with "Mr Dickinson a Copy in manuscript of ['The Dream'] within a year after it was Composed." See Fergusson, *Lania to a Friend*, 41.

49. See 1 Sam. 10:17–25. Of the selection, Samuel notes, "When he stood among the people, he was higher than any of the people from his shoulders and upward" (v. 23). Later, when Samuel must anoint Saul's successor, he is again impressed by physical stature, and God tells him, "Look not on [Eliab's] countenance, or on the height of his stature; because I have refused him: for the Lord seeth not as man seeth; for man looketh on the outward appearance, but the Lord looketh on the heart" (1 Sam. 16:7). Samuel waits instead for the youngest and presumably smallest, David.

50. Fergusson, *Poemata Juvenilia*, [11–12].

51. Ibid., [12–13].

52. Ibid., [13–14].

53. See T. H. Breen, *The Marketplace of Revolution: How Consumer Politics Shaped American Independence* (New York: Oxford University Press, 2004), for more on the connection between the Revolution, patriotic solidarity, and an unprecedented mass consumer boycott.

54. Ophir is a biblical city renowned for its wealth, especially gold. See, e.g., 1 Kings 10:11 and Job 22:24 and 28:16.

55. Fergusson, *Poemata Juvenilia*, [14–15].

56. Ibid., [15–16].

57. Ibid., [18].

58. Ibid., [20].

59. Ibid., [21].

60. Kate Haulman, *The Politics of Fashion in Eighteenth-Century America* (Chapel Hill: University of North Carolina Press, 2011), 5.

61. Fergusson, *Poemata Juvenilia*, [22].

62. Ibid., [28].

63. John Barrell discusses the georgic and its relation to the pastoral. Fergusson, however, downplays the antagonistic relation between nature and humanity by aligning labor with pleasure. See Barrell, *Poetry, Language, and Politics* (Manchester: Manchester University Press, 1988), 114–18.

64. Anthony Low, *The Georgic Revolution* (Princeton, NJ: Princeton University Press, 1985), 8.

65. Fergusson, *Poemata Juvenilia*, [23]. Fergusson identifies her discussion of Virgil as a "Digression" in the table of contents she provides at the beginning of the poem. Interestingly, as with Dickinson, she reserves naming Virgil for a footnote, instead calling him the "Mantuan swain" ([24]).

66. Low, *Georgic Revolution*, 119.

67. Karen O'Brien, "Imperial Georgic, 1660–1789," in *The Country and the City Revisited: England and the Politics of Culture, 1550–1850*, ed. Gerald MacLean, Donna Landry, and Joseph P. Ward (Cambridge: Cambridge University Press, 1999), 164.

68. Ibid., 161.

69. Recall Penn's Quakerism and its more inclusive gender model. Heterosocial balance characterizes the Society's governance structure. See note 43.

70. Fergusson, *Poemata Juvenilia*, [41].

71. Ibid., [37].

72. Ibid., [38].

73. John Milton and Joseph Addison are also associated with the georgic. Low identifies georgic themes in much of Milton's work, including *Paradise Lost*, which has "a broad movement from pastoral to georgic." See Low, *Georgic Revolution*, 310. Dryden's translation of Virgil included an influential introductory essay by Addison.

74. For more on Henry Hugh Fergusson, his British support, and its effects on Fergusson's possession of Graeme Park, see Ousterhout, *Most Learned Woman*, 187–234.

75. Fergusson, *Poemata Juvenilia*, [45].

[III]

THE LEVY AND THE SLAVE

[5]

ZACHARY MCLEOD HUTCHINS

THE SLAVE NARRATIVE AND THE STAMP ACT, OR LETTERS FROM TWO AMERICAN FARMERS IN PENNSYLVANIA

ONE ENDURING LEGACY OF the Stamp Act, 250 years after its passage in 1765, is an ongoing willingness among conservative American politicians and pundits to equate political coercion generally, and oppressive tax policies more specifically, with slavery. As Bernard Bailyn notes, North American Whigs borrowed this conception of slavery from their eighteenth-century counterparts in England and popularized its figurative use during debates over the Stamp Act, Townshend Duties and subsequent crises.[1] In 1764, while Prime Minister George Grenville was still formulating the specific provisions of the Stamp Act, the governor of Rhode Island, Stephen Hopkins, anticipatorily objected that "they who are taxed at pleasure by others, cannot possibly have any property, can have nothing to be called their own; they who have no property, can have no freedom, but are indeed reduced to the most abject slavery."[2] Characterizations of involuntary taxation and other forms of political oppression as bondage proliferated in the decade that followed. Colonists opposed to the Stamp Act reported a public discourse "filled with exclamations against Slavery and arbitrary Power," and declamations against the British imposition of slavery persisted long after the duty had been repealed.[3]

Ironically, no North American did more to propagate this tie between slavery and taxation without representation than the only member of the Second Continental Congress to oppose the Declaration of Independence: John Dickinson. During the winter of 1767–68, in rejection of parliamentary powers first exercised in the Stamp Act of 1765 and then reasserted in the Townshend Duties that followed, Dickinson anonymously published in the *Pennsylvania Chronicle* a series of twelve letters, subsequently entitled *Letters from a Farmer in Pennsylvania*, that were reprinted in nineteen of twenty-three extant North American English-language newspapers.[4] Dickinson's seventh letter declares, "*Those* who are *taxed* without their own consent, expressed by themselves or their representatives, are *slaves. We are taxed* without our own consent, expressed by ourselves or our representatives. *We* are therefore—SLAVES" (*D* 53). These words were consumed silently and read aloud in public spaces, as Caroline Wigginton attests in chapter 4. In just two years Dickinson's *Letters* ran through seven different pamphlet editions, proving so successful that Milton Flower argues, "Until Thomas Paine's *Common Sense* was published early in 1776, no other document earned the acclaim given the *Farmer's Letters*; none reached a wider public. Until the year of Independence, John Dickinson, apart from Benjamin Franklin, was probably the American known to more colonists than any other."[5] More than Hopkins or any other writer, Dickinson and his ubiquitous *Letters* prepared colonial readers to think of oppressive parliamentary governance as a form of slavery, paving the path to revolution.

Despite his central place in North American colonial history and culture, Dickinson and his *Letters* have faded into relative obscurity. This neglect may be in part a product of scholarly patriotism; as Ed Larkin and Philip Gould argue, "[L]oyalism remains one of the last truly invisible categories in the scholarship on early America," and Dickinson's refusal to sign the Declaration allied him with king and Crown, notwithstanding his advocacy of American interests both before and after 1776.[6] Yet Dickinson's downfall is also, at least in part, a matter of genre. While scholars of British literature have long lavished attention on epistolary works, comparatively few have studied early American letters as a literary category. In fact, before Konstantin Dierks's pioneering 2011 account of eighteenth-century epistolary culture, no book-length study of colonial and revolutionary-era American letters had been written. Dierks describes the American eighteenth century as "an infinity of letters," but literary critics have largely limited their inquiries to a handful of epistolary novels and a small sampling of the correspondence between John and Abigail Adams, neglecting Dickinson and the broader sphere of public letters within which he wrote.[7] We frequently reference an eighteenth-century republic of letters but have yet to take that phrase seriously in a generic sense. Editorial epistles filled colonial newspapers with commentary on every public issue of the eighteenth century.[8] And as Clare Brant notes, political pamphlets were also frequently written in letter form "because the dialogic nature of correspondence matched the interrogatory nature of political exchange."[9] The authors of these epistles wrote in a self-consciously literary style, and readers similarly regarded the works as belles lettres, regularly praising or ridiculing a writer's aesthetics as well as his or her politics. Editorial epistles in colonial newspapers popularized an association between taxation and slavery that continues to reverberate in contemporary political discourse and presaged works we have now come to regard as central components of an expanding canon, including J. Hector St. John de Crèvecoeur's *Letters from an American Farmer* (1782).[10]

Crèvecoeur began drafting his epistles in approximately 1769, as a response to Dickinson's critique of parliamentary power and his accompanying representation of colonists as slaves.[11] Although he first put pen to paper at the height of Dickinson's considerable renown, when Dickinson was the most famous of Crèvecoeur's "famous lawyers," the relationship between these two texts has remained concealed over the centuries, for two reasons.[12] First, Crèvecoeur did not find a publisher for his work until he reached England, in 1782, when Dickinson's fame had faded and the questions of taxation underlying both collections of letters had been eclipsed by military matters; parallels that would have seemed obvious and inflammatory to American readers in the 1760s and early 1770s failed to excite English readers in the 1780s.[13] Second, modern readers have long resisted treating Crèvecoeur's epistles as the letters they purport to be. Over the past twenty years, scholars have reframed them as "individual essays," "an early but sophisticated novel," a "loose collection of sketches," "an epic-like venture," "natural history," "parody," "travel narrative," "descriptive geography," a "discursive exposition of the local historian," and literary tiles in a larger "mosaic."[14] In short, it seems that most critics are willing to characterize Crèvecoeur's writings as anything but the letters they purport to be; as Elizabeth Cook notes, the text's "epistolarity—its generic context and codes—is almost always ignored."[15] Crèvecoeur, like Dickinson, wrote letters. That Crèvecoeur responds to or, given the genre, corresponds with Dickinson and other eighteenth-century newspaper editorialists would have been obvious if we had treated the title of *Letters from an American Farmer* as a serious generic claim: "correspondence consists in reciprocal letters" (*C* 18).

Tracing Dickinson's influence on Crèvecoeur foregrounds several features of eighteenth-century epistolary culture, including the quasi-oral immediacy of epistolary exchanges and the genre's uniquely dialogic structure. More important, reading the two in tandem also transforms their letters into a debate over the bounds of another genre: the slave narrative. As previously noted, Dickinson frames political oppression as a form of slavery throughout his *Letters*, and in the ninth epistle he asks, "Is it possible to form an idea of a slavery more *compleat*, more *miser-*

able, more *disgraceful*, than that of a people, where *justice is administered*, *government exercised*, and a *standing army maintained*, AT THE EXPENCE OF THE PEOPLE, and yet WITHOUT THE LEAST DEPENDENCE UPON THEM?" (*D* 69). Dickinson claims that his narration of the historical sufferings and imagined future miseries brought on by imperial coercion and taxation without representation constitutes a slave narrative (*the* slave narrative, even). But when Crèvecoeur responds in his ninth letter with a portrait of slavery more complete, more miserable, more disgraceful than the state of Dickinson's colonists, Crèvecoeur rejects this Whiggish equation between involuntary taxation and slavery, adopting the Royalist strategy so well documented by Peter Dorsey: critiquing "the slavery metaphor as a means of discrediting the patriots' cause."[16]

Scholars produce new work on Crèvecoeur's *Letters* constantly, but little of this scholarship addresses the epistolary character of that text, and our failure to investigate the generic codes of these and other American letters has prevented us from seeing connections between Crèvecoeur and Dickinson that would have been obvious otherwise. Pamela Regis contends that *Letters from an American Farmer* ignores "civil history," and other critics have concurred but only because they are "[l]argely unaware of the literary tradition from which it grew."[17] Civil history—the imposition of the Stamp Act and Townshend Duties, together with a condemnation of colonial responses to these laws—is the primary subject of Crèvecoeur's *Letters*, the disciplining of political rhetoric and Dickinson's representations of slavery a central purpose. The letters of Dickinson and Crèvecoeur highlight the aesthetic prominence and historical impact of an American epistolary tradition while illuminating the contested origins of the North American slave narrative. Long before Frederick Douglass and Harriet Jacobs put pen to paper, Dickinson and Crèvecoeur—with Briton Hammon, Phillis Wheatley, and Olaudah Equiano, among others—worked to determine what forms of oppression constitute slavery and which experiences authorize the composition of a slave narrative. Crèvecoeur's epistolary argument with Dickinson, as to whether the Stamp Act had enslaved American colonists, thus represents one of the earliest attempts to theorize and delimit the racial boundaries of the slave narrative, a genre now central to our conception of American literature.

While many readers of Crèvecoeur's *Letters* have focused on the volume's discussion of revolutionary-era violence in Letter XII, most of Crèvecoeur's preceding epistles consider the philosophical disagreements that preceded war, and especially the legitimacy of Whiggish principles undergirding Dickinson's use of the slave metaphor. As David Carlson helpfully suggests, a "dehistoricization of the text" has led to readings of Crèvecoeur "focused too exclusively on the *manifest* social upheaval . . . in Revolutionary America, rather than on the deeper ideological issues and debates of the period."[18] Until 1776 Dickinson, like Crèvecoeur, accepted and even advocated British governance of the colonies. Both considered themselves loyal British subjects, though they disagreed as to whether Dickinson's aggressive challenge to the exercise of imperial powers and his invocation of slavery were consistent with fealty to the Crown. The letters of Dickinson and Crèvecoeur are more concerned with finding an appropriate metaphor for the fiscal relationship between imperial metropole and colonial outpost—with inscribing a poetics of taxation—than with revolutionary violence.

Dickinson objects to the Stamp Act and Townshend Duties on two grounds. First, he condemns taxation for the purpose of "raising a revenue"—as opposed to taxes regulating trade, "imposed *with design* to restrain the commerce of one part [of the empire], that was injurious to another, and thus to promote the general welfare"—and warns that these new taxes will lead to "a state of the most abject slavery" (*D* 8–9, 69). Second, he rejects Parliament's allegation that the acts are meant to finance debt incurred in protecting colonists during the French and Indian War, insisting the taxes are self-serving and meant to create new revenue streams that will continue after war debt has been repaid, by expanding British rule over "*the conquered provinces of* Canada *and* Florida, *and the* British *garrisons of* Nova Scotia," which "do not deserve the name of colonies" (*D* 56). Colonists will eventually find themselves unable to support this new and unconstitutional tax burden, Dickinson argues, because rates can be raised at any time, without justification; he predicts that taxes will "regularly encrease . . . till at length the inattentive people are compelled to perceive the heaviness of their burthens" (*D* 87). Dickinson prophesies that if England can tax its North American outposts for the sole purpose of raising money, British levies will soon "sink them into slaves" (*D* 39).

Whereas Dickinson complains that British taxes are an insupportable burden, Crèvecoeur contends that colonial taxes are negligible, that a beneficent British Parliament unites colonists "from Nova Scotia to West Florida" (*C* 41). Farmer James, Crèvecoeur's narrative persona, insists that the British "government . . . requires but little from us. I owe nothing but a pepper-corn to my country, a small tribute to my king" (*C* 25). And in the Nantucket letters Farmer James turns to this theme repeatedly.[19] James writes that the colonies pay only "the trifling duties which this community owe to those who protect them, and under the shadow of whose wings they navigate to all parts of the world" (*C* 107). Later, Farmer James praises the British tax code, noting that the "principal benefit it confers is the general protection of individuals, and this protection is purchased by the most moderate taxes, which are cheerfully paid, and by the trifling duties incident in the course of their lawful trade (for they despise contraband)" (*C* 136). These lines, written about an island off the Massachusetts coast at a time when groups promoting Dickinson's Whiggish invocation of slavery were busily importing contraband goods to evade British duties, are more than a little ironic. Crèvecoeur's utopian island—knowingly placed at an inaccurate latitude and longitude—is less a reality than an expression of his desires, a place where the acceptance of parliamentary tax policies has produced prosperity and peace.

If Crèvecoeur's encomiums on Nantucket reflect a willful disregard of dissatisfaction with the Stamp Act and the active resistance prompted by Dickinson's Pennsylvania Farmer, so too does his well-known third letter. In language that any colonist living in the 1760s and 1770s would have found deeply ironic but that modern readers regularly accept at face value, Farmer James writes that Americans "are a people of cultivators, scattered over an immense territory, communicating with each other by means of good roads and navigable rivers, united by the silken bands of mild government, all respecting the laws, without dreading their power, because they are equitable" (*C* 41; see also 108). Ironically, by making colonial unity conditional on a belief in equitable laws and the "silken bands of mild government," Crèvecoeur satirically characterizes Dickinson's epistolary war on the Stamp Act and Townshend Duties, which united colonists as never before, as divisive and disruptive, suggesting that British taxes better resemble the silk collars of high society than the iron manacles of an enslaved African.

During the decade between the Stamp Act's passage and the shots fired at Lexington and Concord, silk became a symbol of both imperial oppression and parliamentary support. Because the Townshend Duties assessed taxes on imported silk, colonial newspapers called for farmers to plant mulberry trees. Until domestic silk production could begin in earnest, editorials instructed women to wear homespun fabrics and warned, "[I]f we meet any of the said Female Sex, dressed in Foreign Silks, and Laces &c. we will pass by them, as persons that have been too free with some Merchant, and are Adulteresses forsaking the interest of their Country."[20] In the interval before the Revolution, individuals who wore silk were presumed to be Tories, while Whigs flaunted their homespun. Crèvecoeur's description of governance both praises the lenient policies of London and implicitly casts the blame for colonial divisions at the feet of Dickinson and others who have allegedly torn the continent apart over trifling duties on silk.

Lest his readers miss the symbolic significance of these "silken bands," Crèvecoeur's third letter follows this praise of British tax law with a more explicit encomium on the Stamp Act. After describing the transformation of poor European immigrants into prosperous American farmers, Crèvecoeur asks:

> By what invisible power hath this surprising metamorphosis been performed? By that of the laws and that of their liberty. The laws, the indulgent laws, protect them as they arrive, *stamping* on them the symbol of adoption: they receive ample rewards for their labours: these accumulated rewards procure them lands: those lands confer on them the title of freemen, and to that title every benefit is affixed which men can possibly require. This is the great operation daily performed by our laws. Whence proceed these laws? From our government. Whence that government? It is derived from the original genius and strong desire of the people ratified and confirmed by the crown. (C 43; my emphasis)

Crèvecoeur could not be more clear: the Stamp Act and other imperial laws governing the colonies are a source of prosperity, without which North America would falter. British tax law affixes the status and benefits of freemen to colonists just as imperial stamps were to have affixed value and legality to colonial paper.

Later, when the third letter considers Native Americans in contact with European colonists, Crèvecoeur simultaneously defends the constitutionality of the Stamp Act and argues that laws of this sort are the primary factor differentiating colonists from their "savage" indigenous neighbors. Comparing the "tender minds" of Indian children with "Europeans, who have not that sufficient share of knowledge they ought to have, in order to prosper: people, who have suddenly passed from oppression, dread of government, and fear of laws, into the unlimited freedom of the woods," Crèvecoeur warns that both groups will "grow up a mongrel breed, half civilized, half savage, except nature *stamps* on them some constitutional propensities" (C 52; my emphasis). In combination with a reminder of colonists who fear government and dread its laws, Crèvecoeur's use of the word *stamp* suggests that he regards Dickinson's crusade against imperial coercion and involuntary taxation as a degenerative influence that will strip colonists of civility and leave them racialized savages rather than freemen; for Crèvecoeur, as Jeff Osborne suggests, "citizenship requires the domination of multiple social segments" through imperial legislation.[21] In Crèvecoeur's *Letters*, it is the question of whether or not colonists accept the Stamp Act and parliamentary power that will determine whether they are savage Creoles or English gentlemen.[22] Dickinson repeatedly describes the Stamp Act and the Townshend Duties on goods such as paper, glass, lead, and silk as a form of "slavery" designed to raise a general revenue (*D* 13); just as often, Crèvecoeur construes the taxes as an ennobling and civilizing pittance gladly paid for protection from racialization as well as domestic and foreign enemies that might otherwise overrun the colonies.

Parliament regularly denied that the Stamp Act was intended to raise general-purpose funds, presenting the tax as a way of recovering British expenses incurred while protecting colonists during the French and Indian War. Dickinson disagreed. In response to the British insistence that colonists should reimburse London for the costs of military protection from French and Native American attacks, Dickinson calls the late conflict "a war *undertaken solely for* [Britain's] *own benefit*. The objects of it were, the securing to herself the rich tracts of land on the back of these colonies, with the *Indian* trade; and *Nova-Scotia*, with the fishery. *These and much more, has that kingdom gained*; but the *inferior animals*, that hunted with the *lion*, have been amply rewarded for all the sweat and blood their loyalty cost them, by the honor of having sweated and bled in such company" (*D* 57). Rejecting the English pretense of "defending, protecting and securing" the colonies, Dickinson describes both colonists and king as animals cooperating in an offensive hunting venture (*D* 56). He condemns imperial taxation with a metaphor that characterizes colonial cooperation as the voluntary association of admittedly inferior animals—perhaps wolves, snakes, or other less impressive predators—with a royal lion reminiscent of the monarch presented by Gilbert Gigliotti (chapter 3). If the colonies are inferior, Dickinson insists that they are nonetheless independent entities whose hunting venture with the lion has yielded few tangible benefits.

When Crèvecoeur refers metaphorically to the British navy as protective "wings" overshadowing colonial commerce, he replies to Dickinson's animal allegory with one of his own, inviting readers to reconsider an anecdote describing the protection kingbirds provide Farmer James by preserving his fields "from the depredation of crows" (*C* 29). In his second letter, James acknowledges practical benefits derived from the oversight of kingbirds, but he also complains that these guardians regularly kill and eat the bees that pollinate his fields. When hundreds of bees unite and attack a kingbird, Farmer James watches them drive the predator off, only to disband soon after. Seeing its assailants separate, the kingbird returns and eats dozens of the bees. Farmer James, for his part, kills the kingbird, cuts open his stomach, and watches in amazement as fifty-four of the bees swallowed by the bird return to life, lick themselves clean, and fly back to their hive. Given Crèvecoeur's later, explicit connection between moderate tax rates, British protection, and wings, this anecdote about kingbirds preserving colonial fields from marauding crows clearly serves, as Christine Holbo once speculated it might, "as an allegorical apology for British rule, pointing out that the crown ('our king-birds') earns the taxes owed it by protecting the colonies against outside invasion."[23] As John Cox notes, the "meaning of these stories becomes clearer in the following paragraph when James explicitly compares himself to the colonial legal system, which, he points out, should protect those who are unable to take care of themselves."[24]

Crèvecoeur, like Dickinson before him, converts the debate over who should pay for the French and Indian War into an allegory involving animals that hunt. Crèvecoeur's kingbird, like Dickinson's lion, is a regal predator credited with protecting colonial property, but Crèvecoeur's allegory differs from Dickinson's in three notable respects. First, Crèvecoeur reaffirms the British perspective of the French and Indian War as a conflict fought to protect colonial prosperity (Farmer James's fields) rather than an attempt to enlarge British dominion, as Dickinson alleged. Second, Crèvecoeur dramatically exaggerates the inferiority of colonial "animals." Whereas Dickinson insists that colonists participated cooperatively in the lion's pursuit of prey, Crèvecoeur suggests that colonists are more likely to become prey themselves than to join in the kingbird's fight against the crows. Third, Crèvecoeur implies that the colonies, far from being the inferior but independent and autonomously governed animals suggested by Dickinson's comparison, are merely parts of the British political body.[25] The kingbird eats the bees precisely because they belong inside of his body, and as Crèvecoeur's allegory suggests, incorporation within the British body politic does not necessarily result in death: a third of the ingested bees continue to live and function within the kingbird's craw.[26] Dickinson rails against taxation as a form of slavery and uses animals symbolically to illustrate the injustice of British claims to reparation for costs incurred during the French and Indian War; Crèvecoeur responds with an animal allegory of his own, downplaying the impact of British taxes and praising the crown's protection of colonial interests.

Notwithstanding the violence of these allegories, both Dickinson and

Crèvecoeur yearned for peace. But Dickinson warns that colonists can never enjoy that peace until Parliament stops attempting to tax colonial wealth, or property, without consent. Quoting from the millennial prophecies of Micah, Dickinson argues "that their property, acquired with so much pain and hazard, should be disposed of by none but themselves—or to use the beautiful and emphatic language of the sacred scriptures, 'that they should sit *every man* under his vine, and under his fig-tree, and NONE SHOULD MAKE THEM AFRAID'" (*D* 34). Dickinson looks forward to a paradisiacal reprieve from oppressive tax policies. Like Dickinson, Crèvecoeur references the millennial promise of Micah; unlike Dickinson, Crèvecoeur suggests that colonists already "enjoy the fruit of their labour under the peaceable shade of their vines and fig trees" (*C* 87). Because the British tax burden is trifling, a mere peppercorn, Crèvecoeur contends that colonists retain "the full rewards of their industry" and that Dickinson's divisive colonial rhetoric is the only obstacle to peace and prosperity in North America (*C* 87). The colonists of Nantucket already enjoy "peace," Crèvecoeur reminds his readers, precisely because they are not affected by "the political commotions which sometimes agitate our continent!" (*C* 138). He acknowledges Dickinson's complaint by quoting Micah but rejects the premise that British taxes deprive colonists of their property. Here, as in other instances, Crèvecoeur has clearly read Dickinson's *Letters* and composes his own epistles in reply, challenging the Whiggish logic that equates taxation and heavy-handed parliamentary governance with slavery.

In crafting his response to Dickinson, Crèvecoeur labors to link his *Letters* to the Pennsylvania Farmer even as he simultaneously works to undermine Dickinson's use of the slave metaphor by drawing distinctions between himself, in the rustic guise of Farmer James, and an urbane Dickinson, whom Crèvecoeur casts as a lawyer hypocritically invoking the specter of slavery to undermine social hierarchies for personal gain. An avaricious attorney and slave owner like Dickinson, Crèvecoeur suggests, supports oppressive systems far more unnatural and burdensome than imperial governance and the Stamp Act.[27]

Beyond the topical correspondences already noted and obvious similarities in the two collections' titles, Crèvecoeur ties his work to Dickinson by describing himself—indistinguishable, at this point, from Farmer James—as "a farmer in Pennsylvania" (*C* 1). This statement is, as several have previously noted, factually inaccurate; Crèvecoeur owned and cultivated land in Orange County, New York—not Pennsylvania. Crèvecoeur's geographical red herring is, in part, a commercial calculation.[28] Dickinson's Pennsylvania Farmer was a character familiar to all of Crèvecoeur's eighteenth-century American neighbors and most British citizens across the Atlantic. Nearly every literate colonist had read Dickinson's letters, and his Farmer reached illiterate Americans through oral tributes and attempts to merchandize his likeness. As Frank Mott recalls: "[T]own-meetings and grand juries commended the Farmer; songs were written in his honor; his likeness was engraved and printed for sale at a shilling, or 'glazed and framed' at five shillings; the College of New Jersey made him a Doctor of Laws. In the lists of toasts at patriotic meeting in the late sixties and seventies—those lists which begin 'The King; The Queen' and run on to a score or more—'The Farmer' was sure to appear not too late in the enumeration."[29] When Crèvecoeur began writing his *Letters*, Dickinson's work was universally known, recently published, and internationally relevant. In describing himself as a Pennsylvania farmer, Crèvecoeur undoubtedly hoped that his readers would associate this second set of letters from a second farmer in Pennsylvania with Dickinson's earlier, best-selling epistles.

Having begun by tying his *Letters* to Dickinson, Crèvecoeur moves to distinguish himself from his predecessor by foregrounding the agricultural authenticity of his own authorial persona. In the summer of 1768, after the public learned that Dickinson wrote the anonymous *Letters from a Farmer in Pennsylvania*, some—aware that Dickinson was first and foremost a Philadelphia lawyer, whose property lay in Maryland and Delaware—attacked his credibility. As Jeffrey Pasley contends, by "disclosing the real identities of newspaper writers," Tories "made the Revolutionary agitation appear to be the illegitimate machinations of a handful of conspirators," and Dickinson's critics launched a concerted attack on his character.[30] Capitalizing on Dickinson's new celebrity as the author of *Letters*, newspapers throughout the colonies republished excerpts from his previous pamphlet against the Stamp Act, *An Address to the Committee of Correspondence in Barbados* (1766), and Philadelphia editorialists worked to discredit Dickinson by accusing him of lying in the earlier *Address*. A "BARBADIAN" suggested that in composing the *Address* and then permitting its resurrection in newspapers, "the author of the *Farmer's Letters*" acted contrary to "common *justice* . . . and if such are his notions of that *divine virtue*, I am sure *he* shall never be my *lawyer*." And "*A* COUNTRY *Farmer*" called attention to the deceitfulness of Dickinson's legally minded "*City-Farmer*" by contrast.[31]

In *Letters from an American Farmer*, Crèvecoeur adopts this last strategy—critiquing the urbane, slaveholding lawyer with the voice of a more authentic "COUNTRY *Farmer*"—and it seems all but certain that he either participated in or read and received inspiration from these editorial exchanges, whose rhetorical strategies he adopts at other moments, as in his attempts to link lawyers like Dickinson to Machiavelli (on which more soon).[32] Indeed, Crèvecoeur calls attention to the avidity with which colonial cultivators such as Farmer James consumed the newspapers that published epistles by Dickinson, his critics, and supporters: "[T]hey will carefully read the newspapers, enter into every political disquisition, freely blame, or censure, governors and others. As farmers, they will be careful and anxious to get as much as they can, because what they get is their own" (*C* 46). Crèvecoeur prefaces his *Letters* with a declaration of authenticity that implicitly contrasts the private epistles of Farmer James with the putatively promotional and deceptive productions of the "*City-Farmer*" Dickinson: "*The following Letters are the genuine production of the American Farmer whose name they bear. They were privately written, to gratify the curiosity of a friend; and are made public, because they contain much authentic information, little known this side of the Atlantic*" (*C* 3). Dickinson's critics alleged that he adopted the persona of a Pennsylvania farmer and wrote his *Letters* only in order to campaign for public office.[33] By claiming to be an actual farmer who writes without any desire for a public readership—or public office—Crèvecoeur disavows the corruption so often associated with publicity in colonial America and positions Farmer James as a more credible correspondent than Dickinson's politically minded Pennsylvania Farmer.[34]

Throughout the *Letters*, as Carlson and others have noted, Crèvecoeur repeatedly contrasts farmers and lawyers, exalting the former and criticizing the latter. Describing his "family and farm" in the third letter, Farmer James asks, "Is it not better to contemplate, under these humble roofs, the rudiments of future wealth and population, than to behold the accumulated bundles of litigious papers in the office of a lawyer?" (*C* 63). Throughout his Nantucket letters, Farmer James identifies lawyers as a cause of economic inequality, scheming practitioners who cheat farmers of their labor's rewards:

> Lawyers are so numerous in all our populous towns, that I am surprised they never thought before of establishing themselves here: they are plants that will grow in any soil that is cultivated by the hand of others; and, when once they have taken root, they will extinguish every other vegetable that

> grows around them. The fortunes they daily acquire, in every province, from the misfortunes of their fellow citizens, are surprising! The most ignorant, the most bungling, member of that profession, will, if placed in the most obscure part of the country, promote litigiousness, and amass more wealth, without labour, than the most opulent farmer with all his toils. (*C* 135)

In the context of editorials castigating Dickinson for masquerading as a farmer to win political office and generate wealth, this portrait of attorneys who take root in the country and mismanage the surrounding soil seems particularly pointed. Legal fees burden Crèvecoeur's cultivators far more grievously than the taxes of which Dickinson's Pennsylvania Farmer complains, and Crèvecoeur suggests that attorneys like Dickinson would do well to leave agriculture and rural politicking to Farmer James or other, more experienced husbandmen.

When James later journeys to Charlestown and sees the atrocities that this lawyerly love of money has induced slave owners to commit, he discovers attorneys at the root of slavery's evils also. Lawyers, he laments,

> are more properly law-givers than interpreters of the law, and have united here, as well as in most other provinces, the skill and dexterity of the scribe with the power and ambition of the prince: who can tell where this may lead in a future day? The nature of our laws, and the spirit of freedom which often tends to make us litigious, must necessarily throw the greatest part of the property of the colonies into the hands of these gentlemen. In another century, the law will possess in the north what now the church possesses in Peru and Mexico. (*C* 152–53)

By accusing attorneys of acting with "the power and ambition of the prince," Crèvecoeur echoes the language of the same editorials that criticized Dickinson the lawyer for masquerading as a farmer. In the eighteenth century, princely power and ambition were widely associated with *The Prince* of Machiavelli, and one of Dickinson's harshest newspaper correspondents adopted the sobriquet "Machiavel"; this anonymous writer suggested that Dickinson was attempting to establish himself as an American emperor after the model of Octavius. Forecasting a political alliance between Dickinson, Boston lawyer James Otis, and the anonymous author of *Considerations upon the Rights of the Colonists* (1766), Machiavel warns that the three will form a new triumvirate: "The Author of the Considerations, is *Anthony*; the Author of the Farmer's Letters, *young Octavius*; and the Author of the Riots at *Boston* (Mr. O—s) is *Lepidus*."[35] When Crèvecoeur wrote, in the voice of a Pennsylvania country farmer, of lawyers profiting politically from slavery and pursuing Machiavellian schemes in order to seize power, he reformulated accusations made against Dickinson, the original Pennsylvania Farmer. A greedy lawyer and slave owner like Dickinson, Crèvecoeur implies, has fostered forms of bondage far worse than the putatively burdensome taxes of the Stamp Act; Dickinson, and not parliamentary power or oppressive tax laws, has transformed the colonists into slaves.

Dickinson, for his part, blamed Grenville, Great Britain's former prime minister, for enslaving the colonists, and in *Letters* he cautions that the Stamp Act's repeal has not freed them from the threat of bondage. His ninth epistle warns that "if Mr. *Greenville*, setting his fertile fancy again at work, can, as by one exertion of it he has stript us of our *property* and *liberty*, by another deprive us of so much of our *understanding* . . . we may bow down our necks, with all the stupid serenity of servitude" (*D* 69–70). Colonists blamed Grenville, often described simply as "the minister," for their fiscal oppression more frequently than they censured Parliament, because they knew that radical members, such as John Wilkes, espoused the colonial cause; indeed, colonial rhetoric often reflected Wilkes's insistence that "he was always ready to take any dutiful, humble or submissive measure, with respect to the King, which should be hinted to him, was agreeable, but would never make an application to any present or future minister." The same patriotic toasts that lauded Dickinson's Farmer began with a tribute to "our rightful sovereign GEORGE the Third" before proceeding to jeers at the Stamp Act, which was described as a "'meerly ministerial' Mandate" or the "Mandates of a minister."[36] In 1768 Grenville, the minister jeered at in these toasts, may have been the least popular person in North America.

Dickinson blamed Grenville for the deteriorating relationship between London and the colonies and, in an argument that Crèvecoeur would respond to, suggested that the problem was epistolary in nature. In a portion of the *Address* widely reprinted after Dickinson's authorship of *Letters* had been revealed, he portrays British ministers as power mongers seeking to construe colonial letters of protest as a rebellion against the monarchy:

> The *British* nation is *wise* and *generous*. They can distinguish between a disgust to *government* and to the *administration* of it; a distinction, which bad ministers are continually striving to confound. *They* set up *their passions* for the *interest of their king and country*; and then, whoever is offended with *their* conduct, is convicted by a very plain deduction of *minis-*

> *terial* logic, of being an enemy to his *king* and *country*. No farmer dislikes the sun; but if it collects such thick clouds as too much intercept its beams, surely the poor man who sees all his hopes sickening and withering, may very innocently dislike the gloom and wish the reviving rays may be felt again.

The farmer of Dickinson's *Address*, here conflated with his Pennsylvania Farmer by colonial newspaper editors, blames a deteriorating relationship with England (the sun) on ministerial interference (the clouds) and specifically accuses the ministry of mishandling colonial correspondence. He complains, "Many of our colonies sent home petitions; others ordered their agents to make proper applications on their behalf. What was the effect? *They were rejected without reading*. . . . The language of the ministry was, that '*they* would teach the insolent *North-Americans*, the respect due to the laws of their mother country.'"[37] Ministers, Dickinson suggests, have sought to destroy the transatlantic relationship between king and colonists by ignoring American letters of protest.

In the first of his letters, Crèvecoeur rebuts Dickinson's complaint by making a figure known only as "Minister" the indispensable intermediary who facilitates an epistolary exchange between Farmer James and his English correspondent, Mr. F.B. (*C* 14–16).[38] Crèvecoeur positions Farmer James as a well-traveled, representative colonist (albeit a firm supporter of king and Parliament, as Larkin argues), and his correspondent, "a great European man, who hath lived abundance of time in that big house called Cambridge" studying science and "never in his life done a single day's work," shares many qualities with George III, who did not attend Cambridge but did live in a palace, study science intensively, and live a life free of physical toil (*C* 12). Like the relationship between king and colonists, James's relationship with his aristocratic correspondent is mediated by Minister, who "lives upward of twenty mile distant" but solicitously visits James often, despite his other, pressing affairs (*C* 12). When James's wife discourages him from replying to F. B., Minister encourages James to write and assures him that F. B. "will read your letters with pleasure" (*C* 13). James, for his part, respectfully accepts Minister's instruction and even asks for more: "Do go on. I always love to hear you talk" (*C* 14). Minister urges James to "begin this correspondence, and persevere. Difficulties will vanish in proportion as you draw near them" (*C* 20); furthermore, he warns James that this correspondence is necessary because "[i]t is good for American farmers to have friends even in England" (*C* 17). Whereas Dickinson's *Address* and *Letters* accuse British ministers of ignoring colonial communications and working to damage American relations with the king, Crèvecoeur's Minister works to improve relations between both sides of the Atlantic and teaches James how to compose effective letters. The benefits of this colonial correspondence with royalty are only reaffirmed in Letter XI, when Crèvecoeur details John Bertram's correspondence with George III and Queen Ulrika of Sweden.

In Crèvecoeur's *Letters*, it is the farmer's Quaker wife—not ministers, as in Dickinson's *Address*—who seeks to prevent communication between James and his correspondent, and here too Crèvecoeur jabs subtly at Dickinson, who, although not a member of the Religious Society of Friends, was a public advocate of Quaker views and often mistaken for a Quaker.[39] James's wife first objects that F.B. cannot seriously desire a letter from James and, in words that Crèvecoeur's readers would do well to heed, insists that James "read this letter over again, paragraph by paragraph, and warily observe whether thee can'st perceive some words of jesting; something that hath more than one meaning" (*C* 13). Crèvecoeur's warning that letters often contain multiple meanings invites readers to think more carefully about his own prose and, in particular, about James's wife, who persists in discouraging James's correspondence with F.B. She objects that if James writes, "[s]ome would imagine that thee wantest to become either an assembly-man or a magistrate" (*C* 21), and rather than James come to be known as "the scribbling farmer," she would prefer that the public pay attention to the condition of their slaves: "Better hear them, as usual, observe. . . . Look how fat and well clad their negroes are" (*C* 22). By diverting attention from the authorship of a farmer's letters to the status of his slaves (prosperous here, sapping the Whiggish political metaphor of its potency) so that others do not construe his writing as an attempt to win political office, and by working to sever epistolary relations between England and North America, James's wife conforms to extant editorial caricatures maligning Dickinson. In Letter I Crèvecoeur has cast American Whigs generally—and Dickinson, more specifically—in the role of James's wife.[40]

From Crèvecoeur's perspective, American Whigs and the Quaker "Farmer" who purportedly leads them have inappropriately censured king and minister, their social, political, and economic superiors; he emphasizes their improper relationship with London by feminizing Whiggish firebrands like Dickinson and allowing James's outspoken wife to advocate a rupture with England.[41] James, of course, ignores his wife's dire warnings—just as Crèvecoeur hoped colonists would ignore Dickinson.[42] Anticipating Washington Irving's shrewish Dame Van Winkle by more than thirty years, Crèvecoeur implies that rebellious colonies are an inferior partner in the political marriage between England and her North American outposts, using entrenched eighteenth-century gender hierarchies to reinscribe colonial subordination.

By effeminizing Dickinson and his allies, Crèvecoeur might even hint that those who characterize the exercise of parliamentary power as enslavement are themselves natural slaves in an Aristotelian sense. Describing the relationship between husband and wife, Aristotle insists that "the male is by nature superior, and the female inferior; and the one rules and the other is ruled; this principle, of necessity, extends to all mankind. Where then there is such a difference as that between soul and body, or between men and animals (as in the case of those whose business is to use their body, and who can do nothing better), the lower sort are by nature slaves, and it is better for them as for all inferiors that they should be under the rule of a master." Aristotle identifies two categories of slavery: slavery by law and slavery by nature.[43] In his critique of the Stamp Act and Townshend Duties, Dickinson insists that tax-burdened colonists have been made slaves by law; Crèvecoeur counters that claim by implying that slavery is a natural state for colonists whose effeminate lack of reason leads them to disregard the advantages of a transatlantic correspondence and the arguments posed by Crèvecoeur's Minister. Dickinson, Crèvecoeur suggests, has forgotten his place, and *Letters from an American Farmer* works to restore social order by reminding readers that wives ought not attempt to control their husbands, that lawyers ought not farm, that colonists ought not criticize their king or his ministers.[44]

In condemning Dickinson's invocation of slavery, Crèvecoeur spoke for the minority. Most colonists identified with the Pennsylvania Farmer's critique of parliamentary oppression, and in the 1770s, the same newspapers that printed Dickinson's *Letters* also adopted and adapted Benjamin Franklin's rattlesnake with its accompanying mottoes ("Join, or Die" and "Don't Tread on Me") as a symbol of the colonies' collective resistance to British tax policy (see figures 5.1 and 5.2). In his tenth letter Crèvecoeur draws on that rattlesnake imagery to demonstrate, in another animal allegory, the dangers of inflammatory Whiggish rhetoric:

> A Dutch farmer of the Minisink went to mowing, with his negroes, in his boots, a precaution used to prevent being stung. Inadvertently he trod on

Figure 5.1. Franklin's woodcut was first published in the May 9, 1754, issue of the *Pennsylvania Gazette.* Courtesy of the Library of Congress.

> a snake, which immediately flew at his legs, and, as it drew back in order to renew its blow, one of his negroes cut it in two with his scythe. They prosecuted their work and returned home: at night the farmer pulled off his boots and went to bed, and was soon after attacked with a strange sickness at his stomach; he swelled, and, before a physician could be sent for, died. (C 167–68)

Crèvecoeur's words—"he trod on a snake"—specifically recall the colonial cry for unity, "Don't Tread on Me." This farmer from the Minisink, a township in Orange County, New York, where Crèvecoeur farmed, might represent Crèvecoeur himself and, more generally, his perception of the Loyalist cause. His death from rattlesnake poison—the inflammatory Whiggish rhetoric of Dickinson and the radicalized woodcut of Franklin—foreshadows Crèvecoeur's twelfth letter, when Farmer James describes the horrors of revolution. Crucially, however, the rattlesnake that bites this farmer also dies, sliced in two; here, as in his earlier description of the conflict between kingbirds and bees, mutual destruction ensues.[45] Crèvecoeur warns that Franklin and other Patriots will suffer from the Revolution, as will Loyalist farmers like himself.

That an enslaved African should slice Crèvecoeur's rattlesnake in two seems appropriate, given Dickinson's divisive claim that an oppressive Parliament will enslave American colonists, and it is in these last four letters that Crèvecoeur directly rejects Dickinson's characterization of taxation as slavery and his right to author a slave narrative. Even more than in *Letters from a Farmer in Pennsylvania*, Dickinson's poetic trope for taxation reached the ears and voices of common people through the chorus of his popular "Liberty Song." After its publication in July 1768, colonists across the continent regularly gathered to sing:

Figure 5.2. The masthead of Isaiah Thomas's newspaper, the *Massachusetts Spy*, was engraved by Paul Revere. Courtesy of the Library of Congress.

> In FREEDOM we're BORN, and in FREEDOM we'll LIVE
> Our Purses are ready,
> Steady, Friends, Steady,
> Not as SLAVES, but as FREEMEN our Money we'll give.[46]

Thus, when Crèvecoeur answers Dickinson's challenge to present "an idea of a slavery more *compleat*, more *miserable*, more *disgraceful*" than that endured by colonial taxpayers, he begins by describing the tortured and enslaved bodies of Africans in South Carolina but concludes by presenting an account of freemen, black men and women liberated from bondage (*D* 69). Crèvecoeur, in considering both enslaved and freed African laborers, shows how the letter always enacts or erodes relational hierarchies by establishing democratic bonds of sympathy on the one hand and asserting prescriptive force on the other. *Letters from an American Farmer* acknowledges that epistles often insist on the subservience of one correspondent but rejects the notion that considerations of genre or politics justify Dickinson's decision to write a slave narrative.

Indeed, in Letter IX Crèvecoeur offers a haunting portrait of slavery that implicitly damns Dickinson for his cavalier usage of the term. While walking through a South Carolina forest, Farmer James

> perceived . . . something resembling a cage, suspended to the limbs of a tree, all the branches of which appeared covered with large birds of prey. . . . I fired at them; they all flew to a short distance, with a most hideous noise: when, horrid to think and painful to repeat, I perceived a negro, suspended in the cage, and left there to expire! I shudder when I recollect that the birds had already picked out his eyes; his cheek bones were bare; his arms

> had been attacked in several places, and his body seemed covered with a multitude of wounds. From the edges of the hollow sockets, and from the lacerations with which he was disfigured, the blood slowly dropped, and tinged the ground beneath. No sooner were the birds flown, than swarms of insects covered the whole body of this unfortunate wretch, eager to feed on his mangled flesh and to drink his blood. (C 163–64)

The sufferer begs first for water and then for death, but Farmer James embarrassedly explains that he can satisfy only his thirst and departs for a dinner appointment with the slave owner who had devised the enslaved African's torment.

In this arresting scene, painted to answer the Pennsylvania Farmer's dare, Crèvecoeur shapes his correspondence with Dickinson into a debate over the meaning of slavery and the right of colonists to invoke the tortured bodies of kidnapped Africans as a moral justification for rebellion against the Crown. At stake is the question of whether distress induced by an oppressive Parliament authorizes the overburdened colonist to narrate an account of slavery. Dickinson conceives of himself and his fellow colonists as slaves pressed into bondage by British duties; his anticipation of stolen labor and colonial suffering in *Letters from a Farmer in Pennsylvania*, when considered from this perspective, might be described as the first North American slave narrative: an account in which one who is "master of my time" experiences an inversion of power and is subjected "to any drudgery, which our lords and masters shall please to command" (*D* 1, 70). Of course, Dickinson's farmer does not till the soil; he reads in the library while "servants" tend his crops, and "a little money at interest" provides a fund for books (*D* 1). But the absence of present labor only heightens the horror of his prospective enslavement when, coerced by parliamentary masters, Dickinson's farmer will lose his own privileged position and join his servants in the fields. And so the Pennsylvania Farmer spends his days synthesizing the narrative of his own future slavery from accounts in his books, a patchwork story of vassals "in wooden shoes, and with uncombed hair" (*D* 15); of Romans suffering under "the cruel and rapacious NERO" (*D* 49); of starving Sardinians; and of "dutiful children, who have received unmerited blows" (*D* 22). Dickinson's composite slave is a curious conflation of those enslaved by nature (children) and by law (Sardinians), and his Farmer seems helpless to redirect the pseudo-masochistic bent of an imagination committed to vicariously enduring the horrors of matted hair and uncouth footwear. He denounces enslavement by parliamentary coercion as a fate equivalent to death (*D* 16) but flounders for anecdotes and illustrations that adequately communicate the gravity of his plight. To compile this synthetic story of bondage from accounts that inspire little sympathy or anguish is to depend on the associative and imaginative powers of colonial readers, assuming that they will supply their own knowledge of chattel slavery, which Dorsey reminds us was "an intimate reality, a common reference point, and thus a unifying experience for those whose economies, climates, and ways of life were frequently quite diverse."[47] Suffering black bodies, such as the one discovered by Farmer James, are implicitly present in the white spaces of Dickinson's *Letters*; they *must* be imported by his readers, or the Farmer's dire warnings of enslavement amount to little more than a laughable forecast of impending bad fashion.[48]

Dickinson never acknowledges the suffering of enslaved Africans, perhaps because—as the largest slave owner in the Delaware Valley at the time he wrote his *Letters*—he knew that this most obvious comparison would undermine the moral authority of his claims. The examples of slavery that Dickinson references by way of comparison are always classical or feudal: peoples ruled by Carthaginian masters or, in more recent history, French and Polish lords. But Crèvecoeur refuses to let Dickinson's omission obfuscate the fact that slavery, in eighteenth-century North America, almost always referred to the bondage of African peoples. Dickinson introduces the metaphor of slavery and the condition of European peasants as a demonstration of that condition in his second letter; Crèvecoeur responds, in his own second letter, by acknowledging that he has received and rejected Dickinson's message. Farmer James thanks "God that my lot is to be an American farmer, instead of a Russian boor or a Hungarian peasant. I thank you kindly for the idea, however dreadful, which you have given me of their lot and condition. . . . Hard is their fate to be thus condemned to a slavery worse than that of our negroes" (C 24). This mention of contrasting experiences of slavery is the only point in *Letters from an American Farmer* when James discloses the content of epistles received from F.B. and is, thus, the moment when Crèvecoeur reveals the underlying theme of his correspondence with Dickinson. Crèvecoeur places the servitude of Dickinson's European vassals within the context of chattel slavery, and while Farmer James writes, here, of enslaved Africans as a relatively privileged class, he will come to reconsider that position after his encounter with the gibbeted man in Letter IX. No matter how often Dickinson references classical or distant models of slavery, Crèvecoeur suggests, colonial readers like Farmer James will always associate the term with contemporary, local practice; he calls

Dickinson to task for evading the most obvious meaning of his metaphor and for exploiting the horrors of eighteenth-century American slavery in the minds of his readers without explicitly acknowledging the suffering of enslaved Africans.

Crèvecoeur rejects the metaphorization of slavery because the realities of that condition, as illustrated by his account of the caged African man, are so troubling that the term cannot be ethically or accurately used to describe any state that does not involve a direct bodily compulsion to labor and to suffer against one's will. An eighteenth-century slave narrative, Crèvecoeur insists, can take as its subject only the plight of brutalized Africans or those whose bondage entails bodily suffering similar to that endured by the gibbeted man of his ninth letter. When the gunshot of Farmer James drives birds of prey away from the caged African, Crèvecoeur reveals the black bodies so carefully concealed in the white space of Dickinson's *Letters*, recentering slavery and the slave narrative around the pain of a confined "negro" body rather than the political distress of a white mind.

After revealing the unspoken premise of Dickinson's tirade against slavery, Crèvecoeur presents a portrait of liberated Africans, freemen whose relationship to their employer, John Bertram, better represents his understanding of the connection between Crown and colonists. In the process of depicting Bertram's happy freemen, Crèvecoeur's eleventh epistle also foregrounds the generic significance of the letter as a medium of imperial and interpersonal reconciliation. Whereas James is the narrative voice in every other epistle, this letter is written to James by a Russian named Iwan, whose visit to Bertram foregrounds the sympathetic bonds forged by correspondence. Bertram engages in "extensive correspondence . . . with the most eminent Scotch and French botanists," with George III, and with a Swedish queen (*C* 173); Iwan's visit is anticipated with pleasure because of "a letter from Philadelphia" (*C* 175), and Bertram assures him that he is "no stranger" (*C* 178). Holbo suggests that by including Iwan's epistle, "Crèvecoeur abandons James's unifying and limiting perspective"—the perspective of a Dickinsonian farmer in Pennsylvania —"to emphasize what we might call the 'letterness' of the letters: the fact that correspondence creates ties of sympathy among people. . . . By thus presenting these communities, Crèvecoeur suggests a model for an ideal American identity, one in which limited and local communities are directly allied with global communities."[49] Letters like his own, Crèvecoeur hopes, might facilitate the reconciliation of local, colonial interests with imperial, British interests: the barrier between colony and Crown is one of communication, not taxation. By reframing the problem as a matter of correspondence both here and in his earlier portrayal of the understanding Minister, Crèvecoeur underscores the political work done by his own letters and, more broadly, all the letters that flooded sympathetic newspapers in response to Dickinson's epistles. If the British government would only subscribe to the *Pennsylvania Chronicle*, Crèvecoeur seems to suggest, they would perceive that a strong chorus of colonial voices had joined together in support of the Stamp Act and in willing subjection to British authority.

Once cordial communications have been restored "by this management" of letters, Crèvecoeur implies, Dickinson and the American Whigs who promoted Dickinson's epistles, like Bertram's happy, formerly enslaved Africans, will "become a new set of beings" who once again "do their work with the cheerfulness of white men" (C 182). Indeed, a peaceful transition from slave to relative, from colonial Creole to English gentleman is implicit in the sympathetic intercourse—both textual and sexual—of Bertram's freed black laborers; formerly enslaved "women breed in our families; and we become attached to one another" (C 183). Before James's descent into revolution, Crèvecoeur provides a last model of appropriate colonial communication and "subordination" as a peaceful alternative to Dickinson's narrative of slavery (C 183). Communicating a desire to obey British laws and respect parliamentary authority, Crèvecoeur promises, will purge colonists of the racializing influence of Dickinson's rhetoric and accompanying acts of resistance, such as the nighttime raids against Stamp Act supporters conducted in blackface and described in chapter 2 by Molly Perry.[50] Inspired, perhaps, by Iwan's epistle, Farmer James finally decides to free the enslaved Africans living on his farm: "I intend to say to my negroes,—In the name of God, be free, my honest lads; I thank you for your past services; go, from henceforth, and work for yourselves." However, this act of emancipation is not to be conflated with support for American independence and the Whiggish use of slavery; James explains, "Lest my countrymen should think that I am gone to join the incendiaries of our frontiers, I intend to write a letter" indicating otherwise (C 207). The letter, which has induced James to follow Bertram's example and free his slaves, is optimistically touted in Crèvecoeur's conclusion as a relational genre that stimulates sympathy and cultivates new forms of community.

Of course, while Crèvecoeur's last two epistles stress correspondence, in its double meanings of equivalence and intercourse, his earlier letters acknowledge that the genre can also reify and legitimize the relational hierarchies that enable slavery as an institution. At the beginning of Letter X, Farmer James, who has previously and pliantly insisted that F.B. is "to give me my subjects, and on no other shall I write, lest you should blame me for an injudicious choice," complains that the demands of his correspondent have effectively enslaved him (*C* 22). When F.B. requests a letter on snakes—symbols of slavery, as I have argued earlier and elsewhere—James asks, "Why would you prescribe this task? you know that what we take up ourselves seems always lighter than what is imposed on us by others" (*C* 166). The letter, in this context, enacts social control, and Crèvecoeur makes visible the ways in which epistles consolidate "covert power significant for its very *invisibility*." As Dierks contends, correspondence cultivates "a *prescriptive force of letter writing* whereby authors in print and especially writers of letters defined the meanings of communication and expression, of personal identity and agency, and of social order and change."[51] Farmer James characterizes the epistolary power wielded by F.B. as a form of bondage, and so, too, did the earliest writers describing the New World for a European elite. At the beginning of the sixteenth century, when Peter Martyr d'Anghiera wrote of Columbus's voyages in a letter to Cardinal Luigi d'Aragona, he expressed dismay that "you haue layde this burden on my backe, in whose power it is to commaunde me to take vppon me more then I am wel able."[52] As it places two parties in relation, the letter works to instantiate power as well as sympathy, and it is this element of the genre that makes the letter an ideal vehicle for accounts of bondage—for the slave narrative.

The slave narrative, as we now understand it, is concerned primarily with making visible and critiquing the various forms of relational authority wielded by white masters in subjugating racialized peoples; the genre performed a function, in the nineteenth-century United States, similar to that of political epistles in the eighteenth century, when the colonial inhabitants of North America came to be considered Creoles by those living in the imperial centers of Europe. Like eighteenth-century letters, slave narratives are "intensely political documents" meant to challenge, as Dickson Bruce argues, the "philosophical underpinnings" of "arbitrary power."[53] In other words, the project of a slave narrative is not only to castigate the obvious and visible injustices of chattel slavery through biography but also to reveal the prescriptive force of traditions—such as liberalism, letter writing, or Whiggish political metaphors—that invisibly or circuitously facilitate, shield, and perpetuate the institution of slavery.[54] *Letters from an American Farmer* unveils the ways in which a letter's generic codes and contexts can enact coercion and anticipates the conclusion of Patricia Bradley, that the figurative use of slavery "gave first evidence that the issue of real slavery was not to have a part in the revolution."[55] In recentering Dickinson's artificial, conglomerate pseudo–slave narrative around the bleeding bodies of black laborers, Crèvecoeur theorizes the limits and functions of the slave narrative while bridging the gap between two genres more closely connected than we have hitherto supposed.

And yet: although Crèvecoeur vehemently opposed Dickinson's description of parliamentary coercion and unjust taxation as a form of slavery, he does not write in anticipation of modern voices decrying that equation as a divisive racialization of politics. Crèvecoeur and other Tories, as much as Dickinson and his compatriots, eagerly embraced inflammatory racial rhetoric as a weapon in their epistolary war for colonial hearts and minds; Alan Gilbert reminds us that "we see enough casual racism and social and racial condescension on both sides to subvert any claims to absolute 'good' or 'bad.'"[56] Just two months after Dickinson's "Liberty Song" had been released, Tory poets responded with "A Parody upon the Well Known Liberty Song":

> In Folly you're born, and in Folly you'll live,
> To Madness still ready,
> And stupidly Steady,
> Not as Men but as Monkies the Tokens you give.[57]

Read in opposition to the Liberty Song's final line ("Not as SLAVES, but as FREEMEN our Money we'll give"), this anonymous poet's characterization of Dickinson and Whigs as lower-order primates is far more racially fraught than Dickinson's characterization of taxation without representation as slavery. Dickinson's "SLAVES" have been replaced with "Monkies," implying that the Africans who have been kidnapped and forced to labor in North American fields are more simian than human. If, as Dickinson alleges, tax-strapped colonists are slaves, his anonymous adversary suggests that mere animals do not deserve their freedom—that both Africans and rebellious colonists are animals whose enslavement, from an Aristotelian perspective, is natural. Tories generally, and Crèvecoeur in particular, were less concerned about the racial implications of Dickinson's metaphor than with defusing its rhetorical charge. Crèvecoeur objects to Dickinson's characterization of slavery because it is politically expedient and not necessarily or even primarily because he conceives of the institution as inherently evil. From a modern perspective, Crèvecoeur's utilization of slavery's horrors may be just as repugnant as Dickinson's, perhaps even more so, since he seems fully conscious that employing the language of slavery exploits human suffering for political gain.

To recover Crèvecoeur's critique of revolutionary rhetoric is not, therefore, to rebrand him as a forebear of contemporary liberals or to unleash a facile (but centuries-old and therefore venerable!) literary attack on the continuing use of Dickinson's tax metaphors by conservative politicians and pundits. In fact, Crèvecoeur's resistance to the equation of slavery and involuntary taxation might just as easily be deployed against the agenda of progressive thinkers like Walter Benn Michaels, who seeks to redirect attention and resources away from calls for reparations for slavery to a more broadly based redistribution of wealth through tax reforms.[58] Rather, reading Crèvecoeur's *Letters from an American Farmer* in the context of Dickinson's *Letters from a Farmer in Pennsylvania* speaks to the casuistic and contingent nature of both political rhetoric and public morals. In the twenty-first century, as in the eighteenth, politicized language linking taxation and slavery only distracts public attention from the fact that human trafficking is a persistent, ongoing problem; like Dickinson and Crèvecoeur, modern pundits and politicians devote more energy to the rhetoric of slavery than its eradication.

Crèvecoeur's contemporaries never responded to his scathing rebuke of Dickinson, because it arrived too late. Instead of sparking a debate over the definition of slavery and the right of Dickinson and the Whigs who adopted his *Letters* to self-identify as slaves, Crèvecoeur's correspondence with Dickinson has languished in relative obscurity. Recovering that correspondence promises to refine our understanding of two genres that shaped national and literary history. The slave narrative was not yet, in the eighteenth century, the exclusive province of racialized peoples laboring as chattel, and white writers of the period argued with each other over the boundaries of slavery as a metaphor and lived experience in an attempt to delimit the genre in politically expedient ways. Pairing the letters of Crèvecoeur and Dickinson thus restores our awareness of the prescriptive force and dialogic structure of an epistolary mode that has shaped popular understandings of that peculiar American institution since the Stamp Act's passage, 250 years ago.

Notes

The author would like to thank Jane Calvert, Sandra Gustafson, and the anonymous readers whose suggestions and queries helped to refine the claims and bolster the evidence in this essay.

1. Bernard Bailyn, *The Ideological Origins of the American Revolution* (Cambridge, MA: Harvard University Press, 1967), 232–46. Bailyn's thesis has been refined and challenged over the years by David Brion Davis, *The Problem of Slavery in the*

age of Revolution, 1770–1823 (Ithaca, NY: Cornell University Press, 1975), 255–62; F. Nwabueze Okoye, "Chattel Slavery as the Nightmare of the American Revolutionaries," *William and Mary Quarterly* 37.1 (1980): 3–28; Patricia Bradley, *Slavery, Propaganda, and the American Revolution* (Jackson: University Press of Mississippi, 1998), 1–24; Peter A. Dorsey, "To 'Corroborate Our Own Claims': Public Positioning and the Slavery Metaphor in Revolutionary America," *American Quarterly* 55.3 (2003): 353–86; and François Furstenberg, "Beyond Freedom and Slavery: Autonomy, Virtue, and Resistance in Early American Political Discourse," *Journal of American History* 89.4 (2003): 1295–330, among others.

2. Stephen Hopkins, *The Rights of the Colonies Examined* (Providence, RI: William Goddard, 1764), 16. For a synthetic account of colonial resistance to the Stamp Act, see Edmund S. Morgan and Helen M. Morgan, *The Stamp Act Crisis: Prologue to Revolution* (Chapel Hill: University of North Carolina Press, 1953).

3. "New-Haven," *Boston Gazette*, 19 August 1765.

4. Although the Stamp Act had already been repealed when Dickinson wrote *Letters*, he invokes its legislative specter in arguing against the Townshend Duties: "[W]hat signifies the repeal of the *Stamp-Act*, if these colonies are to lose their other privileges, by not tamely surrendering *that* of taxation?" He complains that these new laws "are as much *taxes* upon us, as those imposed by the *Stamp-Act*." After some thirty mentions throughout, the phrase "*Stamp-Act*" is also the conclusion of Dickinson's epistles, the last words of his Pennsylvania Farmer. John Dickinson, *Letters from a Farmer in Pennsylvania, to the Inhabitants of the British Colonies*, 3d ed. (Philadelphia: William and Thomas Bradford, 1769) [hereafter *D*], 4, 11.

5. Milton E. Flower, *John Dickinson: Conservative Revolutionary* (Charlottesville: University Press of Virginia, 1983), 69.

6. Edward Larkin, "The Cosmopolitan Revolution: Loyalism and the Fiction of an American Nation," *Novel* 40.1–2 (2006–2007): 62; Philip Gould, *Writing the Rebellion: Loyalists and the Literature of Politics in British North America* (New York: Oxford University Press, 2013), 8.

7. Konstantin Dierks, *In My Power: Letter Writing and Communications in Early America* (Philadelphia: University of Pennsylvania Press, 2009), xiii. Prior to Dierks, Susan Scott Parrish provided the most recent reading of eighteenth-century letters, describing the letters of transatlantic scientific correspondents; see Susan Scott Parrish, *American Curiosity: Cultures of Natural History in the Colonial British Atlantic World* (Chapel Hill: University of North Carolina Press, 2006), 103–35.

8. Charles Clark calculates that in terms of sheer volume, colonists consumed far more newspapers than books, "so that by 1790, it could be said that newspaper issues had comprised 80 percent of all American publications up to that point." Given the number of editorial letters printed in every issue, it seems reasonable to suggest that colonists read many more letters to the editor than epistolary novels. Charles E. Clark, "Periodicals and Politics," in *A History of the Book in America: The Colonial Book in the Atlantic World*, vol. 1, ed. Hugh Amory and David D. Hall (Chapel Hill: University of North Carolina Press, 2007), 361.

9. Clare Brant, *Eighteenth-Century Letters and British Culture* (New York: Palgrave Macmillan, 2006), 171.

10. This essay cites the Oxford edition of Crèvecoeur's 1782 *Letters* rather than the excellent Harvard edition recently edited by Dennis Moore, for two reasons. First, Moore characterizes the 1782 letters as sketches rather than epistles, grouping them with Crèvecoeur's posthumously published essays. Second, by eliding the distinction between Crèvecoeur's published and unpublished work, Moore questions the existence of an overriding artistic vision governing the selection of materials for and the organization of his 1782 volume. This essay emphasizes the epistolarity, unity, and structural integrity of Crèvecoeur's 1782 *Letters*, an emphasis best served by citing the Oxford edition. See Dennis D. Moore, "Introduction to J. Hector St. John de Crèvecoeur," *Letters from an American Farmer and Other Essays* (Cambridge, MA: Belknap Press of Harvard University Press, 2013), xv.

11. James Myers argues that Crèvecoeur worked to advance French interests—not those of the king or rebellious American colonists. This essay is concerned less with Crèvecoeur's personal views or aims than with the political perspective of his public *Letters*, which is staunchly Loyalist. Whatever Crèvecoeur's personal politics, *Letters* advocates Tory positions and repudiates Whiggish thought, as Myers himself seems to acknowledge. See James P. Myers, Jr., "Crèvecoeur: Concealing and Revealing the Secret Self," *Early American Literature* 49.2 (2014): 368, 381.

12. J. Hector St. John de Crèvecoeur, *Letters from an American Farmer*, ed. Susan Manning (New York: Oxford University Press, 1997) [hereafter C], 12.

13. Grantland Rice notes that Crèvecoeur's contemporary readers struggled to understand his *Letters*: "In the two years after its English publication in 1782, *Letters* had been read by European critics as, variously, a portrayal of the exotic, a benign literary hoax, a contribution to the English literary canon, a colonial panegyric, an invective against the Revolution, a Tory panegyric, an immigration tract, a French Catholic deceit, a Rousseauistic conceit, and a true documentary account of the Americas." Grantland S. Rice, "Crèvecoeur and the Politics of Authorship in Republican America," *Early American Literature* 28.2 (1993): 106.

14. Ibid., 109, 93; Norman S. Grabo, "Crèvecoeur's American: Beginning the World Anew," *William and Mary Quarterly* 48.2 (1991): 165; Eric D. Lamore, "Cultivating the Ancient Classical Tradition in Early America: Vergil and J. Hector St. Jean de Crèvecoeur's *Letters from an American Farmer*," *Atenea* 29.1 (2009): 130; Pamela Regis, *Describing Early America: Bartram, Jefferson, Crèvecoeur, and the Influence of Natural History* (Dekalb: Northern Illinois University Press, 1992), 107; Ralph Bauer, *The Cultural Geography of Colonial American Literatures: Empire, Travel, Modernity* (New York: Cambridge University Press, 2003), 211; John D. Cox, *Traveling South: Travel Narratives and the Construction of American Identity* (Athens: University of Georgia Press, 2005), 26; Yael Ben-Zvi, "Mazes of Empire: Space and Humanity in Crèvecoeur's *Letters*," *Early American Literature* 42.1 (2007): 78; Nathaniel Philbrick, "The Nantucket Sequence in Crèvecoeur's *Letters from an American Farmer*," *New England Quarterly* 64.3 (1991): 415; Ed White, "Crèvecoeur in Wyoming," *Early American Literature* 43.2 (2008): 397.

15. Elizabeth Heckendorn Cook, *Epistolary Bodies: Gender and Genre in the Eighteenth-Century Republic of Letters* (Stanford, CA: Stanford University Press, 1996), 141. Other than Cook, the most notable exception to this rule is Eve Ban-

net, who reads Crèvecoeur's first epistle in tandem with letter-writing manuals of the period. See Eve Tavor Bannet, *Empire of Letters: Letter Manuals and Transatlantic Correspondence, 1688–1820* (New York: Cambridge University Press, 2005), 275–87.

16. Dorsey, "To 'Corroborate Our Own Claims,'" 362. Although, as Jane Calvert argues, Dickinson was not a Whig, his political views overlapped with Whig thought. See Jane E. Calvert, *Quaker Constitutionalism and the Political Thought of John Dickinson* (New York: Cambridge University Press, 2009).

17. Regis, *Describing Early America*, 113, 107.

18. David Carlson, "Farmer Versus Lawyer: Crèvecoeur's *Letters* and the Liberal Subject," *Early American Literature* 38.2 (2003): 260.

19. By locating his commentary on the reasonableness of taxes in the Nantucket letters, Crèvecoeur may have subtly reminded Whigs that they faced an *internal* rebellion against locally assessed and administered taxes. As Jennifer Schell explains, "[D]uring both the American Revolution and the War of 1812, Nantucketers negotiated treaties of neutrality openly and independently with the British and refused to pay taxes to the state of Massachusetts." Jennifer Schell, "Figurative Surveying: National Space and the Nantucket Chapters of J. Hector St. John de Crèvecoeur's *Letters from an American Farmer*," *Early American Literature* 43.3 (2008): 584.

20. "To Messr's Greens, Printers," *Connecticut Journal*, 8 April 1768.

21. Jeff Osborne, "American Antipathy and the Cruelties of Citizenship in Crèvecoeur's *Letters from an American Farmer*," *Early American Literature* 42.3 (2007): 541. This comparison between Native Americans and American Whigs becomes the occasion for an allegorical warning against revolution in the Nantucket letters. Discussing Native Americans, Crèvecoeur writes, "It is strange what revolution has happened among them in less than two hundred years! What is become of those numerous tribes which formerly inhabited the extensive shores of the great Bay of Massachusetts?" (*C* 103). Crèvecoeur lists fourteen Native American nations and twelve English towns built on their home sites; when he describes the Native inhabitants of Cape Cod, he lists thirteen "tribes" who live "divided into two great regions" (*C* 104). The number of Native groups in play at any one time—thirteen or fourteen—approximates the number of English colonies in North America, and Crèvecoeur warns that these Native nations "have all disappeared either in the wars which the Europeans have carried on against them or else they have mouldered away, gathered in some of their ancient towns, in contempt and oblivion" (*C* 103).

22. Bauer shows that this question of Creole identity troubled gentlemen farmers such as Crèvecoeur because English observers "referred to the colonials as 'natives,' 'Creoles,' and 'country-born.' As was the case in other parts of the Americas, nature's undesirable effects upon bodily 'humors' in the New World were thus seen as a plausible explanation for the 'extreme choler and passion' that seemed to characterize" colonists. Ralph Bauer, *The Cultural Geography of Colonial American Literatures: Empire, Travel, Modernity* (New York: Cambridge University Press, 2003), 183.

23. Christine Holbo, "Imagination, Commerce, and the Politics of Associationism in Crèvecoeur's *Letters from an American Farmer*," *Early American Literature* 32.1 (1997): 37.

24. Cox, *Traveling South*, 34.

25. Notwithstanding his characterization of the colonies as independent animals, Dickinson also viewed them as an essential part of the British body politic. Dreading the prospect of civil war and independence, Dickinson asks, "But if once *we* are separated from our mother country, what new form of government shall we adopt, or where shall we find another *Britain*, to supply our loss? Torn from the body, to which we are united by religion, liberty, laws, affections, relation, language and commerce, we must bleed at every vein" (*D* 21).

26. This proportion is not coincidental; as Larkin notes, John Adams estimated that Loyalists constituted a third of the population in revolutionary North America. Larkin, "Cosmopolitan Revolution," 57.

27. Although Dickinson was one of the largest slaveholders in the Delaware Valley when he wrote his *Letters* and when Crèvecoeur began drafting his response, by the time Crèvecoeur published his response Dickinson had been speaking out against slavery for several years and had already begun the process of freeing all his slaves unconditionally. Crèvecoeur's caricature of Dickinson as slaveholding hypocrite was, thus, outdated by the time it made it into print. For this insight and other helpful suggestions throughout the essay I thank Jane Calvert.

28. Scholars have explained this diversion from autobiographical similarities between Crèvecoeur and Farmer James in various ways. Larkin notes that some scholars have suggested that Crèvecoeur turned "Pennsylvania into a model for the entirety of British North America" (Larkin, "Cosmopolitan Revolution," 62). White suggests that a Pennsylvania setting represents Crèvecoeur's attempt to contrast the cultural values of New England and the Middle Colonies (White, "Crèvecoeur in Wyoming," 393). White's arguments actually make more sense if Crèvecoeur's *Letters* responds to Dickinson; when Dickinson's *Letters* sparked a spirit of rebellion in New England, some Pennsylvanians angrily sought to dissociate themselves from New England. Larkin, "Cosmopolitan Revolution," 62; White, "Crèvecoeur in Wyoming," 393. On regional factionalism, see "To Messieurs Hall and Sellers," *Pennsylvania Gazette*, 21 July 1768.

29. Frank Luther Mott, *Golden Multitudes: The Story of Best Sellers in the United States* (New York: Macmillan, 1947), 50. An example of these toasts to "The FARMER" can be found in "Boston, August 22. 1768," *Boston Evening-Post,* 22 August 1768.

30. Jeffrey L. Pasley, *"The Tyranny of Printers": Newspaper Politics in the Early American Republic* (Charlottesville: University Press of Virginia, 2001), 35. On the need for anonymity in the development of the eighteenth-century public sphere, see Michael Warner, *The Letters of the Republic* (Cambridge, MA: Harvard University Press, 1990). Francis Walett helpfully reviews the editorial debates over the Stamp Act that preceded Dickinson's *Letters* and established the generic conventions which guided debate over Dickinson's *Letters* in the newspapers; see Francis G. Walett, "The Impact of the Stamp Act on the Colonial Press," in *Newsletters to Newspapers: Eighteenth-Century Journalism*, ed. Donovan H. Bond and W. Reynolds McLeod (Morgantown: West Virginia University, 1977), 157–69.

31. "Mr. Goddard," *Pennsylvania Chronicle*, 1 August 1768; "For the Pennsylvania Chronicle," *Pennsylvania Chronicle*, 8 August 1768. See also "To the Printer of the

Pennsylvania Chronicle," *Pennsylvania Chronicle*, 1 August 1768; and "To the Printers," *Pennsylvania Gazette*, 4 August 1768. Editorials from 1769 repeatedly drew a distinction between writers from Philadelphia and Delaware even though the two colonies were commonly combined, as John Munroe argues, into a single political entity. See John A. Munroe, *The Philadelawareans, and Other Essays Relating to Delaware* (Newark, NJ: University of Delaware Press, 2004), 44–46.

32. Norman Grabo first noted that Crèvecoeur's "prose is mainly that of the newspaper essayists of the time. . . . St. John assumes the same kind of dignity in his prose, an almost foreign formality of grammar and diction—long sentences, highly subordinated, heavily Latinate." Beatrice Fink, for her part, reminds us that Crèvecoeur wrote editorial epistles to New York newspapers during his service as the French consul in the 1780s and signed them "Agricola." Crèvecoeur's contributions to European newspapers are noted in the biography by Gay Allen and Roger Asselineau. Grabo, "Crèvecoeur's American," 160; Beatrice Fink, "Saint-John de Crèvecoeur's Tale of a Tuber," *Eighteenth-Century Life* 25 (2001): 231. See also Gay Wilson Allen and Roger Asselineau, *St. John de Crèvecoeur: The Life of an American Farmer* (New York: Viking, 1987), 72, 200.

33. See "Mr. Goddard, Pray Give the Following a Place," *Pennsylvania Chronicle*, 19 September 1768; and "To Our 'Patriotic' FREEMEN," *Pennsylvania Chronicle*, 22 August 1768.

34. Cook, *Epistolary Bodies*, 155.

35. "To the Printer of the Chronicle," *Pennsylvania Chronicle*, 15 August 1768.

36. "London, April 26," *New-York Gazette, or Weekly Post-Boy*, 20 June 1768; "Boston, August 22. 1768," *Boston Evening-Post*, 22 August 1768.

37. John Dickinson, "Extracts, from a Pamphlet Published by the Author of the Farmer's Letters," *Boston Evening-Post*, 1 August 1768.

38. The minister of Crèvecoeur's first letter is a clergyman, not an officer of government, but this distinction between civic and religious ministers collapses in the larger trajectory of *Letters*. In his well-known third letter, Farmer James explains that the profits of an American farmer cannot be "claimed, either by a despotic prince, a rich abbot, or a mighty lord. Here religion demands but little of him; a small voluntary salary to the minister" (C 44). Proximity conflates, in Crèvecoeur's prose, the payment to a clergyman with that which might be offered to a prince, lord, or abbot—another religious leader whose inclusion speaks to the alignment of church and state power and officials; the word *minister* slips between its civic and religious meanings.

39. Calvert, *Quaker Constitutionalism*, 16–17. As Moore notes, James's wife uses speech patterns characteristic of Quaker grammar consistently, but James only briefly adopts a Quaker dialect when speaking with his wife (C 17–18); furthermore, James's reliance on a minister and his ownership of slaves would be uncharacteristic of a Friend, suggesting that only James's wife is a Quaker. Dickinson, like Farmer James, married a Quaker woman and was often mistaken for a Quaker himself. See Moore, "Introduction," xiii.

40. Placing Dickinson's views in the mouth of a Quaker wife advocating separation from England is ironic, given that Dickinson's peers in the Second Continental Congress, as Calvert notes, "claimed that Dickinson's Quaker mother and wife 'were

continually distressing him with their remonstrances'" and preventing him from embracing the Patriot cause. Calvert, *Quaker Constitutionalism*, 239.

41. Crèvecoeur also tweaks Dickinson for advocating aggressive behavior not in keeping with his position in the second letter, when he describes a wren who steals a swallow's nest: "The peaceable swallow, like the passive Quaker, meekly sat at a small distance, and never offered the least resistance. But, no sooner was the plunder carried away, than the injured bird went to work with unabated ardour, and, in a few days, the depredations were repaired. To prevent, however, a further repetition of the same violence, I removed the wren's box to another part of the house" (*C* 37). Crèvecoeur insinuates that Dickinson's aggression is inappropriate for a Quaker; he also suggests that Dickinson is fighting over a paltry sum easily regained "in a few days."

42. As if to reinforce the insignificance of Dickinson in his guise as a Quaker woman, Crèvecoeur offers us a second portrait of a Quaker woman ignored by her auditors in Letter XI. At the beginning of a Quaker meeting "profound silence ensued, which lasted about half an hour; every one had his head reclined, and seemed absorbed in profound meditation; when a female friend arose." This Quaker woman speaks for forty-five minutes, during which time "I did not observe one single face turned toward her; never before had I seen a congregation listening with so much attention to a public oration" (*C* 184–85). Crèvecoeur's narrator seems to suggest that her discourse is captivating, but the locutionary force of his language leads to the opposite conclusion: "so much" is the rhetorical equivalent of *so little*. Here, as throughout the *Letters*, Crèvecoeur writes sarcastically, tongue in cheek; auditors with "reclined" heads, who never look at a speaker, are hardly rapt with attention—they are sleeping!

43. Aristotle, *Aristotle's Politics*, trans. Benjamin Jowett (Oxford: Clarendon Press, 1908), 34–35.

44. As Osborne contends, Crèvecoeur's *Letters* promotes a hierarchical perspective, insinuating that "prosperity is a product of division and hierarchy . . . not of equality and interchangeability." My reading of James's wife diverges from a tradition, initiated by D. H. Lawrence and updated by James Bishop, that emphasizes her compliance; Lawrence calls her "Amiable Spouse" and Bishop emphasizes her "unwavering compliance." Anna Carew-Miller, however, has anticipated my more aggressive reading of James's wife, suggesting that "[h]er assertion of authority outside her housewifely duties threatens his position in the domestic partnership." Osborne, "American Antipathy," 532; D. H. Lawrence, *Studies in Classic American Literature* (New York: T. Seltzer, 1923), 25; James E. Bishop, "A Feeling Farmer: Masculinity, Nationalism, and Nature in Crèvecoeur's *Letters*," *Early American Literature* 43.2 (2008): 370; Anna Carew-Miller, "The Language of Domesticity in Crèvecoeur's *Letters from an American Farmer*," *Early American Literature* 28.3 (1993): 249.

45. I have elsewhere suggested that by slicing the rattlesnake in two Crèvecoeur anticipates the colonies' eventual division over slavery, a reading in keeping with the division of thirteen Native American nations in Letter IV. As Christopher Iannini notes, Crèvecoeur deeply absorbed the views of Abbé Guillaume-Thomas-François Raynal, who repeatedly prophesied slave insurrections; thus, the rattlesnake cut in two by "negroes" may also reflect fears that had less to do with a division between North and South than the possibility of a slave insurrection in the South. See Zachary McLeod

Hutchins, "Rattlesnakes in the Garden: The Fascinating Serpents of the Early, Edenic Republic," *Early American Studies* 9.3 (2011): 696, 683–84; and Christopher Iannini, "'The Itinerant Man': Crèvecoeur's Caribbean, Raynal's Revolution, and the Fate of Atlantic Cosmopolitanism," *William and Mary Quarterly* 61.2 (2004): 221–22.

46. "A Song," *New-York Gazette, or Weekly Post-Boy*, 11 July 1768.

47. Dorsey, "To 'Corroborate Our Own Claims,'" 361.

48. That a "direct connection . . . was seldom drawn between chattel slavery and the slavery that Americans feared" is an insufficient reason to assert, as John Reid has, that "most commentators of the eighteenth century thought slavery the opposite of liberty without equating it with chattel slavery." Leaving that connection implicit was, rather, an unsuccessful attempt to avoid Loyalist allegations of hypocrisy. John Phillip Reid, *The Concept of Liberty in the Age of American Revolution* (Chicago: University of Chicago Press, 1988), 45.

49. Holbo, "Imagination, Commerce, and the Politics of Associationism," 49–50.

50. On the raids against British officials conducted in blackface, see also Morgan and Morgan, *The Stamp Act Crisis*, 41–53.

51. Dierks, *In My Power*, xii, 5.

52. Richard Eden, *The First Three English Books on America*, ed. Edward Arber (Birmingham, 1885), 73.

53. Dickson D. Bruce, Jr., "Politics and Political Philosophy in the Slave Narrative," in *The Cambridge Companion to the African American Slave Narrative*, ed. Audrey Fisch (New York: Cambridge University Press, 2007), 28, 38.

54. François Furstenberg forcefully contends that liberalism, like letter writing, obscured the exercise of authority and force in chattel slavery: "The liberal tendency to individualize power trapped slaves in a double bind. It erased the power relationships embedded in chattel slavery and replaced them with the fiction that each individual *chooses* slavery or freedom, thus shifting the moral burden of slavery onto the slave. By attributing moral agency to slaves—by holding them to standards of rational, autonomous subjectivity—it made slaves responsible for their condition. Even people born into slavery at some point made a choice to submit. At the very least they could have chosen death over slavery. This liberal formulation—by not resisting, slaves had consented to their enslavement—grounded both citizenship *and* slavery in consent." Furstenberg, "Beyond Freedom and Slavery," 1310.

55. Bradley, *Slavery, Propaganda, and the American Revolution*, xxiv.

56. Alan Gilbert, *Black Patriots and Loyalists: Fighting for Emancipation in the War for Independence* (Chicago: University of Chicago Press, 2012), xi.

57. "A Parody upon the Well Known Liberty Song," *Boston Evening-Post*, 26 September 1768.

58. See Walter Benn Michaels, *The Trouble with Diversity: How We Learned to Love Identity and Ignore Inequality* (New York: Metropolitan Books, 2006), 122–40.

[6]

ALEXANDER R. JABLONSKI

"PROVIDENCE NEVER DESIGNED US FOR NEGROES": SLAVERY AND BRITISH SUBJECTHOOD IN THE STAMP ACT CRISIS, 1764–1766

ON THE MORNING OF May 30, 1765, Francis Bernard took the floor of the Massachusetts General Court to speak of filial and civic duty. His tenure as the royal governor of that province had always been a rather fitful one, involving regular disputes over judicial appointments and provincial taxes. But the spring of 1765 brought something new in the Stamp Act. The proposed tax, which would not take effect for almost six months, had already inspired a sort of restless assertiveness that went well beyond the typical parochialism and tightfisted intransigence of colonial legislatures. Since its first hearing in Parliament, the tax had met with stiff opposition in the North American colonies. Still saddled with a sizable debt from the French and Indian War, colonists decried the imposition. At the furthest extent, some had even begun to question whether Parliament had any right to levy the tax at all, let alone impose it upon the colonies. On the same day that Bernard took the floor in Boston, a young and excitable lawyer in Virginia named Patrick Henry pushed a series of terse, incendiary resolutions through the half-empty House of Burgesses. That provincial assembly, he declared, held "the only exclusive Right and Power to lay Taxes . . . upon the Inhabitants of this Colony." Lacking the approval of colonial representatives, and so lacking colonial consent, all other taxes became "illegal, unconstitutional, and unjust."[1] Although Bernard had yet to learn of Henry's remarks, he knew a firm defense of Parliament could not come too soon.

Brushing quickly past a few recommendations about hemp and potash, Bernard arrived at the real purpose of his address. "The general Settlement of the *American* Provinces," he remarked, "must necessarily produce some Regulations, which, from their Novelty only, will appear disagreeable." Novelty was important here. Few in either England or the colonies would argue that the Stamp Act trod familiar ground. But if only the colonists would trust in the Parliament, and if only they would accept for a moment the right of Parliament to implement the tax, Bernard was quite certain they would see it operate for the "Benefit and Advantage of the Colonies." After all, any empire as "extended and diverse as that of *Great-Britain*" required some kind of supreme legislature to which all its far-flung parts were subordinate. Britons should count themselves lucky that Parliament "is the Sanctuary of Liberty and Justice; and that the Prince, who presides over it, realizes the Idea of a Patriot King." The colonists could hardly find themselves in safer hands. "In the meantime," he concluded, "a respectful Submission to the Decrees of the Parliament is their Interest, as well as their Duty."[2]

These were hardly empty words, and they did not fall upon an entirely sympathetic audience. When word of the Stamp Act had first arrived in early 1765, the people of Boston turned out to voice their discontent. The taverns filled with talk of the British Constitution. Printers took up the cause of "English liberty." And the provincial assembly did little to remind its constituents of their duty to a respectful submission. Among those attending the governor's speech was James Otis, Jr., a representative of Boston and by turns a brilliant and—many were certain—mentally imbalanced lawyer. An early and relentless opponent of the governor, by the middle of 1765 he had already proved himself perhaps the most prolific pamphleteer in the colonies.[3] Otis loved nothing so much as an argument, and during the previous year alone he had turned out at least three pamphlets for the colonial defense, each more breathlessly invective than the last. In the first, a long-winded and circuitous romp through the origins of civil society, he had declared the imposition of taxes without consent "absolutely irreconcilable with the rights of Colonists as British subjects, as men."[4] No government, and certainly not one that claimed such love of natural liberty as that of Britain, could abridge its subjects' rights of life or property without courting tyranny. Though the British Parliament might have the power and perhaps even the jurisdiction to impose such a tax, doing so would strike at whatever made it truly *British*. To those like Bernard who pressed for colonial obedience to Parliament, Otis retorted that there was a fair distance between "a blind slavish submission, and a loyal generous and rational obedience, to the supreme authority of the state."[5]

However Bernard hoped that a call for submission would land, with such men as James Otis for an audience it did not. In the months that followed his address, the people of Boston arose with others across North

America in anything but dutiful obedience. Stamp officers responsible for administering the tax resigned their posts en masse, and by August, mobs in Boston had even destroyed the homes of prominent officials associated with the Stamp Act. All testified, as the townsfolk of Weymouth declared, that "these taxations and the extraordinary power of the admiralty judges, [were] so many 'Novelties' that time itself will never reconcile us to." While Bernard had insisted they trust in Parliament through unfamiliar circumstances, many regarded the Stamp Act only as an attack on "our particular rights and privileges," which struck "at the very foundations of the English constitution."[6]

From the front page of the *Boston Gazette* in October, "Americanus" joined the din with a word of advice to his countrymen and a word of censure for their governor. "It is a common opinion here that *British Subjects* are *British Subjects*," he opened with caustic sarcasm. "Vain imagination! Be not deceived. Instead of looking upon yourselves merely as subjects of the K[ing] of Great Britain, you should remember that you are *subjects of the subjects* of that monarch." Do not resist, he advised, but "rather hug the chains which you cannot throw off, and then you may hope for more peaceable times." In the final lines of his address, Americanus traded sarcasm for dire prophecy and remarked that if any wondered what a "respectful submission" would entail, they need only look to the plight of their "brother Americans, the black inhabitants of the West India Islands." There were abject slaves who knew no other purpose but, "with the sweat of their brow, to support [their masters] in luxury and grandeur" and who knew to bear the lash "without muttering" for fear that it would bring only further punishment.[7]

At the center of this controversy lay competing visions of subjecthood within the expansive British Empire. On the one side, defenders of Parliament, like Bernard, described its extensive and sovereign jurisdiction as the most basic condition of imperial happiness; out beyond its influence lay both tyranny and licentiousness. Accordingly, dutiful submission to that authority was incumbent upon every subject, in whatever circumstances—and however represented—he might find himself.[8] On the other side, resplendent in their outrage, opponents of the Stamp Act insisted that any meaningful sense of British liberty required restraints upon that jurisdiction and that far from submission—tantamount to slavery—the British subject had a duty to resist whenever tyrannical designs threatened the inalienable right of consensual government. "Providence never designed us for Negroes," John Adams wrote in the colonial defense, "and so never intended us to be slaves."[9]

On the surface of things, the imperial crisis occasioned by the Stamp Act was a constitutional one, in which these divergent notions of subjecthood supported opposing conceptions of the "imperial constitution."[10] The Stamp Act set unprecedented taxation upon untested claims of parliamentary jurisdiction, and so provoked a decade of increasingly unsatisfying attempts to square a doctrine of parliamentary supremacy with colonial traditions of self-governance and an "ancient constitution" that seemed to guarantee consensual government to its subjects. This constitutional interpretation has a venerable place in the scholarship, and its most recent advocate, Eric Nelson, leaves considerable space for the British subject at the center of the revolutionary period.[11] By the late 1760s, he argues, a great number of Patriots actually broke with the Whig defense of legislative sovereignty they had long espoused and revived a constitutional "Royalism" of extensive prerogative powers and a single, superintending monarch—the very same doctrine advanced by the Stuarts in the seventeenth century. As discussed in greater detail later in the chapter, American colonists envisioned an empire of equal subjects pledged to a common king rather than a multi-tiered structure built atop "virtual representation" in Parliament.

Nelson's work, like others in that vein, hews strictly to constitutional theory. But as advocates and opponents of the tax contested subjecthood in the colonies with competing demands of submission and calls to resistance, they pulled that debate out beyond its narrow base in constitutional doctrine. The British subject, as either side understood the term, was remarkably synthetic; it wove particular assumptions of governmental order together with prescriptive ideas about British identity and character.[12] This essay takes its expanded view from two bodies of scholarship. First, it looks to works of political culture by Richard Bushman and Brendan McConville, which demonstrate the central role of monarchy—and so of subjecthood—to colonial life.[13] Second are those works that explore the pliability of subjecthood in the British context. Provocative essays by T. H. Breen and Chris Beneke demonstrate how individual American colonists could draw upon a shared language of subjecthood to critique imperial policy or express the sorts of radical ideas that would pour forth during the Revolution.[14] These scholars have recovered the forgotten potential of subjecthood in the mid-eighteenth century, which at its broadest could stretch far wider than the citizenship that would follow.[15]

British subjects derived their political nature from the British Constitution, but their status as Britons, however implicated in that constitutional order, depended just as importantly upon cultural concerns about heritage and race, which together informed the character of the present generation. And as either of those categories remained uncertain, foundering upon the ambiguities and troubling diversity of so extensive an empire, British subjecthood proved quite pliable. Under the pressures of crisis, a shared vocabulary of subjecthood supported two directly opposed visions of the British Empire and of its membership. Each traced the bounds of the imperial community with cultural assumptions or prescriptions of character and in the process drew clear lines between those subjects who could rightfully claim the benefits of being British and so many slaves who, either by their intransigence or their abject submission, decidedly could not.

The Subject and the Slave

Beyond legal and constitutional studies, the "subject" has rarely taken center stage in the history of the British Empire or of the early United States.[16] Instead, the considerably more modern "citizen," its seeming opposite, draws much of the attention. David Ramsay, an early historian of the American Revolution, exulted in 1789 that at the stroke of a pen "nearly three million people who had been subjects became citizens," a change of political and personal identity nothing short of "immense." The Declaration of Independence, which dredged a new American republic from the state of nature, also inaugurated a new sort of political individual that was fundamentally distinct from—and far superior to—what had preceded it. "Subject," Ramsay explained, described one who was "*under* the power of another," subjected to that authority and far removed from the government that ordered his life. "Citizen," by contrast, described "an *unit* of a mass of free people, who, collectively, possess sovereignty." Where the subject looked up to a master, the citizen found himself only in the company of his fellows, each possessed of "as much common sovereignty as the other," and all more exalted in their condition than any "noblemen."[17] So it looked in the first years of the early Republic: the American citizen stood in stark contrast to the British subject, the former vested in every measure of legislative influence and constitutional liberty that the latter conspicuously lacked.

Over the past decade, a number of historians have undertaken a fruitful conversation about the nature of citizenship in the early United States and moved in important ways beyond Ramsay's simple account. Citizenship certainly did not come at the stroke of a pen, but rather emerged fitfully, haltingly alongside the structures of a new American state, as capacious republican ideals ran squarely into prevailing notions of gender, race, and status. Citizenship proved not so much a promise of collective sovereignty as a powerfully contested and intensely pliable language of rights and identity, a means at once to restrict the political community and demand access to it. As many scholars have demonstrated, the scope of American citizenship steadily contracted in the wake of the American Revolution, until only the propertied white men who had always held power lay entirely within its bounds.[18] For all their insight, though, even the most recent studies rehearse Ramsay's fundamental distinction between subject and citizen. However restrictive, the voluntary nature of American citizenship and the democratic potential it at least implied sharply distinguished it from the permanent and hereditary status of subjecthood. With citizenship a defining feature of modern politics, subjecthood remains its rather uncomplicated foil, left behind as an oppressive fixture of the ancien regime.

There has been another, perhaps more basic reason than republican hindsight to overlook subjecthood. "Subject" rings generic to our ears, especially when it concerns the early modern period, while "citizen" has an air of declared purpose about it. Citizens, after all, emerged from a string of consciously republican revolutions in government and distinguished themselves explicitly from the subjects they had once been. Prior to that distinction, there had been few alternatives to the subject—save, perhaps, the alien and the slave—and so the term proved quite expansive. It simply acknowledged allegiance to some kind of political order, however virtuous or tyrannical that government happened to be. Indeed, it might even function just as the republicans employed it by the end of the eighteenth century. One could speak, as John Locke certainly had, of the benighted subject, "or rather Slave of an Absolute Prince," whose life under arbitrary government lacked any security of life or property.[19]

In the same breath, however, when turned upon themselves British writers meant something quite different by the word *subject*. Challenging advocates of divine right absolutism with a notion of consensual government, Locke argued that Britons "could never be safe or at rest, *nor think themselves in Civil Society*, till . . . every single person became subject, equally with other Men, to those Laws, which he himself, as part of the Legislative had established."[20] Far from a mark of subjection as we might understand the word, British subjecthood was something precious, well worthy of defense, as it distinguished Britons from those tenant-subjects around them in France, Spain, or Turkey. British subjecthood entailed the peculiar benefits of the British Constitution, an order of government and society uniquely disposed to protect its subjects' basic, natural rights since at least the Glorious Revolution, and it envisioned a people active in the defense of those rights. As James Otis argued, in a bit heavily cribbed from Locke, the basic principles of government—legitimacy derived from the consent of the governed, an abiding concern for life and property—had been inscribed in nature by "the unchangeable will of God." Nothing in the state of nature laid a foundation for the slavery of arbitrary government, though few had ever experienced that natural equality. Everyone, except for a handful of hermits and misanthropes, came into a world of human societies and subject to whatever compact their ancestors had drawn up to govern them. Only Britons had exercised their sovereign right, thrown off their shackles, and created for themselves a constitutional order uniquely in keeping with the laws of nature. Much as Locke described, and not too far from Ramsay's praise of the citizen, the revolutionaries of 1688 had been animated by "a professed and real view . . . to put the liberties of the people, out of the reach of arbitrary power in all times to come."[21]

Throughout the empire, metropolitan and colonist alike embraced a common language of British subjecthood and joined with Otis in celebrating the constitution that guaranteed it. "It is our happiness under English government to enjoy whatever we have a natural right to," David Rowland told his congregation in Providence, Rhode Island. "Such is it's [*sic*] constitution, that the honor and dignity of the crown and legislative body, the property and liberty of the subject, are each secured, protected, and defended."[22] Indeed, "it was God who gave us our natural liberty," Rowland's colleague in Halifax, Massachusetts, explained, and "it was his kind providence that fixed us under the british constitution, rather than under that of France, or Spain, or Turkey, where the gripe of tyranny occasions an almost total insensibility to liberty."[23] Much like the republican citizen who would emerge by the end of the eighteenth century, the British subject stood at the head of a revolutionary heritage and surrounded by a system of government that made him, as one London writer put it, "the envy of Slaves and Bigots."[24]

It was not a more perfect citizen, but rather the abject slave who opposed the British subject. For the most part, slavery figured into a common language of British politics much as Locke had used it, shorthand for the sort of despotic government that trod freely upon its subjects' natural rights. This was the *political* slavery warned of in John Dickinson's *Letters from a Farmer in Pennsylvania*, which recalled the tragic death of republican Rome, the plight of the Israelites, and the tortured lives of subjects in Turkey and France.[25] Britons of whatever stripe, whether the strongest advocate of the Stamp Act or its most ardent critic, understood liberty and the will to maintain it as the defining features of British subjecthood, a grant of virtuous ancestors and a mixed constitution, and the chief distinction between them and so many slaves who surrounded them. The ancient Britons, so the story went, had been a liberty-loving people until the Norman Conquest brought "the Rape of Despotism," which broke the people's spirit and condemned them for centuries to "the most abject vassalage." Common enslavement, though, bred unity and inspired resistance to Norman tyranny. "By the boldest opposition," they broke free of their enslavement, restrained an unchecked monarchical prerogative, and "never stop'd 'till they had secured the most valuable Privileges which are now said to be the Birth-Right of Englishmen."[26] Continually defended from the Magna Carta through the Glorious Revolution, it was those privileges "which, in an especial Manner, denominate the *British* subjects a free People."[27]

In North America and the West Indies, the presence of enslaved Africans lent the language of political slavery a colonial inflection.[28] Colonists could hardly have ignored one of the most conspicuous features of their lives, and indeed the plight of black slaves provided colonial writers and activists a rich, nightmarish vocabulary with which to condemn parliamentary taxation. The Stamp Act threatened to rivet "Shackles" upon the wrists of every American colonist.[29] Effigies and stamped papers hung and burned, as Molly Perry recalls in chapter 2, suspended by "an iron chain."[30] Stamp officers, each of them native to the colony in which they would administer the stamp tax, came over as "Negro Overseers," who "in order to please their Masters . . . are more severe to their own Colour in their Exactions and Whippings . . . and consequently are more abhorred and detested."[31] And the advocates of passive obedience, as Americanus described Francis Bernard, advanced a wholly slavish doctrine: "When your neck has been accustomed to the yoke, it will not feel so galling; when your backs are grown callous by repeated flagellation, the whip will make but little impression."[32] At least in the early days of the imperial crisis, however, this language generally fell far short of black slaves themselves, whose distinct ancestry and assumedly passive disposition kept them well beyond any conversation about British subjecthood. Though a rhetoric of natural liberty would in short order provoke harsh criticism of the paradoxical relation between American slavery and American freedom, it did not do so in 1765. Instead, reflecting upon the Stamp Act, a respected minister of Boston like Johnathan Mayhew could recall, without a hint of irony, that "even our bought *Negro* slaves apparently shared in the common distress" and recoiled at the thought of being "the *servants* of *servants*, [rather] than of free men." Upon repeal, those same slaves rejoiced, "as tho' they had received their own manumission," to see their masters freed from bondage.[33] "Slavery," however it recalled the plight of black slaves, worked initially and primarily as the foil of British subjecthood and clarified by its terrible prospect what it meant to possess liberty and remain free of tyrannical government.

The Stamp Act provoked an imperial crisis that saw this common language of British subjecthood fracture into two nearly irreconcilable dialects. As in the controversy between Francis Bernard and his opponents that opened this essay, a shared pride in the British subject and a common dread of the slave informed two fundamentally distinct notions of subjecthood as it operated in the American colonies. Variously defined, subjecthood at once entailed duty and right, implied hierarchy and equality, and justified the Stamp Act even as it obliged resistance to it. Either side martialed its particular vision against the slavish doctrines of the other.

The debate over subjecthood in the American colonies began, while the Stamp Act was just an abstracted dread, with a look backward. Unsurprisingly for a people whose whole system of government ran on accumulated custom and usage, either side looked to the early days of colonial settlement to support its particular vision of the empire, and each came away with a wildly different notion of the imperial constitution and of the ostensible Britons who lived in the colonies. As the Stamp Act shifted from abstraction to reality and as colonial resistance spread from printing houses into the streets, the debate over subjecthood shifted as well, from heritage to new elements of character. Neither the subject nor the slave was a simple, static category in this period; both were, to the last degree, performative.[34] And it was ultimately character that, from either direction, would divide the truly *British* subjects from slaves.

Ancient Rights and Modern Obligations

Heritage supplied the basic outline of subjecthood in the American colonies. Just as common veneration for British subjecthood sprang from ancient Britons and the Glorious Revolution, so subjects along the colonial periphery relied upon a motley cast of "first adventurers" for the terms of their subjecthood. Those early settlers staked out the first British settlements in the Americas, traced the first imperial lines across the Atlantic, and from them advocates and opponents of the Stamp Act drew branching conclusions about the nature of the imperial constitution and the relation of the far-flung colonists to those who had stayed behind in England. It was with an eye to historical precedent that a divide between parliamentary and colonial visions of subjecthood first emerged.

When they recalled those early settlers, proponents of the Stamp Act told a story of ancient debt and modern obligation. Decrying the "petulancy of spirit," the "Tumult and Sedition" that gripped the colonies by the end of 1765, one London writer wished that the Americans might remember "by whose nurture and paternal indulgence they have arrived at the greatness of such a people." Those first adventurers, wrote another, had left neither as "convicts exiled to a foreign land, nor orphans destitute of a tender parent, willing and able to protect them." Planted in "an uncultivated country of numberless difficulties," besieged by "a set of barbarians, uncivilized and jealous of their property," they relied upon the vital assistance of England "for the establishment of their colony in times of peace and the defense of it in times of war." No subjects of Britain, this writer concluded, "could be more dependent on the mother country, than the first planters were."[35] From the pages of the *Public Ledger*, "William Pym" marveled at the colonists, who could ignore any "numberless favors" of England and be "to the last degree offended, because we are not doing a great deal *more*."[36] A long history of indulgence and support, traced from the first settlement of North America through the most recent war with France and even into the troops who would secure its peace, invested British subjecthood in the colonies with a heavy measure of debt and obligation. For what other purpose had Britain "lavish[ed] away her blood and treasure?" demanded a contributor to the *London Chronicle*. For only "an ideal right to barren territory?" Or was it "to feed and cherish an Alien?"[37] No, the American colonists, as filial dependents, owed a dutiful submission in return for the regular and costly support that secured their livelihoods in America.

Colonists and their advocates told an entirely different story, one of toil and suffering, of service to empire, and of a subjecthood that entailed right far more than obligation. As often as the defenders of Parliament claimed indulgence, colonial writers firmly denied it. Richard Bland recalled that his Virginian ancestors had settled an "uncultivated and almost uninhabited" land "without any Expense to the Nation."[38] The assembled representatives of Connecticut agreed, declaring that the conquest of a hostile country and of its barbarous inhabitants had come only "with much difficulty, and at the only Endeavours, Expence, and Charges of our Forefathers."[39] It was a purchase, wrote James Otis, "sealed by the blood of their ancestors."[40] By their own expense, at the cost of their own lives, the first adventurers had added considerably to the British dominions and secured for their posterity not debt and obligation, but a subjecthood that entailed constitutional rights and the name of "Briton" in common with those back in England.

In New England, a Puritan heritage turned the story of the first adventurers into something of a Homeric epic, luridly detailed as it echoed through churches, meetinghouses, and printing offices. John Adams, a regular compatriot of Otis, recounted how the civil and ecclesiastical tyranny of "the execrable race of Steuarts" had sent the first settlers across the Atlantic. Bearing "an utter contempt of all that dark ribaldry of hereditary power and indefeasible right," they fled European despotism and preserved in their new home "a love of universal liberty" that had passed unsullied on to their descendants.[41] In Plymouth, where "the Foundations of the British Empire" had first been laid in New England, the townsfolk celebrated forefathers who had disdained slavery and established an "Asylum of Liberty" in North America.[42] William Patten, the town's Congregationalist minister, recounted how "our fathers were treated as though they had forfeited the common rights of Englishmen." Though "grievously harassed" and even "martyred," they had nonetheless planted themselves in America as Britons: "They dared plow the atlantic, and enter on a wild, uncultivated wilderness inhabited by savage animals and more savage men." And at the risk of all they had, "even to life itself," they had secured that land for England and secured for themselves a basic assurance of their rights. "They fulfilled their engagements, and acquitted themselves of their obligations." We may infer, Patten concluded, "that we, being the offspring of such progenitors, are born free."[43]

Across the colonies, the story of the first adventurers opened long histories of colonial service to the British Empire. Colonists touted an extensive trade across the Atlantic that, structured by the Navigation Acts, operated "to the infinite advantages and emolument of the mother state."[44] Most importantly, and most often, they pointed to colonial participation in the French and Indian War. Imperial debts from that war helped to justify the Stamp Act, and colonists responded with their own debts, which had never been "so pressing in the memory of man," and with a peace whose favorable terms depended upon "the general exertion *of the colonies of North-America*."[45] All asserted, as John Dickinson proclaimed, that the "FOUNDATIONS OF THE POWER AND GLORY OF GREAT-BRITAIN ARE LAID IN AMERICA."[46] And that fact, which lay atop the hardships of the first adventurers and more than a century of colonial service to the empire, testified that the colonists "rather merit Favour, than a Deprivation of [their] Rights."[47]

From these directly opposing views of the first adventurers, the one entailing obligation and the other bestowing right, sprang two fundamentally opposed visions of the imperial constitution. Colonists argued that a string of royal charters, which compensated their ancestors with local government, provided their only guarantees of *British* subjecthood in any way that distinguished them from the slaves of more arbitrary princes. James Otis described all those who had crossed the Atlantic, of whatever nation, as "the noble discoverers of a new world," from whose labors, "as from an endless source, wealth, and plenty, the means of power, grandeur and glory, in a degree unknown to the hungry chiefs of former ages," had poured into Europe. In return, however, all but the Britons had received "nothing but ill-usage, slavery and chains, as fast as the riches of their own earning could furnish the means of forging them." Only the Britons, by way of their colonial charters, might claim equality with those back in the mother country.[48] Even as it sat upon Stuart heads, Daniel Dulany added from Virginia, the Crown had recognized the necessity of such constitutional guarantees, else the colonists would lack any security of life or property and find themselves reduced to "meer tenants at will." Their charters provided the only bases by which the British Constitution could effectively span the Atlantic: "The granting them powers of government was not mere *favor*, but that which was *right*, *fit*, *equitable* . . . for without it, they must be deprived of that right, which others enjoyed who were no more than their equals."[49]

The colonists built a model of the empire upon their charters that secured their subjecthood—and so their British rights—by setting explicit bounds to the jurisdiction of Parliament. In their view, all British subjects owed allegiance to a common monarch, but enjoyed their natural right of consent through local, representative government.[50] At the furthest extent, on display in the provocative *Constitutional Courant*, this interpretation denied the authority of Parliament to tax or even legislate within the colonies: "Let the British parliament be treated with all possible respect, while they treat us as fellow subjects; but if they transgress the bounds prescribed them by the constitution, if they usurp a jurisdiction to which they have no right . . . if they pursue such measures as will infallibly end in Turkish despotism . . . we owe them no more subjection, in this regard, than the Divan of Constantinople." To acknowledge that authority, and so to deny the constitutional guarantee of colonial charters, "would be to court our chains" and welcome the slavery of tyrannical government.[51] Through a series of provincial resolves, where the familiar mantra of "no taxation without representation" took shape, colonists declared it "the indisputable Privilege of every British subject" to have a say in the disposal of his property. And they condemned the Stamp Act, which claimed sweeping parliamentary influence in the colonies, as flatly "UNCONSTITUTIONAL," as "an Abolition of that Constitution under which [we] have so long and happily enjoyed the Rights and Privileges of Englishmen."[52]

The proponents of the Stamp Act put little stock in royal charters. Instead, they drew their understanding of the imperial constitution from a revolutionary past, which seemed one long march of the British Parliament against the tyrannical pretensions of English kings and their overwrought prerogative. The advocates of parliamentary taxation argued that if any royal decree could actually grant an exemption from the obligations of subjecthood, the royal prerogative might stretch so far as to bind the Parliament, nullify the Glorious Revolution, and in a stroke welcome back monarchical tyranny. Whatever the phrase actually meant, Soame Jenyns, an arch-defender of Parliament, felt sure that the "Liberty of an *Englishman*" could never mean "an Exemption from Taxes imposed by the Authority of the Parliament of *Great Britain*."[53] No charter of the Crown—particularly a Stuart crown—could possibly stand above the sovereign legislature. William Pym was even more direct, as he declared that "a resolution of the British Parliament can at any time set aside all the charters that have ever been granted by our monarchs." Certainly, he admitted, the first adventurers had received a few "particular indulgences" from the Crown to assuage their hardships, but these were no more than "casual inconveniences" to the Parliament, whose responsibility lay with the welfare of the empire as a whole. Anyone who would contend that royal charters set bounds upon the sovereign legislature proved himself "unacquainted with the nature of the Colonies and the constitution of this Kingdom."[54] Parliament, wrote the erstwhile agent of Georgia, "has a full and compleat jurisdiction over the property and person of every inhabitant of a British colony."[55]

As a number of parliamentary writers had it and as their particular vision of colonial settlement attested, it was only the authority and influence of Parliament unrestrained that meant colonial prosperity. Francis Bernard had called Parliament the "Sanctuary of Liberty and Justice" in his speech before the Massachusetts General Court, and plenty of others joined in to sing praises of its wisdom and protection. One particularly incensed contributor, who mused that a standing army might "rub off the rust of puritanism" from the colonies, outlined the evils that would follow parliamentary restraint. From within, a spirit of petty factionalism, the same that had "kindled the flames of civil war in [England]," awaited only a spark to set the colonies ablaze. From without, the factious colonists would then find themselves exposed to all manner of foreign threats and would fall, as had the ancient Greeks to Philip of Macedon, into the hands of some despotic prince. "How then," the writer asked, "do you expect to remain free from slavery?"[56] Martin Howard of Rhode Island feared that by denying the jurisdiction of Parliament, his fellow colonists would "take leave of the common law," the font of parliamentary authority, "and thereby with equal temerity and folly strip ourselves of every blessing we enjoy as Englishmen."[57] Howard knew that the greatest danger to colonial liberty came not from the overwrought powers of Parliament, but from the licentiousness, the veritable slavery, that would arise in their absence: "While we lament how thin the partition is between excess of liberty and absolute tyranny, it should be a pleasing consideration, to every man in the colonies, that his liberty and property are subject, in the last resort, to the care and animadversion of the mother country."[58] Proponents of the Stamp Act described an empire almost entirely reversed from what their opponents imagined. All British subjects owed their allegiance to a common sovereign, they agreed, but sovereignty lay with the supreme legislature—the king-in-Parliament—and not with the king alone. Some even went so far as to declare that representative government was a positive privilege rather than a basic right and that the constitution itself was "confined to the island of Great Britain, and does not, and cannot operate in its full force in our Colonies."[59] On display here was a clear distinction between subjects in the colonies and those in England, supported already by a history of imperial indulgence. Though some attempted to assuage that difference with a contrivance of "virtual representation," it never disappeared entirely. Colonists owed a dutiful submission to the legislature that secured their prosperity, though denied any actual presence within it.

Race and Subjecthood

A belief in the difference between metropolitan and colonial subjects sprang from deeper roots than constitutional theory. Just as the first adventurers had bound their descendants to a particular system of government, they had also invested them with a certain racial heritage that set them apart from England. Significantly, these were racial notions drawn up in the comfortable ambiguity of the eighteenth century rather than the stern phenotypical categories of the nineteenth; racial identity arose from ancestry and blood ties, certainly, but depended just as heavily on the mediating influence of environmental factors and behavior.[60] Race was at once inherited, molded by circumstance, and performed in the eighteenth century. And from the perspective of many parliamentary writers, each facet made the American colonists distinct from their relations in England. Their ancestors had come from the margins of English society, one London writer explained, a disordered crew of "independents and Anabaptists, presbyterians and quakers, convicts and felons, savages and negro-whippers."[61] In the foreign wilderness of America, close contact with Indian "savages" and far too heavy an investment in chattel slavery had done them little good, as J. Hector St. John de Crèvecoeur warned in his response to John Dickinson (chapter 5). The most common characterization of the American colonists was that of undutiful children, too long indulged by their doting parent. One writer described "a giddy multitude" of "truant children," while others derided their easy susceptibility to emotional, demagogic rhetoric of the sort that held sway among "that more numerous Part of Mankind, who have ears but no understanding."[62]

A few went further and described the utterly corrupted nature of American colonists. The people of Massachusetts, "Pacificus" wrote from London, were "a crabbed Race, not very unlike their Half Brothers, the Indians, for unsocial Principles, and an unrelenting Cruelty." And in Virginia, settled as it was upon a swamp, he found men "whose emaciated Bodies and pale Faces, prove at first Sight the Degeneracy of their Morals, and the consumptive state of their natural Constitutions." They were, in short, "yellow Shadows of Men."[63] Metropolitan writers laid particularly heavy emphasis on the deleterious effects of chattel slavery upon colonial morals and character. "Unused to constraint, and unacquainted with reprehension," William Pym explained, American slave owners were "naturally haughty and overbearing . . . callous to the nicer feelings of humanity, as well as insensible to the proper regulations of Government." And when he considered the consequences of colonial growth, Pym feared that the locus of empire might eventually shift, and "in another century . . . our posterity will be broiling on the sands of America," subject to the jurisdiction of the descendants of "African Negro[s]" and "Mulattoes."[64]

American colonists, in their turn, roundly denied that they had been corrupted by life in the colonies or that they were anything less than true Britons and deserving of full British subjecthood. "Every drop of my blood is British," wrote John Dickinson in 1766, "and that heart is animated with as warm wishes for her prosperity, as her truest sons can form."[65] American writers rejected the idea that they were somehow less than English, that generations in the American colonies had enervated their spirits and turned them from Britons to degenerate cast-offs. However the common people of England might "foolishly imagine" North America to be filled with "a compound mixture of English, Indian, and Negro," James Otis described the colonists all "free born British white subjects, whose loyalty has never been suspected."[66] "What a strange animal must a *North American* appear to be," huffed Daniel Dulany, "to the generality of *English* readers, who have never had an opportunity to admire, that he may be neither black, nor tawny, may speak the *English* language, and, in other respects, seem, for all the world, like one of them!"[67]

As the Stamp Act shifted from abstracted threat to pressing reality in the fall of 1765, North American colonists seeking the rights of subjecthood drew this defense of their racial heritage into demonstrations of their truly British character. Where parliamentary writers paired demands of submission with notions of racial difference, colonists founded their claims of British subjecthood on the virtuous example of their forefathers and their own jealous defense of liberty. "How would our glorious ancestors have behaved at this juncture?" demanded a writer in the *Pennsylvania Journal*. "Would those renowned worthies, who with such infinite toil . . . delivered to us their generous plan of liberty, have stood hesitating and trifling when an outrageous attempt was made to subvert it?" They would have resisted even the smallest encroachments of arbitrary power, came the answer, and given not "one inch of ground to the insults of despotism." Nothing would be "so degenerate" as to abandon their example.[68] Amid public demonstrations and impassioned calls to resistance, character drew the clearest line between subject and slave. Nothing better identified the British subject than an active and jealous defense of liberty. And nothing revealed a slavish disposition quite like the willingness to give passive obedience to tyranny. "The *British* nation," John Dickinson asserted, "aims not at empire over vassals." They would "be better pleased to have their children speaking the language of freemen, than muttering the timid murmurs of slaves."[69]

Beginning in the summer of 1765, agitated colonists exhorted their more complacent neighbors to a principled resistance, not in opposition to the British Constitution, but to the "adamantine chains" that would deny them its benefits.[70] In early October, shortly before the Stamp Act was to take effect, a skull and crossbones appeared on the front page of the *Boston Gazette*, there to mark out space for the new stamp (see figure

6.1). Just above it, an open letter addressed the people of Massachusetts. Though certainly incensed by corrupted ministers and a few "mercenary Placemen" newly arrived in the colonies, the anonymous author fixed the greatest part of his wrath on those in his community who seemed content to stand by or, worse, to abet the tax: "The time is not I trust yet come that Indolence has so enervated your Powers that you will neither bestir yourselves . . . nor make a stand, when Oppression, like Poverty, *invades as an armed man*." "Behold your Offspring," the letter exclaimed, "bred up in Bondage! Behold the Province swarming with Slaves and Beggars, and your lands, those Lands you now so much delight in, all owned by haughty and domineering Lords."[71] All would attend inaction. Sons of Liberty throughout the colonies declared it the duty of every British subject to avert such disaster. In Norfolk, Virginia, they opposed the quiet submission that would wreck civil liberty in the colonies and make them all "absolute slaves." And in Wallingford, Connecticut, of all places, they pledged unending opposition to the Stamp Act, "even to take the field."[72]

However colonists traced the line between subject and slave within their own communities, that distinction emerged with the most striking clarity in the comparison between North Americans and the "Creole" planters of Jamaica and Barbados. Relations between North America and the West Indian sugar islanders had never been particularly amicable. West Indians had the luxury of several representatives in Parliament, and North Americans saw their hands at work in the Molasses Act of 1733 and the Sugar Act of 1764.[73] More than that, they found the "Creoles" twisted by the heat, luxurious and corrupted planters at the head of a brutal and exploitative slave regime, not unlike the ways in which parliamentary writers viewed the North Americans. But when, in early 1766, word began to make its way northward that most of the Caribbean colonies had given in and enforced the Stamp Act, colonists in North America arose in outrage at the "Creole slaves." "Meeching, sordid, stupid Creatures," John Adams fumed in his diary, "below Contempt, below Pity. They deserve to be made Slaves to their own Negroes."[74] Sons of Liberty in several colonies began to organize boycotts to deprive the planters of their much needed provisions—one can eat only so much sugar—and hoped, as did the editors of the *Boston Gazette*, to bring them "to a State of Despondency, without Cash, without any Thing but stinking Fish and false Doctrines."[75]

Whenever a piece of stamped paper arrived in northern ports, North Americans were ready with chains and effigies to dispose of those "Ignominious Ensigns of Creole Slavery." When a stamped let-pass from Barba-

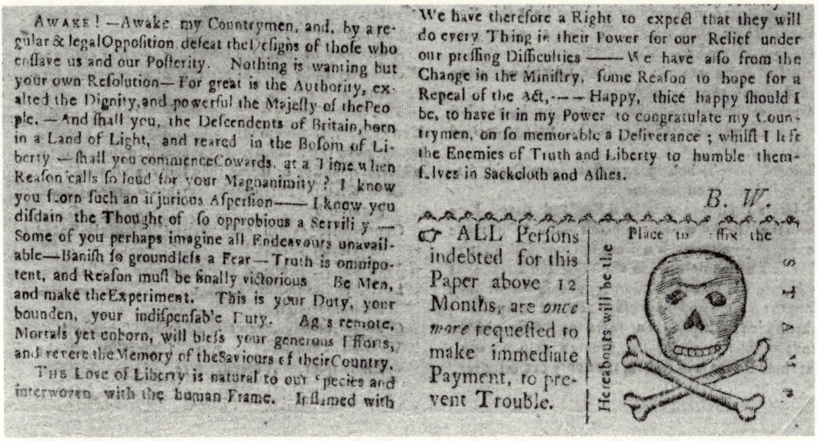

AWAKE!—Awake my Countrymen, and, by a regular & legal Oppoſition defeat the Deſigns of thoſe who enſlave us and our Poſterity. Nothing is wanting but your own Reſolution—For great is the Authority, exalted the Dignity, and powerful the Majeſty of the People.—And ſhall you, the Deſcendents of Britain, born in a Land of Light, and reared in the Boſom of Liberty—ſhall you commence Cowards, at a Time when Reaſon calls ſo loud for your Magnanimity? I know you ſcorn ſuch an injurious Aſperſion——I know you diſdain the Thought of ſo opprobious a Servility—Some of you perhaps imagine all Endeavours unavailable—Baniſh ſo groundleſs a Fear—Truth is omnipotent, and Reaſon muſt be finally victorious. Be Men, and make the Experiment. This is your Duty, your bounden, your indiſpenſable Duty. Ages remote, Mortals yet unborn, will bleſs your generous Efforts, and revere the Memory of the Saviours of their Country.

THE Love of Liberty is natural to our Species and interwoven with the human Frame. Inflamed with

We have therefore a Right to expect that they will do every Thing in their Power for our Relief under our preſſing Difficulties——We have alſo from the Change in the Miniſtry, ſome Reaſon to hope for a Repeal of the Act,——Happy, thice happy ſhould I be, to have it in my Power to congratulate my Countrymen, on ſo memorable a Deliverance; whilſt I left the Enemies of Truth and Liberty to humble themſelves in Sackcloth and Aſhes.

B. W.

☞ ALL Perſons indebted for this Paper above 12 Months, are *once more* requeſted to make immediate Payment, to prevent Trouble.

Figure 6.1 . From the front page of the *Boston Gazette* of October 7, 1765. Such imagery was quite common in colonial papers on the eve of the Stamp Act. After the act had gone into effect on November 1, a few printers draped their pages in black mourning for the death of British liberty. Courtesy of the American Antiquarian Society.

dos arrived in Portsmouth, New Hampshire, much of the town turned out in protest. On the morning of January 3, several Sons of Liberty bound an effigy of George Grenville in chains—"the true emblem of that servile state"—and carried it through the snowy streets of town, through a din of whatever insults the townsfolk could muster for the architect of the Stamp Act. Before the crowd, they tacked the repulsive pass just above Grenville's heart, to indicate his commitment to the enslavement of his fellow subjects, and cast the whole thing into a waiting bonfire. The Sons of Liberty even composed a poem to commemorate the event and to distinguish themselves as subjects from the corrupted slaves of the southern islands:

> Come view [George Grenville] with attention,
> Mark this vile STAMP, his rare invention,
> And here, behold him at the Stake,
> Observe how ev'ry Limb does shake,
> His guilty Countenance betrays
> His meaness in a thousand Ways;
> His fav'rite ACT Barbadian Slaves
> Adopted have, such menial Knaves
> Slavery may suit, but not these Climes,
> Where Freedom reigns and Honor shines.[76]

Portsmouth was not alone. In nearby Boston, another pass drew a crowd of two or three thousand in late February, and the Sons of Liberty in Philadelphia seem to have made a regular evening of burning stamped papers in their coffeehouse, hung from the rafters "not by a golden, but an iron chain."[77] All turned to the West Indian "Creoles" as a foil of American subjecthood; their acquiescence to slavery only cast in sharper relief the British resolve of the North Americans, a distinction preserved in modern scholarship that ignores Caribbean protests and North American supporters of parliamentary power.

As they sought to justify themselves, the sugar islanders actually exaggerated the growing conceptual divide between British subjects and Creole slaves. In the spring of 1766, for example, the committee of correspondence in Barbados pleaded for redress from the Stamp Act in terms that, on the surface, echoed the arguments of their neighbors in North America. The Barbadians claimed the same right of representation—"that *seeming birthright* of every Briton"—as the colonists farther north. And they even shared in the general economic discontent: stagnated trade and declining specie. They staked their pleas for redress, however, not in solidarity with the North Americans, but in distinction from them. The Barbadians complained of their being punished, by tax and boycott, "for the present *REBELLIOUS opposition given to authority by our fellow subjects on the Northern continent*." They condemned the "violent spirit" raised against the act, the "excesses of *popular fury*," and offered their own supplication instead. Barbados had submitted to the act, had refused to clear any ships without stamped documents, and, along with Jamaica, had begun to bring in a sizable revenue. So, they reasoned, their submissive loyalty made a better case for relief—and a better show of subjecthood—than the rebellion of their neighbors.[78]

The letter from Barbados, which made its way into North American newspapers, drew a flurry of criticism. American writers certainly agreed with a difference in character, but insisted the fault lay with submissive Barbadian slaves and not assertive British-American subjects. A fiery response in the *Boston Gazette* declared that "if they were content to be Slaves," at least common decency might have kept them from "bestowing the very pretty Epithet of Rebels on those, who have exerted a glorious Spirit to preserve their just Rights and Privileges." The writer wondered at their "astonishing Imprudence to call us *Fellow-Subjects*" and asked that the printers publish his remarks to "let them know, that we disdain the Relation, that we are the Fellow Subjects of Freemen, not the Fellow Subjects of Slaves."[79] Similarly, John Dickinson rejected the ties of fellow subjecthood: "Could not your 'principle of loyalty' sink you to a satisfactory depth of humiliation, unless you flung yourselves down with such a rage of prostration as to splatter all around you?" North Americans resisted, he argued, not only for themselves, but for their posterity, who would otherwise have been born "to a condition that would have rendered their birth a curse," that of "perpetual slavery."[80]

When repeal finally came to the colonies in the late spring of 1766, it came as a validation for rebellious American colonists, evidence that assertive British subjects and not abject slaves had gotten it right in their understanding of subjecthood. Like many of his fellow ministers, Charles Chauncy of Boston cast the repeal—"good news from a far Country"—as cold waters that refreshed a "thirsty Soul." "No news handed to us from Great-Britain," he said, "ever gave us a quicker sense, or a higher degree of pleasure. It rapidly spread through the Colonies, and, as it passed along, opened in all hearts the springs of joy."[81] The reasons for thanksgiving were manifold, but all reflected a close and reciprocal bond revived between the colonies and the mother country. Repeal demonstrated the kind regard of Parliament to the general commercial good, a triumph of public spirit over private interest and an incorporation of colonial woes into imperial well-being. It removed a grievous burden that had compounded the already sizable task of settling, expanding, and maintaining the colonies, costs that largely devolved to the colonists themselves. And it validated the "vast expence of blood, treasure and labor" already committed to that project. Most important, it further guaranteed the claim of Americans to the rights and privileges of British subjects. Americans stood vindicated in their belief that those rights were "their righteous due in consequence of what they, and their fore-fathers, had done and suffered." With repeal, Chauncy celebrated the return of common affection between equal subjects, of the "tender sympathy" that had waned under the threat of slavery. Now was an opportunity for both civic and religious thanksgiving, a chance to praise the wisdom of Parliament, venerate the constitution, and see God at work behind "a spirit . . . raised in all the Colonies nobly to assert . . . freedom as men, and English-born subjects."[82] Of course, that relief would prove transitory, as the Declaratory Act and the taxation that followed it kept alive the alternative vision of subjecthood. For the moment, though, North Americans prided themselves on having successfully defended, in the tradition of their ancestors, their essential liberty as Britons.

What did it mean, then, to be a British subject in the American colonies? That question lay at the heart of the Stamp Act Crisis, but however forcefully either side made its case, competing visions never gave way to a definite answer. Instead, British subjecthood worked far better as a language, a common vocabulary and syntax that wove shared veneration of the British Constitution and equal claims of British heritage into conflicting—and all but irreconcilable—expressions of the British Empire. Quite like republican citizenship that would take shape in the next decade, subjecthood organized rights and obligations as a means to chart the outer reaches of the imperial community and to police its borders. Each invocation of the British subject entailed certain assumptions about the precise order of the imperial constitution and the extent of British identity. Debated amidst an imperial crisis, those assumptions became prescriptive. Working forward from a doctrine of parliamentary supremacy, and bolstered by records of colonial debt and lingering suspicions of racial difference, advocates of the Stamp Act expected that colonial subjects would pay the sovereign legislature their dutiful obedience. At the same time, of course, colonial opponents of the act envisioned bounds to Parliament's authority, denied so heavy a balance of debt, and met seemingly tyrannical pretensions in government with a notion that truly *British* subjects—not abject slaves—had a duty to resist. Implicit in both arguments were ideas about the emergent British Empire, divided between those ostensible Britons who merited the name of "subject" and those who—by distance, difference, or defect of character—decidedly did not. North Americans set themselves against abject slaves in their own communities and in the Caribbean, while metropolitan writers joined with Creole planters in condemning the rebellious colonists who, lured by demagoguery and their own consumptive character, would trade subjecthood for the slavery of licentiousness. Over the next decade, this dynamic sense of British subjecthood, which could credibly support such countervailing interpretations, only hardened the divisions first drawn up around the Stamp Act and drove the crisis toward a final rupture.

Notes

1. *Newport Mercury*, June 24, 1765.

2. *Boston Gazette*, June 3, 1765.

3. T. H. Breen, "Subjecthood and Citizenship: The Context of James Otis's Radical Critique of John Locke," *New England Quarterly* 71.3 (1998): 378–403.

4. James Otis, *The Rights of the British Colonies Asserted and Proved* (Boston: Edes and Gill, 1764), 38.

5. James Otis, *A Vindication of the British Colonies* (Boston: Edes and Gill, 1765), 8. For an excellent treatment of this colonial position, see Barbara Clark Smith, *The Freedoms We Lost: Consent and Resistance in Revolutionary America* (New York: New Press, 2010).

6. *Boston Gazette*, October 21, 1765.

7. Ibid.

8. This essay pointedly uses male pronouns when referring to the British subject. Whatever else they may have disagreed upon, advocates of Parliament and of the colonies shared a common assumption that the typical British subject was male. That is not to say that women could not count themselves as subjects or that women could not find in their subjecthood a means to press for public influence—as Caroline Wigginton attests in chapter 4. But that is a story that falls beyond the scope of this short essay.

9. *Boston Gazette*, October 15, 1765.

10. The phrase as it appears here comes from the work of Jack P. Greene, who uses it to signify the poorly understood relation of metropolitan to colonial governments that came up for fierce debate in the 1760s and 1770s. Greene's concept has had a profound influence on my thinking, and the competing definitions it entails have helped to frame the competing notions of British subjecthood that structure this essay. See, in particular, Jack P. Greene, *Peripheries and Center: Constitutional Development in the Extended Polities of the United States* (Athens: University of Georgia Press, 1989).

11. Eric Nelson, *Royalist Revolution: Monarchy and the American Founding* (Cambridge, MA: Harvard University Press, 2014). Other important contributions to this constitutional school include C. H. McIlwain, *The American Revolution: A Constitutional Interpretation* (New York: Macmillan, 1923); the voluminous works of Jack Greene and J. P. Reid; and the more recent entries by Mary Sarah Bilder and Daniel Hulsebosch. On the "ancient constitution," an influential reading of the English common law that envisioned parliamentary rule as an inheritance from ancient (i.e., pre-Norman) Britons, see J. G. A. Pocock, *The Ancient Constitution and the Feudal Law: A Study of English Historical Thought in the Seventeenth Century* (Cambridge: Cambridge University Press, 1957); and Daniel Hulsebosch, "The Ancient Constitution and the Expanding Empire: Sir Edward Coke's British Jurisprudence," *Law and History Review* 21.3 (2003): 439–482.

12. On the fruitful association of legal institutions and identity, see Jack P. Greene, "'By Their Laws Shall Ye Know Them': Law and Identity in Colonial British America," *Journal of Interdisciplinary History* 33.2 (2002): 247–260.

13. McConville in particular insists that allegiance to the British monarch, more than any latent republican or proto-democratic convictions, set the tenor of American political culture right up to the revolutionary break. Crucially, too, he explains the imperial crisis as a moment in which colonial attachments to the monarch, played out in public ritual and political practice, took on a subversive tone as they exposed a yawning gulf between provincial and metropolitan perspectives. See Brendan McConville, *The King's Three Faces: The Rise and Fall of Royal America, 1688–1776* (Chapel Hill: University of North Carolina Press, 2006), 8–10, 249–280; and Richard Bushman, *King and People in Provincial Massachusetts* (Chapel Hill: University of North Carolina Press, 1985).

14. Breen, "Subjecthood and Citizenship"; Chris Beneke, "The Critical Turn: Jonathan Mayhew, the British Empire, and the Idea of Resistance in Mid-Eighteenth-Century Boston," *Massachusetts Historical Society* 10 (2008): 23–56.

15. Hannah Muller's new work extends that story into the newest parts of the empire after 1763 and demonstrates that, as even Catholics in Quebec and Grenada pressed for their British rights, the pliable form of the British subject proved essential for binding together increasingly diverse groups of people. See Hannah Weiss Muller, "Bonds of Belonging: Subjecthood and the British Empire," *Journal of British Studies* 53.1 (2014): 29–58.

16. James Kettner's work, which traces the divergence of perpetual subject and volitional citizen from the fragmented nature of British naturalization policy in the eighteenth century, remains the standard legal approach to the topic. *The Development of American Citizenship, 1608–1870* (Chapel Hill: University of North Carolina Press, 1978).

17. [David Ramsay], *A Dissertation on the Manner of Acquiring the Character and Privileges of a Citizen of the United States* (South Carolina, 1789), 3–4.

18. Especially Kettner, *The Development of American Citizenship*; Joan Gunderson, "Independence, Citizenship, and the American Revolution," *Signs* 13.1 (1987): 59–77; Douglas Bradburn, *The Citizenship Revolution: Politics and the Creation of the American Union, 1774–1804* (Charlottesville: University of Virginia Press, 2009); Peter Thompson and Peter S. Onuf, *State and Citizen: British America and the Early United States* (Charlottesville: University of Virginia Press, 2013).

19. John Locke, *Two Treatises of Government*, ed. Peter Laslett (New York: Cambridge University Press, 1988), 326.

20. Ibid., 329–330.

21. Otis, *Rights of Colonies*, 10–16.

22. David S. Rowland, *Divine Providence Illustrated and Improved* (Providence, RI, 1766): 27.

23. William Patten, *A Discourse Delivered at Halifax* (Boston, 1766), 20–21.

24. *Good Humour, or a Way with the Colonies* (London, 1766), 26.

25. For slavery in Dickinson's writing, refer to Zachary Hutchins, chapter 5, this volume. The language of political slavery pervaded Dickinson's *Letters*, but its clearest expression came in a tidy syllogism: "*Those* who are *taxed* without their own consent, expressed by themselves or their representatives, are *slaves. We are taxed* without our own consent, expressed by ourselves or our representatives. *We* are therefore—SLAVES." John Dickinson, *Letters from a Farmer in Pennsylvania, to the Inhabitants of the British Colonies*, 3d ed. (Philadelphia: William and Thomas Bradford, 1769), 53.

26. *Considerations upon the Rights of the Colonists to the Privileges of British Subjects* (New York, 1766), 2–4.

27. [Thomas Fitch], *Reasons why the British colonies . . . should not be charged with internal taxes* (New Haven, CT, 1764).

28. The precise relevance of chattel slavery to political slavery has been the subject of some scholarly debate. At one end of the spectrum, J. P. Reid flatly denies that "slavery" as applied to despotic government and as Americans leveled it against parliamentary taxation had anything to do with enslaved Africans; rather, it was *political*

slavery. Others, such as, Patricia Bradley and Okoye Nwabueze argue that American invocations of slavery could hardly have avoided the actual slaves in their midst and that complaints against British tyranny exposed deep-seated anxiety about chattel slavery and troubling hypocrisy in American political thought. And finally Mary Nyquist carefully trods the middle way by connecting the language of political slavery to a sort of "antityrannicism" that might be traced all the way back to Greece and Rome, a mode of outrage by which ostensibly free people condemned corruption in their government and society. However Britons working in this idiom might have relied on the imagery of chattel slavery, Nyquist argues that by the very act of using it, they assumed a basic distinction between themselves and chattel slaves. Okoye Nwabueze, "Chattel Slavery as the Nightmare of the American Revolutionaries," *William and Mary Quarterly* 37.1 (1980): 3–28; J. P. Reid, *The Concept of Liberty in the Age of the American Revolution* (Chicago: University of Chicago Press, 1987); Patricia Bradley, *Slavery, Propaganda, and the American Revolution* (Jackson: University Press of Mississippi, 1998); Mary Nyquist, *Arbitrary Rule: Slavery, Tyranny, and the Power of Life and Death* (Chicago: University of Chicago Press, 2013).

29. Richard Bland, *An Inquiry into the Rights of the British Colonies* (Williamsburg, VA, 1766), 109.

30. *Boston Gazette*, December 23, 1765.

31. *Boston Gazette*, June 3, 1765.

32. *Boston Gazette*, October 21, 1765.

33. Jonathan Mayhew, *The Snare broken. A Thanksgiving-Discourse* (Boston, 1766), 17, 23.

34. For a particularly insightful discussion of the differences between "active liberty" and "abject slavery," see François Furstenberg, "Beyond Freedom and Slavery: Autonomy, Virtue, and Resistance in Early American Political Discourse," *Journal of American History* 89.4 (2003): 1295–1330.

35. *The Rights of Parliament Vindicated* (London, 1766), 17–18.

36. *Public Ledger*, August 23, 1765.

37. *London Chronicle*, November 28, 1765.

38. Bland, *An Inquiry*, 116.

39. *Boston Gazette*, November 11, 1765.

40. *Boston Gazette*, December 16, 1765.

41. *Boston Gazette*, August 12, 1765.

42. *Boston Gazette*, November 4, 1765.

43. Patten, Discourse, 14–15.

44. [Stephen Hopkins], *The Rights of Colonies Examined.* (Providence, RI, 1765), 8.

45. *Portsmouth Mercury*, September 23, 1765; [Daniel Dulany], *Considerations on the Propriety of Imposing Taxes in the British Colonies* (New York, 1765), 17.

46. [John Dickinson], *The Late Regulations Respecting the British Colonies on the Continent of America Considered* (Philadelphia, 1765), 31.

47. Edmund Morgan, ed., *Prologue to Revolution: Sources and Documents on the Stamp Act Crisis, 1764–1766* (Chapel Hill: University of North Carolina Press, 1959), 60–62.

48. Otis, *Rights of Colonies*, 24–25.

49. *Boston Gazette*, March 17, 1766.

50. Kettner, *Development of American Citizenship*, 131–172. As already noted, Eric Nelson ties these arguments to a Royalist constitutionalism that became popular in the late 1760s, a defense of the royal prerogative drawn from the Stuarts of the seventeenth century. There is much to recommend Nelson's case, especially as he connects it to the powerful executive that became central to American constitutionalism in the 1780s, but in his close attention to constitutional theory he leaves unaddressed a central tension in colonial discourse. At the same time that they brandished their charters, and so the theories of empire that underlay them, colonial writers continued to recall the hardships and—in the case of New England—persecutions that had attended the first adventurers. Colonial writers defended the prerogative to bolster the power of the king, certainly, but with the ultimate intention of securing the constitutional rights that their ancestors had earned and guaranteed to them. Nelson, *Royalist Revolution*.

51. [William Goddard?], *The Constitutional Courant*, in *Tracts of the American Revolution, 1763–1776*, ed. Merrill Jensen (New York: Bobbs-Merrill, 1967), 84–85.

52. *Boston Gazette*, November 18, 1765; Morgan, *Prologue to Revolution*, 60–62.

53. [Soame Jenyns], *The Objections to the Taxation of our American Colonies* (London, 1765), 10.

54. *Public Ledger*, August 19, 1765.

55. [William Knox], *The Claim of the Colonies to an Exemption from Internal Taxes . . . Examined* (London, 1765), 1–2.

56. *The Justice and Necessity of Taxing the American Colonies* (London, 1766), 27–28.

57. [Martin Howard], *A Letter from a Gentleman at Halifax* (Newport, RI, 1765), 11.

58. [Martin Howard], *A Defence of the Letter from A Gentleman at Halifax* (Newport, RI, 1765), 29.

59. *Constitutional Considerations on the Power of Parliament to Levy Taxes on the North American Colonies* (London, 1766), 7–8.

60. On the issue of environmental influences and the "creolization" of American colonists, see Ralph Bauer, *The Cultural Geography of Colonial American Literatures: Empire, Travel, Modernity* (New York: Cambridge University Press, 2003), 179–199.

61. *Justice and Necessity*, 22–23.

62. Knox, *Claim of the Colonies*, 3, 36; Jenyns, *Objections to the Taxation*, 4.

63. Morgan, *Prelude to Revolution*, 100–102.

64. *Public Ledger*, August 30, 1765.

65. [John Dickinson], *An Address to the Committee of Correspondence in Barbados* (Philadelphia, 1766), 10.

66. Otis, *Rights of British Colonies*, 24.

67. Dulany, *Considerations*, 31.

68. Quoted in *Boston Gazette*, February 27, 1766.

69. Dickinson, *An Address*, 10.

70. *Boston Gazette*, October 21, 1765.

71. *Boston Gazette*, October 7, 1765.

72. Morgan, *Prelude to Revolution*, 116, 114.

73. Andrew Jackson O'Shaughnessy, *An Empire Divided: The American Revolution and the British Caribbean* (Philadelphia: University of Pennsylvania Press, 2000), 81–110.

74. John Adams, Diary, January 2, 1766, in *Diary and Autobiography of John Adams*, vol. 1: *Diary, 1755–1770*, ed. L. H. Butterfield (Cambridge, MA: Harvard University Press, 1962), 285.

75. *Boston Gazette*, January 6, 1766.

76. *Boston Gazette*, January 13, 1766.

77. *Boston Gazette*, December 23, 30, 1765; February 24, 1766.

78. Dickinson, *Barbados*, iii–vi. John Dickinson included the full text of the letter in his pamphlet condemning it. While not wholly trustworthy, given his intentions, this was the version of the Barbardian argument with which most North Americans became familiar.

79. *Boston Gazette*, May 19, 1766.

80. Dickinson, *Barbados*, 3, 14–15.

81. Charles Chauncy, *A Discourse* (Boston, 1766), 6–7.

82. Ibid., 7–18, 28.

[IV]

INDIANS ACROSS THE ATLANTIC

[7]

TODD NATHAN THOMPSON

"HOMESPUN," "INDIAN CORN," AND THE "*INDIGESTIBLE* . . . STAMP ACT": AN EMPIRE OF STEREOTYPE IN FRANKLIN'S LETTERS TO THE LONDON PRESS

For climes oblique, that fear the sun's full rays,
Chill'd in their fogs, exclude the generous maize;
A grain whose rich luxuriant growth requires
Short gentle showers, and bright ethereal fires.
But here, tho' distant from our native shore,
With mutual glee we meet and laugh once more,
The same! I know thee by that yellow face,
That strong complexion of true Indian race, . . .

—Joel Barlow, from The Hasty-Pudding: A Poem, in Three Cantos (1793)

ON FEBRUARY 13, 1766, Benjamin Franklin stood for four hours before the House of Commons to answer questions about the Stamp Act and to urge its repeal. He ended his testimony with the following answers to questions that had probably been pre-circulated:

Q. What used to be the pride of the Americans?
A. To indulge in the fashions and manufactures of Great-Britain.
Q. What is now their pride?
A. To wear their old cloaths over again, till they can make new ones.[1]

Of course, Franklin was famously wary of pride. He would later joke in his *Autobiography* that "there is perhaps no one of our natural Passions so hard to subdue as *Pride* . . . even if I could conceive that I had compleatly overcome it [pride], I should probably by [be] proud of my Humility." And, as Jack Greene has noted, in Franklin's view excessive English "pride" was the "principal animating force behind . . . deep-rooted and widespread prejudice against the colonies and the posture of hostility it expressed."[2]

Equally important, Franklin's responses before the House of Commons also asserted the power in American subjects' dual roles as producers of raw materials and consumers of vast quantities of manufactured British goods, roles heretofore considered to signify only economic dependence. Like Poor Richard vowing to wear his old coat "a little longer," Franklin emphasized the political consequences of simple domestic choices: frugality on a mass scale amounted to provincial boycotts of British textiles at a time when British merchants could least afford them.[3] Franklin's folksy threat that colonists would boycott British textiles and instead wear homespun clothes highlighted just how integral the American colonies were to the British economy; precisely because of their provincialism and distance from the metropole, they craved British manufactures as markers of Britishness but, in a pinch, could do without them quite easily.[4] In this way Franklin underscored the paradoxical clout of colonial provinciality by refiguring domesticity as economic power that could be wielded equally in the service of the British Empire (through the purchase of English goods) or in resistance to it (via colonists making their own clothes).

Franklin's performance at the House of Commons represented the culmination of his attempts to resuscitate his damaged reputation back home in the aftermath of the Stamp Act Crisis. Though Franklin had lobbied against the passage of the Stamp Act, his reaction to it—all but condoning the tax as inevitable and taking advantage of the situation by getting his friend John Hughes appointed as stamp distributor—angered even his supporters back home. When Franklin's *Pennsylvania Gazette*, published by his printing partner David Hall during Franklin's absence in Europe, maintained its standard of neutrality and did not print indignant reactions to the Stamp Act, the *Gazette* lost subscribers, and a mob threatened Franklin's Philadelphia home. This was a microcosm of the situation in the colonies: mob violence and an almost entirely unified response from the popular media in America (the *Gazette* excepted) prevented the Stamp Act from ever being successfully implemented. (As Molly Perry notes in chapter 2, English traders, too, protested the act. Petitions from twenty-five English trading towns flooded the House of Commons during the move to repeal it, detailing the commercial damage caused by a precipitous decline in exports to North America.) But the damage to Franklin had been done, and by November 1765 he realized just how severely tarnished his political reputation was back home. So he began "a herculean public relations campaign," including writing scores of letters to key supporters explaining his position and assuring them that he was working to get the Stamp Act repealed.[5]

Even before his House of Commons testimony, Franklin had written a slew of letters to the British press aimed at convincing British readers of the harm to both British and colonial interests if the stamp tax were enforced. These letters provide a tonal and ideological counterpoint to Franklin's official duties as a colonial agent and to his private letters to friends and family. Because Franklin wrote most of these "clearly pro-American" letters under various pseudonyms that protected his identity from British ministers, we cannot dismiss them as cynical attempts to recoup the affections of American colonists. In fact, Franklin's political rivals at home decried what they perceived as his silence on the subject. For instance, an anonymous entry in the *Pennsylvania Journal* asked, "But why does not the Pennsylvania Agent write? He has leisure and a masterly pen."[6] Despite the fact that readers did not know who wrote them, Franklin's defenses of colonial American rights in the London newspapers reached a wider audience than had his American newspaper articles and even his almanacs. The *Gazetteer and New Daily Advertiser*, which printed his "Homespun" letters in early 1766, had a circulation of five thousand, and the more popular letters were widely reprinted in British monthlies as well as in American newspapers. His "[I]nvectives . . . against Americans" and the "Homespun" letters, for example, appeared alongside other Franklin letters in the *Pennsylvania Chronicle* in February and March 1867, slightly more than a year after their original publication in London. Franklin's mostly satirical arguments in defense of colonists' rights, then, reached a large and broad transatlantic readership.[7] The satiric letters that Franklin wrote and published during the Stamp Act Crisis enabled him to test and circulate ideas—in London, in America, and in his own mind—that he dared not speak in his official, diplomatic capacity.

If the Stamp Act, as historian Ned Landsman claims, led colonists to question their "self-image as full contributors to British security and prosperity," Franklin sought to defend that self-image through these pseudonymous writings.[8] Linda Colley has argued that Britishness as a political and cultural identity did not arise from a blending of English, Scottish, and Welsh culture or from English imposition of its values onto a "helpless and defrauded Celtic periphery." Instead, "Britishness was superimposed over an array of internal differences in response to contact with the Other, and above all in response to conflict with the Other."[9] Colley does not extensively treat the relationship between Britain and the British American colonies, but her formulation puts into relief colonists' anxieties about their place within the British Empire. In short, during and after the Stamp Act Crisis, American colonists felt that they were consistently characterized as the "Other" rather than part of a British coalition defined in opposition to an "Other." Specifically, according to T. H. Breen, colonists responded to a mid-eighteenth-century "intensification of British nationalism" with "powerfully exclusionary tendencies" by echoing it, "protesting their true 'Britishness,' their unquestioned loyalty to king and constitution." For American colonists, nationalism meant a commitment to seeing themselves as an integral part of the imperial project. "Loyalty to colony," John Murrin writes, "meant loyalty to Britain. The two were expected to reinforce one another." But as Breen attests, as does Alexander Jablonski in chapter 6, during the Stamp Act Crisis it became obvious to colonists that this heightened British nationalism was really "English nationalism writ large," and this "aggressive patriotism" tended to define "colonial Americans as 'other,' as not fully English, or as persons beyond the effective boundaries of the new national imagination."[10] Americans were suddenly on the outskirts of empire not just geographically but also culturally. Exclusionary English nationalists thus rhetorically colonized the colonists themselves during and after the Stamp Act Crisis.

So, in his widely read letters to the London press, Franklin sought to separate *English* from *British* nationalism, denouncing anti-Americanism while claiming a space for American participation in the imperial project of British nationalism. To navigate these competing nationalisms, Franklin's letters attempted to deny the "otherness" of Americans (thus reclaiming their Britishness) while defending the very "American" characteristics on which English nationalists based their "othering" attacks. In short, the intensification of a culturally exclusive English nationalism required that Franklin combine his claims for the unity of American and British interests with satirical defenses of Americans themselves. In these letters, Franklin used cultural pride as political resistance by defensively embracing the very Americanness that English writers had stereotyped pejoratively, in effect overlaying a positive identity onto a negative, "othering" stereotype.

To achieve this, Franklin resorted to what I will call *ironic essentialism* —a tongue-in-cheek performance of an exaggeratedly provincial Americanness that was both meant and not meant, that questioned the creation of a separate "American" identity but highlighted virtues latent in stereotypes painted by English writers.[11] Philosopher Richard Rorty characterizes ironists as those who realize "that anything can be made to look good or bad by being redescribed" and as such are "always aware that the terms in which they describe themselves are subject to change, always aware of the contingency and fragility of their final vocabularies, and thus their selves."[12] In his letters to the press Franklin, through ironic reoccupation of humiliating stereotypes, mitigated the negative effects of British "othering" of colonists while accepting, to a certain extent, a separate cultural-as-political American identity.

For eighteenth-century writers generally, and for Franklin in particular, the donning and doffing of multiple personae in pseudonymous writings was a perfect way to demonstrate the contingency of identity. Franklin, who as a teenager wrote for the *New-England Courant* as "Dr. Janus" and had already caused a stir in the colonies and Europe as "Silence Dogood," "Poor Richard Saunders," and even "Polly Baker," used satiric personae throughout his career to voice and interrogate vastly different subject positions.[13] Similarly, in several of Franklin's letters to the London press in the months leading up to his stamp tax testimony before the House of Commons, his pseudonymic personae responded defensively to British correspondents who had impugned American colonists with stereotypic epithets. As short epistles to printers, these letters were not fully conceived literary satires; nevertheless, they did employ satiric devices —most notably defensive irony and the out-of-context isolation of his opponent's argument—in order to rebut English nationalism. Appearing in the *Gazetteer and New Daily Advertiser* in December 1765 and January 1766, several of these letters directly addressed a writer with the pseudonym "Vindex Patriae," a correspondent whose anti-American writings embodied the "aggressive patriotism" described by Breen. The "insolence, contempt, and abuse" for which Franklin chided Vindex Patriae was a manifestation of the English nationalism that by the mid-1760s consistently employed the term "American" as a consciously "external construction, a term in some measure intended to be 'humiliating and debasing.'"[14]

In a piece appearing December 28, 1765, as in most of his letters to the British press, Franklin posed as an Englishman (here, "N.N.") to make his defense of American interests seem a plausible English position. Quoting portions of Vindex Patriae's arguments in order to dismantle them in isolation, Franklin interrogated the extremism of British taxation and *epithetical tyranny*: that is, a performance of English nationalism through verbal abuse of American colonists. Franklin began his "N.N." letter with a paragraph consisting almost entirely of rhetorical questions that ask, "[W]hat good purpose can be answered, by the frequent invectives published in your and other papers against the Americans[?]" In doing so, Franklin briefly inhabited pro–Stamp Act logic, only to push that logic to an untenable extreme and then ridicule it. In a sense, Franklin accomplished what Terry Eagleton has described as a critique that is "'immanent,' installing itself within the very logic of that order's own most cherished values."[15] He simultaneously performed and questioned the "flimsey arguments" of pro–stamp tax correspondents when he wrote, "Can it be supposed that such treatment will make them rest satisfied with the unlimited claim set up, of a power to tax them *ad libitum*, without their consent; while they are to work only for us, and our profit; restrained in their foreign trade by our laws, however profitable it might be to them; forbidden to manufacture their own produce, and obliged to purchase the work of our artificers at our own prices?"[16] This long sentence piles clause upon clause, in effect syntactically mimicking the taxes and abuse the British piled upon the colonists. Franklin's negative but restrained diction (e.g., "*ad libitum*," "forbidden," "obliged") allowed him to make the justification for British arguments for the taxes—that is, the need to raise revenue to pay off huge debts from the Seven Years' War—sound initially logical but ultimately ridiculous and inhumane.

Franklin also briefly embodied the "othering" language of the English nationalism he sought to refute in the pains he took to re-voice some specific "invectives" that other correspondents had levied against the colonists. He wrote, "The gentle terms of *republican race*, *mixed rabble of Scotch*, *Irish and foreign vagabonds*, *descendants of convicts*, *ungrateful rebels* &c. are some of the sweet flowers of English rhetorick, with which our colonists have of late been regaled." By recontextualizing disparate quoted epithets into list form, Franklin created a cumulative effect that made such name-calling seem excessive and rude, especially when sarcastically labeled "sweet flowers." As the list implies, colonists in British America were in the awkward position of identifying themselves as active agents of empire while being represented as a colonized other. English nationalists culturally excluded Americans by figuring them, as Homi Bhabha has described the workings of colonial discourse in another context, "as a fixed reality which is at once an 'other' and yet entirely knowable and visible."[17] Franklin took shrewd advantage of this effect to chastise English writers, claiming that "if we [the English] are so much their superiors, we should shew the superiority of our breeding by our better manners!"[18] As an American writer-diplomat masquerading as an Englishman, Franklin mocked the "superiority" of English "breeding" through a persona who claimed it.

Indeed, it is emblematic of Franklin's conception of the transatlantic elasticity of identity that he would write—during the same time period—both as a "true" Englishman and, as we will see, as an Indianized American. Franklin's English persona differed from his American personae—Silence Dogood, Poor Richard, Obadiah Plainman, and Homespun—in that N.N. was snooty instead of humble in his manner, learned instead of homely in his syntactical formulations. But the letter ended on a conciliatory note, assuring readers that the colonists "have not the least desire of independence" and lauding the generosity of "Britons, as a people," who are "by no means niggards of those rights, liberties and privileges, that make the subjects of Britain the envy and admiration of the universe." This shift in tone, however, was less a surrender to Vindex Patriae than an attempt to shame the English into living up to their constitutional ideals and to undermine statements of English nationalism that increasingly defined any "Americanness" as a deviation from the proper English norm. Thus, the satiric defensiveness of Franklin's letters to the London press had two simultaneous (and seemingly contradictory) goals. First, he hoped to mitigate the "invectives . . . against the Americans," often by defending cultural characteristics commonly assumed to be "American," and thus tacitly agreeing to the existence of a separate "American" character.[19] For Franklin, "American" was tied to a kind of homespun provinciality: Americans were practical and economically savvy because able to fend for themselves in times of need but still resolutely connected and committed to the metropole, even if removed from it geographically and, during the Stamp Act Crisis, commercially. But, second, he also reasserted American claims that bonds of race, language, culture, and imperial destiny continued to link England and America.

Six years earlier, in *The Interest of Great Britain Considered*, Franklin had made a similar rhetorical gesture toward imperial community, characterizing the Seven Years' War in self-consciously British terms, in part to cast the conflict as of imperial instead of merely American interest: "The inhabitants of them [the colonies] are, in common with the other subjects of Great Britain, anxious for the glory of her crown, the extent of her power and commerce, the welfare and future repose of the whole British people. They could not therefore but take a large share in the affronts offered to Britain, and have been animated with a truly British *spirit* to exert themselves beyond their strength, and against their evident interest." Franklin strained to identify both Americans and the English as equally British. He described colonists "in common with the other subjects of Great Britain," reinforced the implication that Americans were a part of the "whole British people," and characterized colonists as "animated with a truly British *spirit*." But, Franklin complained, despite their efforts to promote British interests, the Americans' "virtue has made against them" in representations of the late conflict with France and its Native allies, as British officials viewed them as "supposed authors of a war carried on *for their advantage only*."[20] As Franklin's plea demonstrates, as early as the Seven Years' War, American colonists strained to claim their patriotic Britishness even as the metropole viewed them as outsiders seeking refuge under the Crown. Franklin's self-consciousness in attempting to bridge the gap between two separate (though not yet mutually exclusive) notions of self—even as he blamed Britons for blaming Americans—revealed the problematic nature of American provincial identity. Such competing notions of Americanness and Britishness have long been a subject of debate among historians and literary scholars. Landsman, for example, calls attention to the centrality of "provinciality" to American self-identity in the eighteenth century. He argues that, while the American colonies' original settlers "had largely defined themselves with reference to their particular colonial experience, as New Englanders or Virginians or Barbadians, for example . . . during the eighteenth century provincial Americans increasingly came to view themselves as Britons and as Protestants, whose positions were secured by a system of British liberty." Significantly, though, this new cultural identity was not particularly English but rather British and provincial; in this way colonists came to see themselves as linked to each other and to provinces in the growing British Empire. But the more colonials began to assert themselves as contributors to the empire with the same rights and liberties as the inhabitants of the English metropolis, the more imperial authorities fretted about budding American economic strength.[21] Hence, the colonists' identification with the British Empire also, paradoxically, helped estrange them from it.

For Franklin, smug English "invectives . . . against the Americans" circulating in newspapers served to widen this divide. Writing again as "N.N." in a January 11, 1766, letter, Franklin chastised Vindex Patriae for threatening that cultural unity and therefore the advantages of favorable trade conditions with the colonies, bemoaning the

> *impropriety* and *imprudence* of angry reflections on the Americans in the public papers, as more than half the trade of this country is with them; and that trade depends greatly on the regard they have for us, and in consequence for our fashions and fineries, which are by no means necessary to their subsistence; the Northern Colonies having among themselves the natural means of furnishing, by a little additional industry, every convenience and ornament of life; and to that industry I apprehended a resentment of harsh and contemptuous treatment might naturally provoke them.[22]

In this admonition, Franklin turned the interdependence of colonial and English commerce into a portent of boycotts that would both hurt English trade and engender a sense of colonial unity. Franklin posed this economic threat in defensive response to "angry reflections on the Americans in the public papers"; in this way, he answered cultural degradation with the specter of punitive economic measures that would also foster colonial pride in the "industry" and frugality of republican simplicity. This was, Franklin's Englishman N.N. warned, the power of provinciality.

In his two winter 1766 letters to the *Gazetteer and New Daily Advertiser* under the pseudonym "Homespun," Franklin embraced a provincial American identity but also repudiated Vindex Patriae and other English nationalist writers for promoting "American" as a viable identity. To put it another way, for Franklin and his persona any notion of a separate "American" category was a mistake, though the contents of that category—that is, the very character traits that English nationalists tended to mock—were themselves praiseworthy. Franklin pursued this double project of imperial chastisement and provincial praise through his discussion of domestic concerns as political issues (i.e., via a lengthy discussion of food, substituting gastronomy for a national identity), thus mirroring in print the tactics of colonial boycotts.

The Homespun persona was fairly unique in Franklin's letters to the London press in that it offered a proud and distinctly American voice, not entirely unlike the satiric creations—the chatty widow Silence Dogood and the folksy philomath Poor Richard Saunders—of his earlier career as a printer-journalist in Boston and Philadelphia. The very name "Homespun," of course, calls to mind the frugal Poor Richard, who, in the preface to the 1758 edition of *Poor Richard improved*, had decided to wear his old secondhand coat "a little longer." For Poor Richard as for Homespun, taxes provided the impetus both for frugality and for colonial unity. Poor Richard's preface had begun with Pennsylvanians at the market asking Father Abraham, "*[W]hat think you of the Times? Won't these heavy Taxes quite ruin the Country? How shall we be ever able to pay them?*" Here frugality was not merely a virtue of individualism and capitalism; it was a pragmatic response to imperial hardship. Such combinations of the practical and the political were common to colonial almanacs, especially during the Stamp Act Crisis. For example, the 1765 *Poor Richard improved* combined home economy with current events at a time when "the utilization of native products was necessary and 'American'" in suggesting that colonists avoid high taxes by making their own products and providing readers with a recipe for homemade Madeira;

the 1766 edition printed an abstract of the Stamp Act to help inform its readers of its consequences. Boston printer Nathaniel Ames was more pointed in his 1765 response to the Sugar Act in *An Astronomical Diary: or an Almanack*, written in anticipation of the Stamp Act. Ames's aphorisms explicitly connected personal thrift to the hardships created by British taxes and offered domestic advice for effectively sustaining boycotts against British goods. Examples include "It is better to wear a homespun Coat, than to lose our LIBERTY," "It's time to think of raising Hemp & Flax, if we've a Mind to save a Tax," and "New England Luxury cannot be supported, unless more of her Commodities are Exported."[23] Such practical counsel was entirely appropriate to an almanac, but took on a political edge in the wake of the taxation crises of the 1760s. These loaded aphorisms demonstrate the special political-aesthetic function of the almanac—by nature a hybrid genre joining the domestic with the civic—in times of political turmoil. *Poor Richard* and other colonial almanacs showed their readers how political decisions affected their everyday lives, and vice versa.

Similarly, in the "Homespun" letters, Franklin shifted back and forth between domestic and national (or, more accurately, domestic *as* national) concerns that captured the essence of the colonists' boycotts of British goods. For instance, in the January 2, 1766, Homespun letter, Franklin alternated between defiant and humorous tones in addressing potential military action to end the boycotts and enforce the Stamp Act. He wrote, "I question whether the army proposed to be sent among them, would oblige them to swallow a drop more of tea than they chuse to swallow; for, as the proverb says, though one man may *lead* a horse to the water, ten can't *make him drink*."[24] This sentence combines fierce pride in the resolve of the boycotting colonists with a folksy, Poor Richard-esque aphorism that reinforces the colonies' status as geographically distant from the metropole and thereby at some ease to accept or reject its dictates. It is in this equation of American colloquialism with the politicization of the domestic that Homespun's rhetorical force resides. Through Homespun, Franklin could articulate explicit connections between the everyday concerns of modest characters and critiques of overzealous English pride.

Vindex Patriae had written that Americans could not continue their boycotts of imported tea because their standard diet of Indian corn did not provide "an agreeable, or easy digestible breakfast." One scholar has traced the "English contempt for Indian corn" to preconceptions about its coarseness as well as the "relatively poor conductive properties of the grain (compared to wheat), which necessitates abandoning any significant depth in the product." Of course, Vindex Patriae's dismissals of American breakfast sound much more like demeaning national insults than discursions on cooking propriety. Franklin responded as Homespun by defending Indian corn as tasty and nutritious in its various manifestations, such as "*samp*, *hominy*, *succatash*, and *nokehock*," all of which he claimed were "better than a Yorkshire muffin."[25] Franklin chose a litany of Indian terms, proudly claiming them as American, even though Vindex's intention in discussing "Indian corn" in the first place was to associate colonists with metropolitan preconceptions of savagery.

By the time of the Stamp Act Crisis the Indian had become an extremely common symbol of the American colonies. For instance, between 1765 and 1783 British cartoonists personified the colonies as an Indian in satiric cartoons at least sixty-five times, four times as many as the other main symbols of America, the child and the snake. Equating British creoles with the Indians they were displacing in America helped mainland Britons to defamiliarize them, even as it called attention to the fact that the colonies' "white inhabitants had yet to evolve a recognizable identity of their own," separate from their British ancestry and cultural ties.[26] Vindex Patriae, in pretending that "Indian corn" was the staple food and culture of the American colonies, tapped into European colonialist discourse about "creolization": that is, a deterministic understanding of the American environment that assumed the gradual degradation of colonists. Such logic allowed the English to represent colonials as uncivilized others instead of equal participants in the British Empire.[27]

Franklin had felt the sting of this prejudice personally during his time in England. As Carla Mulford notes, though Franklin as a colonial agent in London "got to know many of the merchants and printers, and his scientific and intellectual interests brought him in contact with the most noted English intellectuals and scientists, yet he had a frustrating time of it, all things considered, because wherever he went, he might be reminded that he was, after all, just a colonial. He was, in other words, constructed in part as a barbarian who had come to the metropolis."[28] But Franklin, as Homespun, instead of denying his barbarian status and claiming his right to a proper English breakfast, to a certain extent accepted the designation and proliferated it by bringing in other Native American–named foods. Philip Deloria, in *Playing Indian*, claims that the "presence of Indian words in prerevolutionary language . . . can be seen as more than simply a borrowing of the exotic or the quaint. . . . As Indian words and expressions spread into proto-American discourse, they subtly shifted the way in which colonists understood themselves and their world." Of course, such a representation of "Indianness" as "Americanness" was strategic instead of authentic. Specifically, Franklin responded to Vindex Patriae's ethnocentric delineations of Americans as savage others by laying claim to the familiar eighteenth-century tradition of the "noble savage" that philosophers like Montaigne and Rousseau had used to critique European social institutions, norms, and customs. Such ironic essentialism proved useful to colonial creoles because notions of noble savagery created "values that could be assigned to Indians and that could be reflected back upon a Self, either as cultural critique or colonial legitimation"[29] Additionally, in "taking up the role of a hybrid Indian-colonist," as Rafia Zafar has described Joel Barlow's project in the mock-epic celebration of corn, *The Hasty Pudding* (1793), Franklin could claim "the high ground of the unlawfully dispossessed and disenfranchised."[30] In other words, Franklin was "self-othering" in print in ironic response to English insolence while reaffirming the colonists' usurpation of Indian lands.

But if Franklin was willing to play along, in part, with English depictions of Americans as menacing Indians, his own preferred visual imagination pictured the colonies as integral parts of Great Britain, not savage others.[31] Franklin's conception of the connection between England and the colonies was made clear in his engraving "Magna Britannia: her Colonies Reduc'd" (figure 7.1), which Franklin designed in late 1765 and printed in early 1766.

He had the image printed on small cards that he sent or handed to Parliament members and other public figures with messages written on them. In portraying the colonies as the severed arms and legs of Magna Britannia, Franklin updated the message of political unity and the dangers of severing a unified body that originated in his famous "Join, or Die" cartoon by linking the colonies to a larger British body politic (see figure 5.1). He imagined the colonies as vital appendages of the British body republic and attempted to show that by injuring the colonies Britain only hurt itself, as demonstrated by the lance piercing New England, represented as her leg. Shorn of its colonial appendages, the image implies, the head and torso of the metropolis could not survive. As the idle ships in the background attest, the damage to Britain was also economic in nature.[32] Franklin explained this in a letter to his sister Jane Mecom in March 1766, writing, "I send you a few of the Cards on which I wrote my Messages during the Time [Stamp Act Crisis], it was debated here whether it might not be proper to reduce the Colonies to Obedience by Force of Arms: The Moral is, that the Colonies might be ruined, but that

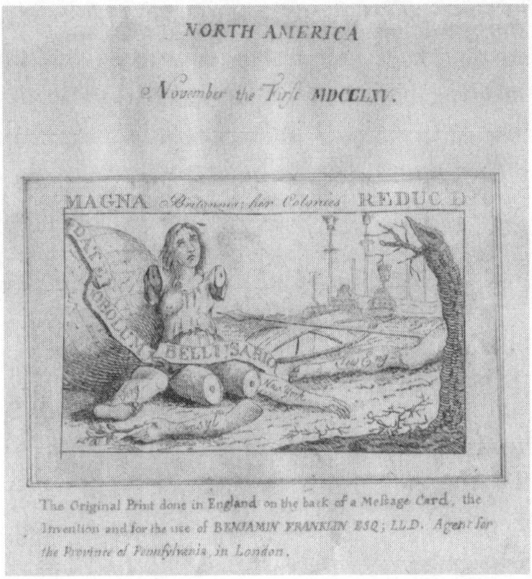

Figure 7.1. "Magna Britannia: her Colonies Reduc'd." Courtesy of the Library Company of Philadelphia.

Britain would thereby be maimed." Franklin saw England, in taxing the colonies unfairly, as lacking both in moral authority and in trade power (as the docked ships illustrate), and thereby slipping from her perch on top of the world. As Franklin put it in the accompanying "Moral":

> The ordaining of laws in favor of *one* part of the nation, to the prejudice and oppression of *another,* is certainly the most erroneous and mistaken policy. . . . These measures never fail to create great and violent jealousies and animosities between the people favored and the people oppressed: whence a total separation of affections, interests, political obligations, and all manner of connections, necessarily ensue, by which the whole state is weakened, and perhaps ruined for ever![33]

In this "Moral," as in his other political and satiric writings during the Stamp Act Crisis, Franklin first posited subjects in the colonies and the metropolis as one people rent into two separate groups ("the people favored and the people oppressed") as the result of unjust laws, and then threatened that such a forced distinction necessarily resulted in a "total" and perpetual separation. In imagining the colonies' wounds as self-inflicted by Britannia, the engraving maintained Franklin's trope of the colonies as an essential part of the British Empire while chastising English nationalists for asserting otherwise.

As a diplomat and visual satirist he stressed commercial partnership with and cultural bonds to the British Empire, but in the "Homespun" letters Franklin abdicated his authority and embraced the outsider status with which Vindex Patriae had smeared Americans. This disavowal of status allowed him to launch sarcastic critiques that he needed to avoid as a self-styled insider at the House of Commons. In accepting Vindex Patriae's "othering," he set up his Homespun persona as a "foreign visitor" to the metropole (another common eighteenth-century trope that played with notions of civilization and savagery), questioning the self-evidence of English cultural assumptions. For example, he represented British food with a "Yorkshire muffin," thus nationalizing diet by identifying English food with an English place name. Food here served as a stand-in for more noxious political and cultural squabbles and allowed Franklin to approach sensitive political topics from a less threatening, private-sphere vantage point.

Of course, diet has always been tied up with cultural politics. If "language of what may be eaten and what may not is transferable to designate who may be eaten with and who may not," then how people describe food choices can be used to include or to exclude, and descriptions of food are often "drawn upon as a privileged means of stereotyping and subordinating others."[34] Representations of food thus can serve to belittle and repress—as in Vindex Patriae's sneering denunciation of Indian corn—or they can offer "occasions of resistance"—as in Homespun's defensive response.[35] Franklin took advantage of the political undertones of food to transform what seemed a bland justification of American dietary habits into a staunch defense of American fortitude in the face of the hardships imposed by the British government, immediately jumping from the "*hoecake*" versus "Yorkshire muffin" debate to the Stamp Act. "But if Indian corn were as *disagreeable* and *indigestible* as the Stamp Act," he wrote, "does he [Vindex Patriae] imagine we can get nothing else for breakfast?"[36] This abrupt shift hardened Franklin's tone and signaled his underlying agenda, allowing him to mock the Stamp Act but, in the very next clause, immediately back away from the subject and return to lauding American foodstuffs.

Franklin employed a similar tactic in his second Homespun letter (January 15, 1766), which once again responded to Vindex Patriae's attacks on colonists' culinary habits. Franklin began by accusing "JOHN BULL" of performing, through "his attorney VINDEX PATRIAE," an arrogant cultural nationalism that made it "the constant topic of his contempt for other nations, that *they do not eat so well as himself.*" In situating his adversarial correspondent Vindex Patriae as an attorney and John Bull as his client, Franklin implied that Vindex Patriae's attacks on Americans were representative of a widespread English desire to exclude the American colonies from full membership in the British Empire (thus cordoning them off as mere far-flung stashes of raw materials and markets for English-made goods). Franklin had advocated strongly for imperial reform and consolidated union that recognized America as a partner in empire with representation in Parliament, and thus decried what he saw as counter-productive "othering."[37] After noting similar insults that Englishmen often made regarding the food of other British provinces (Scotland, Ireland, and Wales), Homespun lamented that John Bull planned to "fix upon me and my countrymen for ever, the indelible disgrace of being *Indian corn-eaters.*" If, then, Vindex Patriae spoke for England in lampooning the American diet as a proxy for America, and Homespun spoke for America, a joke at the end of the second Homespun letter took on considerably more meaning than a mere "trifling . . . dispute" between newspaper contributors. Homespun asked Vindex Patriae why he should see fit to decry the taste of corn "when you never in your life have tasted a *single grain* of it? But why should that hinder you writing on it? Have you not written even on *politics*?"[38] Through Franklin's rhetorical sleight of hand, this snarky personal barb became a broader accusation that the English did not understand the Stamp's Act disastrous ramifications on the British Empire as a whole.

Franklin hinted at the potential consequences of English "othering" when he began to address directly "Master JOHN BULL" as a personification of England, instead of his lawyer Vindex Patriae. What started as a self-defense against arrogant English attacks on the savor of American food became a broader indictment of the way England was "far from being civil even to your own family," by which Franklin meant the Welsh, the Scotch, the Irish, and the colonists. Along with this shift in address came two serious and direct threats to England. First, Homespun chided John Bull for his exclusionary nationalism and tendency "to affront and abuse other nations." Franklin wrote, "[Y]ou have mixed with your many virtues, a pride, a haughtiness, and an insolent contempt for all but yourself, that, I am afraid, will, if not abated, procure you one day or other a handsome drubbing."[39] Franklin's rebuttal to national pride—with a promise of a "handsome drubbing"—revealed a new level of confrontational boldness. Homespun offered a second barely veiled threat in response to a claim by Vindex Patriae that provincials were unable to speak "Plain English"; Franklin wrote, "It is my opinion, Master BULL, that the Scotch and Irish, as well as the colonists, are capable of speaking much *plainer English* than they have ever yet spoke, but which I hope they will never be provoked to speak."[40] Vindex Patriae's demeaning call for "Plain English" echoed the populist (and virulently anti-Scottish) English nationalism of John Wilkes, who in his newspaper, the *North Briton*, wrote that he would "endeavour to write in plain English, and to avoid . . . Scotticisms" and who had complained about the terms "Great Britain" and "Briton" (using "England" to describe the entire island and "Englishman" to describe its people).[41] Franklin's formulation countered Wilkite Anglocentrism: in rhetorically leaguing with Scotland and Ireland as similarly offended members of the British Empire, he situated them all as powerful, connected parts of Britain rather than separate objects of English scorn. In addition to an implied threat of violence as communication (or, conversely, communication as a form or harbinger of violence), Franklin's threat also rendered colloquial or non-"standard" English as a weapon against the mother country. His identity protected by a satiric persona, Franklin as Homespun reveled in co-opting the language and content of anti-American insults for use against the English nationalists who wielded them. Through ironic reoccupation and refraction of humiliating stereotypes, Franklin in his letters to the press deflected the negative effects of British "othering" of colonists while taking political advantage of the cultural unification such stereotyping suggested.

Franklin accomplished this satiric reoccupation more graphically in a short piece that he wrote in February or March 1766, shortly after the Homespun letters appeared. "The Frenchman and the Poker" (reprinted in the *Pennsylvania Chronicle*, March 16–23, 1767) played on English anti-French sentiment and employed shocking visual imagery in an allegory describing British attempts after the Stamp Act's repeal to require "Americans to pay for all the Stamps they ought to have used" when the law was in effect. Franklin (who signed the letter "F.B.," reversing his initials) wrote:

> The whole Proceeding would put one in Mind of the Frenchman that used to accost English and other Strangers on the Pont-Neuf, with many Compliments, and a red hot Iron in his Hand; *Pray Monsieur Anglois*, says he, *Do me the Favour to let me have the Honour of thrusting this hot Iron into your Backside*? Zoons, what does the Fellow mean! Begone with your Iron, or I'll break your Head! *Nay, Monsieur,* replies he, *if you do not chuse it, I do not insist upon it. But at least, you will in Justice have the Goodness to pay me something for the heating of my Iron.*[42]

In this crudely illustrative joke, Franklin rendered painfully physical the economic burden of the Stamp Act on colonists. He made this imposition more immediate to English readers by putting them ("*Monsieur Anglois*") in the colonists' position, and the hated French, of all peoples, in the "accost"-ing role. In this way, Franklin leveraged English prejudices for use against them, repositioning them as the butt of their own joke. But, since Franklin did this indirectly through an anecdotal metaphor, he was able to remove Americans from the stigma associated with a treasonously direct attack on the English. Specifically, since it is not a colonist but a Frenchman who vengefully wields the hot poker, the joke transfers this aggression to the French. This transference is important because, as Colley has argued, British identity had, even before the Seven Years' War, been forged in large part by collective self-definition in opposition to France and Catholicism.[43] Franklin's initial formulation to set up the analogy—"The whole Proceeding would put one in Mind"—is the only connective tissue to colonial American anger at the Stamp Act.

In setting his joke on the Pont Neuf, the oldest bridge in Paris and a well-known hotspot for indigents and criminals, Franklin also raised the possibility that the "Frenchman" could be either a con man posing as a gentleman *or* a government official engaging in state-sanctioned punishment of crimes. In eighteenth-century France it was common practice to brand criminals—"foreigners and Frenchmen alike"—with a "red hot Iron." The impression of the French *fleur de lys* on a criminal's back was a literalizing inscription of state power on the body, and thus a "performative gesture that publicly reclaimed the deviant body for the King" and "marked the convict as the monarch's possession." Tellingly, the irons used for these brandings were very similar to the "strong metal *poincon*, or punch, used to produce Roman type" and were often made by the same artisans who designed and built types.[44] Franklin's allusion to physical imposition of the printing punch onto the body, then, may have derived from his conception of the castigatory power of print: both the punitive measure of stamping paper and retributive satiric discourse used to protest it. In publishing this joke, however, Franklin in essence performed a reversal of such punishments. That is, instead of using a brand to make the body into a text, he used the satiric text as a brand to mark and shame the English as petty criminals. The fact that this piece later resurfaced as a Franklin joke in a 1797 joke book, *The Merry Fellow's Companion: Or American Jest Book*, reveals how Franklin's satiric production could remain in the American consciousness as popular culture ephemera, both keeping its ideas in circulation and adding to the Franklin legend.

But such recirculation could also yield more immediate results. At the end of the first Homespun letter, Franklin warned that "Mr. VINDEX's very civil letter will, I dare say, be printed in all our provincial news papers, from Nova Scotia to Georgia; and together with other *kind*, *polite*, and *humane* epistles . . . contribute not a little to strengthen us in every resolution that may be of advantage, to *our* country at least, if not to *yours*." Franklin's sarcastic pun about Vindex Patriae's "civil letter" again portrayed assaults on Americans as national instead of personal; it also reversed charges of colonists as savages to be measured against a metropolitan norm of civilization. Additionally, his claim that newspapers "from Nova Scotia to Georgia" would reprint Vindex Patriae's letter was a threatening expression of intra-colonial unity that most Britons had taken for granted did not exist. In warning that Vindex Patriae's remarks would be widely reprinted in the colonies, Franklin also emphasized the power of print media—"all our provincial news papers"—to shape public opinion and to engender political action or, in the case of a tea boycott, strategic inaction.[45] In Franklin's warning, the "provincial" media thus functioned as an emergent, unified entity, and, in the last sentence of the letter, "*our* country" is italicized to differentiate it from "*yours*." Franklin made a similar assertion in his "N.N." letter, in which his English persona warned that essays abusing Americans "are unfortunately reprinted in all *their* papers." In both cases, Franklin's mention of the American press showed his awareness (as a printer-politician) of the media's consensus-building potential.[46] On the one hand, newspapers "made it easier to imagine Great Britain as a whole" because they reminded their readers "that their lives were bounded by a wider context," as such fostering a sense of imperial interconnectivity; but on the other, the practice of reprinting meant that screeds like Vindex Patriae's would do more than local damage.[47] By reprinting English insults slandering Americans, the colonial press could use its influence to rupture the imperial unity it had helped create and conversely to foster a colonial community united in its anger at England. In reminding his correspondent of this fact, Franklin was taking advantage of the paradox of English nationalism as it manifested itself in works that dealt in stereotypes of Americans. Such "othering" attacks, when read by American colonists in the mass media, could lead them to develop and embrace a shared American identity—an identity grounded in the power of its very provinciality.

Notes

An earlier version of this essay was published as "'Invectives . . . against the Americans': Benjamin Franklin's Satiric Nationalism in the Stamp Act Crisis," *Journal of the*

Midwest Modern Language Association 40.1 (2007): 25–36. It appears here, much revised and expanded, with express written permission of the MMLA.

This essay's epigraph comes from Joel Barlow, *The Works of John Barlow*, 2 vols. (Gainesville, FL: Scholars' Facsimilies & Reprints, 1970), 2: 89–90.

1. Benjamin Franklin, *The Papers of Benjamin Franklin*, ed. Leonard W. Larabee, 38 vols. (New Haven, CT: Yale University Press, 1969), 13: 159. For more on Franklin's testimony, see Fred Anderson, *Crucible of War: The Seven Years' War and the Fate of Empire in British North America, 1754–1766* (New York: Alfred A. Knopf, 2000), 706–707.

2. Benjamin Franklin, *The Autobiography* (New York: First Vintage Books, 1990), 89–90; Jack P. Greene, "Pride, Prejudice, and Jealousy: Benjamin Franklin's Expectation for the American Revolution," in J. A. Leo Lemay, ed., *Reappraising Benjamin Franklin: A Bicentennial Perspective* (Newark: University of Delaware Press, 1993), 134.

3. Franklin, *Papers*, 7: 350. Fred Anderson notes that the Stamp Act worsened a depression in England that had lasted since the end of the war. By the end of 1765 Americans owed London merchants "vast sums. If colonial commerce, or at least the regular collection of colonial debts, was not soon restored, financial catastrophe would ensue. Unless the colonists began to consume British manufactures again, workers in the industries that fed colonial markets—and those prominently included the cloth-makers in Rockingham's own Yorkshire—would be thrown out of work." Anderson, *Crucible of War*, 695.

4. T. H. Breen has argued that the broad popularity of British manufactures helped to standardize material culture in the colonies; see his "An Empire of Goods: The Anglicization of Colonial America, 1690–1776," *Journal of British Studies* 25.4 (1986): 496.

5. David T. Morgan, *The Devious Dr. Franklin, Colonial Agent: Benjamin Franklin's Years in London* (Macon, GA: Mercer University Press, 1996), 100, 106, 120; Jacob M. Price, "Who Cared about the Colonies: The Impact of the Thirteen Colonies on British Society and Politics, circa 1714–1775," in Bernard Bailyn and Philip D. Morgan, eds., *Strangers within the Realm: Cultural Margins of the First British Empire* (Chapel Hill: University of North Carolina Press, 1991), 412; Gordon S. Wood, *The Americanization of Benjamin Franklin* (New York: Penguin Press, 2004), 111. For a media-history perspective on the colonial American press's role in unifying protests to the Stamp Act, see William David Sloan and Julie Hedgepeth Williams, *The Early American Press, 1690–1783* (Westport, CT: Greenwood Press, 1994), 124.

6. Morgan, *Devious Dr. Franklin*, 118; quoted in Verner W. Crane, "Certain Writings of Benjamin Franklin on the British Empire and the American Colonies," *Papers of the Bibliographical Society of America* 28 (1934): 2. Franklin published 143 letters to the press between 1758 and 1775, most of them in London. See Bruce Ingham Granger, *Benjamin Franklin: An American Man of Letters* (Ithaca, NY: Cornell University Press, 1964), 77.

7. Richard E. Amacher, *Benjamin Franklin* (New York: Twayne, 1962), 70; Bruce Ingham Granger, "Franklin as Press Agent in England," in J. A. Leo Lemay, ed., *The Oldest Revolutionary: Essays on Benjamin Franklin* (Philadelphia: University of Pennsylvania Press, 1976), 30.

8. Ned C. Landsman, *From Colonials to Provincials: American Thought and Culture, 1680–1760* (Ithaca, NY: Cornell University Press, 1997), 180.

9. Linda Colley, *Britons: Forging the Nation: 1707–1837* (New Haven, CT: Yale University Press, 1992), 6.

10. T. H. Breen, "Ideology and Nationalism on the Eve of the American Revolution: Revisions *Once More* in Need of Revising," *Journal of American History* 84.1 (1997): 19–29; John M. Murrin, "A Roof without Walls: The Dilemma of American National Identity," in Richard Beeman, Stephen Botein, and Edward C. Carter II, eds., *Beyond Confederation: Origins of the Constitution and American National Identity* (Chapel Hill: University of North Carolina Press, 1987), 338.

11. The term "ironic essentialism," of course, plays on Gayatri Chakravorty Spivak's term "strategic essentialism" as a politically motivated, temporary acquiescence to culturally created identity categories; I should note, however, that Spivak herself has "thoroughly repudiate[d] the idea of 'strategic essentialism.'" See *Other Asias* (Malden, MA: Blackwell, 2008), 260.

12. Richard Rorty, *Contingency, Irony, and Solidarity* (New York: Cambridge University Press, 1989), 73–74. For Rorty, the deployment of such irony is ultimately personal instead of political. But, in creating distinct personae who call attention to the political valences and repercussions of others' vocabularies and either substitute different terms or, in the case of Franklin as "Homespun," attempt to redefine those terms with alternative meanings, ironists' pretended personal disputes in the print public sphere become precisely political.

13. On Franklin's use of ironic personae, see Ralph Lerner, "Dr. Janus," in Lemay, ed., *Reappraising Benjamin Franklin*, 415–424; see also Todd Nathan Thompson, "Representative Nobodies: The Politics of Benjamin Franklin's Satiric Personae, 1722–1757," *Early American Literature* 46.3 (2011): 449–480.

14. Franklin, *Papers*, 12: 414; Breen, "Ideology and Nationalism," 30. The Latin "Vindex Patriae" translates roughly as "Vindicator of the Fatherland."

15. Terry Eagleton, "Nationalism: Irony and Commitment," in Terry Eagleton, Frederic Jameson, and Edward W. Said, *Nationalism, Colonialism, and Literature* (Minneapolis: University of Minnesota Press, 1990), 31.

16. Franklin, *Papers*, 12: 413–414.

17. Homi K. Bhabha, "The Other Question," *Screen* 24.6 (1983): 23.

18. Franklin, *Papers*, 12: 414.

19. Ibid., 416, 414, 413.

20. Ibid., 9: 72.

21. Landsman, *From Colonials to Provincials*, 3, 7.

22. Franklin, *Papers*, 13: 20.

23. Ibid., 7: 340, 350; Barbara Stowell, *Early American Almanacs: The Colonial Weekday Bible* (New York: Burt Franklin, 1977), 184; quoted in Allan R. Raymond, "To Reach Men's Minds: Almanacs and the American Revolution, 1760–1777," *New England Quarterly* 51.3 (1978): 373.

24. Franklin, *Papers* 13: 8.

25. Ibid., 7; Glynis Ridley, "The First American Cookbook," *Eighteenth-Century Life* 23.2 (1999): 118.

26. Philip J. Deloria, *Playing Indian* (New Haven, CT: Yale University Press, 1998), 28–29; Colley, *Britons*, 134–135.

27. Ralph Bauer, *The Cultural Geography of Colonial American Literatures* (Cambridge: Cambridge University Press, 2003), 25–26.

28. Carla Mulford, "Benjamin Franklin, Native Americans, and European Cultures of Civility," *Prospects: An Annual of American Cultural Studies* 24 (1999): 60.

29. Deloria, *Playing Indian*, 34, 20–21. On the noble savage in the eighteenth century, see also Robert F. Berkhofer, *The White Man's Indian: Images of the American Indian from Columbus to the Present* (New York: Vintage, 1979), 74–78. As Carla Mulford skillfully reminds us, fictionalized versions of the noble savage risked "a sort of textual colonization within the culture. . . . Native peoples' lifeways are doubly colonized, it would seem, in the Europeans' desire to critique their own biases." See Mulford, "Civility," 53.

30. Zafar's analysis of Barlow's "adoption of the role of native subaltern" in his poem parallels my own reading of Franklin's appropriation of Indian corn to claim a particular kind of American past. See Rafia Zafar, "The Proof of the Pudding: Of Haggis, Hasty Pudding, and Transatlantic Influence," *Early American Literature* 31.2 (1996), 143–145.

31. On the subtext of the menacing Indian image as portraying British anxieties of a shift in power from England to America, see Clay Zuba, chapter 8, this volume, and Colley, *Britons*, 134–135.

32. Michael Wynn Jones, *The Cartoon History of the American Revolution* (New York: G. P. Putnam's Sons, 1975), 32; Joan D. Dolmetsch, *Rebellion and Reconciliation: Satirical Prints on the Revolution at Williamsburg* (Williamsburg, VA: Colonial Williamsburg Foundation, 1976), 43. For an extensive visual analysis of this image, see Lester C. Olson, *Benjamin Franklin's Vision of American Community: A Study in Rhetorical Iconology* (Columbia: University of South Carolina Press, 2004).

33. Franklin, *Papers*, 13: 189, 71. For more on Mecom and her lifelong correspondence with Franklin, see Jill Lepore, *Book of Ages: The Life and Opinions of Jane Franklin* (New York: Vintage, 2014).

34. Roger Abrahams, "Equal Opportunity Eating: A Structural Excursus on Things of the Mouth," in Linda Keller Brown and Kay Mussell, eds., *Ethnic and Regional Foodways in the United States: The Performance of Group Identity* (Knoxville: University of Tennessee Press, 1984), 21–22.

35. As the editors of *Edible Ideologies* note, "[B]uying, consuming, and serving food are acts of signification through which people construct and sustain their identities. At the same time these acts—and the broad range of cultural representations that support and are supported by them—also serve as vehicles through which ideological expectations about those very identities are circulated, enforced, and transgressed." See Kathleen LeBesco and Peter Naccarato, "Introduction," in Kathleen LeBesco and Peter Naccarato, eds., *Edible Ideologies: Representing Food and Meaning* (Albany: State University of New York Press, 2008), 1–2.

36. Franklin, *Papers*, 13: 7.

37. The Stamp Act Crisis seems to have led him to change his mind. By 1768–1769 Franklin distrusted Parliament's ability to legislate for the colonies and shifted to de-

scribing the colonies as a separate state under the same king. For a discussion of Franklin's evolving views on imperial politics, see Christopher Pearl, "Franklin's Turn: Imperial Politics and the Coming of the American Revolution," *Pennsylvania Magazine of History and Biography* 136.2 (April 2012): 117–139.

38. Franklin, *Papers*, 13: 45, 49.

39. Ibid., 47. On familial rhetoric as used to characterize Anglo-American relations in the eighteenth and early nineteenth centuries, see Jay Fliegelman, *Prodigals and Pilgrims: The American Revolution against Patriarchal Authority, 1750–1800* (Cambridge: Cambridge University Press, 1982).

40. Franklin, *Papers*, 13: 48.

41. Colley, *Britons*, 116.

42. Franklin, *Papers*, 13: 183–184.

43. Colley, *Britons*, 5.

44. Katherine Dauge-Roth, "Textual Performance: Imprinting the Criminal Body," in Faith E. Beasley and Kathleen Wine, eds., *Intersections: Actes du 35e congrés annuel de la North American Society for Seventeenth-Century French Literature*, Dartmouth College, May 8–10, 2003 (Tübingen: Gunter Narr Verlag, 2003), 128, 129, 134.

45. Franklin, *Papers*, 13: 8. In fact, all of Franklin's letters to the London press discussed in this essay were reprinted in February and March 1767 in the *Pennsylvania Chronicle*, published by William Goddard in partnership with Franklin's Philadelphian political ally Joseph Galloway. The introduction to these letters in the *Chronicle* claims that the paper reprinted them mostly to counter charges by Franklin's enemies of his inactivity during the Stamp Act Crisis and seeming acquiescence to the law. In the February 2–9 issue, the anonymous writer who had sent the letters to the *Chronicle* and identified them as authored by Franklin tried to show that the charge of Franklin's "*not employing his Pen in Behalf of America, at that critical Juncture*" was "groundless." He sent "some *English* News-Papers, containing a considerable Number of Pieces, wrote and published by the Doctor" as evidence. But the author went on to say that the essays, while exonerating Franklin from these charges, would also entertain and instruct: they would, "from the just Strictures, and humorous Strokes they contain, afford no small Satisfaction and Entertainment to many of your Readers." The appeal of these reprintings lay not simply in their resuscitation of Franklin's image in Pennsylvania. The Stamp Act remained a hot topic in the colonies a year after its repeal, and Franklin's defenses against English "othering" could be generalized as satiric arguments against new taxation measures and continuing English pride.

46. Franklin, *Papers*, 12: 414. As Landsman notes, the press had played a key role in helping to "foster a consciousness of the status of colonials as provincial citizens in an extended empire." See Landsman, *From Colonials to Provincials*, 34.

47. Colley, *Britons*, 41.

[8]

CLAY ZUBA

REDNESS AND THE CONTEST OF ANGLO-AMERICAN EMPIRES

WHILE LONDON EDITORIALISTS REFERRED to the colonists as consumers of Indian corn during the Stamp Act Crisis, London engravers went a step further, picturing the colonies as a red Indian. The first British political print to protest the Stamp Act, the London engraving *The Deplorable State of the America, or Sc—h Government* (figure 8.1), depicts the British colonies in North America as a dark, half-naked American Indian. This male figure, further identified as an Indian by his feathered headdress, as well as a bow and arrow strung across his back, stands at the center of the print. This engraving was published as a broadside in 1765 on the very same day as the passage of the Stamp Act itself. Like most such prints, *The Deplorable State of America* situates the figure of the Indian amid an array of well-known, emblematic figures that date back to the Renaissance. This emblematic tradition made political prints readily accessible to illiterate viewers, as well as those without expertise in political theory.[1] A female figure identified by her shield as Britannia proffers a box labeled "Pandora's Box," which Britannia's speech balloon designates the Stamp Act, to the Indian. The Indian states that he "abhor[s]" the act "as death" and appeals to Minerva, an emblem of wisdom, who stands at left with helmet and spear, for aid. Minerva urges the Indian to reject the Stamp Act, advising him to "take it not." Mercury, symbolizing commerce, tells the Indian, "It is with reluctance I leave ye," while Liberty, on the ground beneath the figures, bemoans, "It is all over with me."[2] Through this blend of textual and visual rhetoric, the print decries the Stamp Act for destroying commerce and liberty throughout the empire. By depicting all of these emblematic figures of values that bind British subjects—not only those that we might attribute to national values, such as wisdom, but also those that structure empire, such as liberty and commerce—as vehemently opposed to the Stamp Act, this print rejects the Stamp Act as antithetical to the ideals of British imperial identity.

Figure 8.1. *The Deplorable State of America, or Sc—h Government.* Etching. London, 1765. British Museum. © Trustees of the British Museum.

In popular culture and scholarly studies alike, passage of the Stamp Act of 1765 has long been viewed as the first in a series of events that led inevitably to the War of American Independence.[3] Between the imposition of the tax and the Declaration of Independence, British colonists masqueraded as American Indians in response to the Tea Act of 1773 and threw the Boston Tea Party. Since at least the 1830s, the Boston Tea Party has been considered an originary moment in the development of a uniquely American consciousness, where British colonists played Indian to celebrate their distinctness from European ideas.[4] But the trajectory of intra-imperial conflict that began with the Stamp Act inspired a very different case of colonists dressed as Indians: the allegorical figure of the Indian as America. This racialized, printed symbol of the colonies rooted colonial identity and, later, national identity for citizens of the United States in a consciousness that was not uniquely American, but rather grounded in European conceptions of creolization and colonial inferiority.

Disseminated primarily through the work of printers and engravers at the British metropole, the image of the Indian crisscrossed the eighteenth-century British Atlantic world in prints like *The Deplorable State of America* as a means to signify the colonies in popular debates over the proper structure of authority within the British Empire. Within this transatlantic print network, the red Indian body served as a vital signifier that tethered the diverse British colonies in North America to the imperial metropole. As a key symbol of the colonies, the figure of the Indian functioned as part of the metropolitan project to justify imperial authority by configuring British imperial identity through racial hierarchies. Benedict Anderson has argued that the print culture which produced these political prints fostered the emergence of national identities by connecting individuals who might never meet but shared the same language and reading experiences.[5] Anderson developed his theories of imagined community in part to explain the emergence of New World nationalism. However, as Edward Larkin has argued, "the logic of empire . . . understood as a structural relationship between a series of discrete peoples that could be, but need not be, hierarchical, provided the basis for the conceptualization of the U.S. from the very beginning."[6] This revision of Anderson's theories of New World collective identity formation raises important questions about the symbolic role the figure of the Indian played in the construction of British imperial identities in the Atlantic world, as well as the relationship between nation and empire. As numerous scholars, including Anderson, Paul Gilroy, and Linda Colley have argued, collective identities such as those linked to nation and empire typically bind populations through conceptions of racial or ethnic purity.[7] In his study of the African diaspora, Gilroy writes that according to Euro-American conceptions of modernity, the nation-state is founded on the idea of the "thinking 'racial' self that is encountered . . . within the fortified frontiers of . . . discrete ethnic cultures which also happen to coincide within the contours of the sovereign nation-state which guarantees their continuity."[8] Colley expands formulations such as Gilroy's when she argues that the expansion of the British Empire, accompanied by inter-imperial wars with France and other European powers, stimulated the unification of Welsh, Celtic, Scottish, and English peoples under a common national identity. On the basis of these theories of nation and empire, we would expect Britons at the metropole to assert racial and ethnic continuity with their diasporic settlers on the frontiers of the empire. However, by visually depicting British colonists as Native Americans, illustrators and engravers created difference between colonial and metropolitan populations that within the borders of the British nation would otherwise have been considered homogeneously European and "white." In the act of visualizing the colonial political body through redness, printers and engravers united colony and metropole in a vision of empire grounded in racial difference—not only between Native Americans and Britons, but between white populations within the empire.

By representing the colonial political body with an Indian, British metropolitans visually marked their colonial kinsmen as creoles—Europeans who, according to metropolitan theories of natural development, inevitably degenerated as a result of exposure to the New World environment.[9] In depicting such degeneration through the figure of the Indian, metropolitans employed the image of a racialized other to picture difference between whites within the empire. Although the concept of the creole originated in the metropole, its impact extended across the Atlantic to the colonies, compelling diasporic colonists to assert their purity through conformity with European culture. At the same time that this depiction served to subordinate colonists within the empire, the use of the Indian to portray the culturally and economically diverse British colonies clustered along the Atlantic rim unintentionally contributed to the colonists' growing sense of a shared identity distinct from that of British metropolitans. The figure of the Indian thereby functions as a transnational symbol that obstructed the inclusion of British colonists within British national identity. From this perspective, the nascent U.S. empire would be born of a racialized difference that relied on emerging conceptions of redness as a means to produce hierarchies between populations who both considered themselves white.

Redness and the Structure of Empire

British printers employed the pictorial image of the colonies as an Indian with greatest frequency during the empire-wide debates over the limits of metropolitan authority that followed the Stamp Act and continued through the War of American Independence. Political prints carried the image of the American Indian from their point of primary production in London to the colonies in order to disseminate news about important events in Europe or debate matters of imperial policy. Colonial printers, for their part, often reproduced and modified the imagery and text of metropolitan prints. In this way, political prints like the *Deplorable State of America* reached a wide population of readers across the British Empire. These illustrations were printed and reprinted in magazines and newspapers such as the *Gentleman's Magazine* in London and the *Pennsylvania Gazette* in Philadelphia. Most often, though, Britons encountered the figure of the Indian in the form of broadside prints.[10] In this format, political prints could be purchased by individual consumers at print shops to hang in residences or, more frequently, by the owners of coffeehouses and taverns for public consumption.[11] These establishments displayed prints prominently on the walls of the common room, where they could be viewed and discussed by men across class lines, "from aristocracy to laborers."[12] Thus, the circulation of political prints depicting the figure of the Indian joined colonial and metropolitan communities in a common readership.

Such prints shaped colonial identity within the empire through a complex interplay of race and gender. In racial terms, engravers consistently visualized the colonies as a half-naked Indian with dark skin attired in feathered headdress and skirt, and often grasping a bow or wielding a tomahawk. In terms of gender, at the commencement of the Stamp Act Crisis artists overwhelmingly pictured this Indian as female. Imagined as a daughter of Britannia, this feminine figure dubbed the "Indian Princess" by art historian E. McClung Fleming emphasized consanguinity between the inhabitants of colony and metropole. Yet by visualizing the colonies through redness, metropolitan illustrators portrayed British colonists as inferior and subordinate to white metropolitans.[13] The Indian Princess thereby registers a conflicted effort by artists to picture the colonies at once firmly linked to metropolitans within the empire by filial bonds and yet alien from the British national identity that colonists would otherwise presumably share with metropolitans. Although the Indian Princess remained the primary symbol of the colonies following the Stamp Act, artists and engravers began to depict this Indian as male as a part of their protest against what the British public increasingly regarded as an unconstitutional oppression of the colonies. Prints that employ a male Indian, like *The Able Doctor*, portray the colonies as growing stronger and more capable of political resistance, even though dress and skin color continue to mark the colonies as culturally subordinate. Such prints additionally weaken the filial bonds between metropole and colony, since engravers and printers did not identify the male Indian as a blood relative of Britannia.

The figure of the Indian first emerged as a symbol of the British colonies in North America as a collective political body during the French and Indian War of 1754–1763. During this period metropolitan soldiers were deployed in North America in significant numbers for the first time, and conflict with the French Empire disrupted trade on global levels.[14] Since this North American war served as an extension of long-standing European conflicts between France, England, and eventually Spain as emerging global imperial powers, British illustrators and engravers required a symbol for the colonies in political cartoons that communicated news of important events across the empire. *British Resentment, or the French Fairly Coopt at Louisbourg* (figure 8.2), printed in London in 1755, em-

Figure 8.2. *British Resentment, or the French Fairly Coopt at Louisbourg.* Etching. Published by T. Bowles, L. Boitard artist, J. June etcher. London, 1755. British Museum. © Trustees of the British Museum.

ploys the most common iteration of this figure of the Indian between the French and Indian War and the War of American Independence.

British Resentment dramatizes a complex fantasy of a British Empire that has already eclipsed France as North America's preeminent imperial power. The etching depicts an impending British capture of the French Fort Louisbourg in New France (although the British would not actually capture the fort until 1758). It visualizes Britannia as a monarch newly enthroned in New France to signify British dominion, while two Indian women—with darkened skin, scant clothing, and feathered adornments—kneel at her feet to depict colonial submission to metropolitan power. By representing the colonies as two physically similar Indian Princesses, the artist depicts the British colonies as separate political entities, equally subordinate to metropolitan authority. At right, the French are imprisoned in a cage that is being towed westward to Europe. The print envisions the British Empire forcibly removing the French from North America. Below the border of the illustration, the artist has explained important sections of the image by indexing them with matching numbers and corresponding textual explanations. The first numbered point explains that Britannia is here "attending to the complaints of her injur'd Americans" and that she "receives them into her protection." The third point indicates that the British Lion, a figure that would reappear in epistles and poems discussing the Stamp Act, is "keeping his dominions under his paw safe from invaders." *British Resentment* thereby constructs the French Empire as an invader of North America mercilessly attacking vulnerable colonists. The illustration makes colonial dependency on the metropole explicit by pairing the visual image of Indians kneeling with a textual explanation of Britannia's role as protector of the colonies from the French. The artist thereby guides viewers to understand that Britain is sending thousands of troops to North America for war in New France primarily to protect helpless colonial subjects. The colonies can be saved, the print implies, only if the French are exiled from North America.[15]

By symbolizing the colonial polity with the figure of the Indian in such political prints, metropolitans drew colonists into a visual discourse of racial difference that had been evolving for centuries in two parallel, yet increasingly entangled trajectories. On one hand, an ethnographic pictorial tradition developed in early modern promotional tracts, such as Theodore de Bry's *A Briefe and True Report of the New Found Land of Virginia*. The images created by De Bry and other engravers were instrumental in producing European knowledge of the "New World."[16] The image of Native Americans as primitive savages played a central role in the construction of such knowledge. By depicting the indigenous peoples of the North American continent as inferior to civilized, technologically advanced Europeans, such images justified European conquest of the Americas, as well as the exploitation and genocide of Native Americans. On the other hand, in a tradition that began almost concurrently, European engravers used the female Indian as an emblem of the American continent itself alongside the other established emblems of the three continents of Europe, Africa, and Asia.[17] Artists depicted this figure, dubbed the "Indian Queen" by art critics, as a Native American "tawny" in skin tone, partly naked and wearing a feathered skirt and headdress, often carrying a bow and arrow.[18] In order to convey the exoticism and danger with which Europeans viewed the Americas, the Indian Queen was sometimes depicted riding an animal such as an armadillo, an alligator, or even a stegosaur and surrounded by scenes of cannibalism and human sacrifice.[19] This figure of the Indian as America circulated prominently throughout western Europe in the multimedia forms of prints, textiles, ceramics, and even theater.[20] In these two traditions, then, this depiction of an Indian held divergent significations. The ethnographic figure of the Indian signified Native Americans, while the emblematic figure signified the lands inhabited by Native Americans and desired by European empires. Because Europeans sought to exploit both the indigenous peoples of the Americas and the land itself for its resources, the logic of imperialism embedded in the figure of the Indian applied equally well to both purposes.

Yet this logic does not explain why metropolitans chose this red figure as a symbol of their white kinsmen who settled North America as part of the British imperial project. Metropolitans strategically chose the figure of the Indian to symbolize the British colonies in their political prints as a means to visually convey the metropolitan belief that colonists were creoles. Even though metropolitans considered colonists to be British, they also believed that exposure to the New World environment, as well as proximity to Native Americans and Africans, left colonists vulnerable to creolization. In what metropolitans theorized as an inescapable process, Europeans degenerated culturally when they resided or were born in North America. Creoles became less like Britons and more like savages.[21] Within this context, the figure of the Indian locates colonists outside the boundaries of British national identity. Metropolitans relied on the concept that creoles were culturally degraded to justify limitations on colonial participation in imperial government.[22] Despite the fact that the colonists in North America shared the same ancestry, homeland language, religion, and culture as metropolitans, each colonist was, as Benedict Anderson has put it, "irredeemably a creole."[23] The colonial subjects described in in chapter 6 by Alexander Jablonski thus occupied a liminal position within the empire. Their British descent theoretically allowed them the full rights of Englishmen and, of course, allowed them much greater respect and mobility than would have been granted to Native Americans. But because the logic of creolization portrayed white colonists as culturally degraded, it reconfigured them as, much like Native Americans, savages within the empire.

British political prints interpellated colonists, now separated by the Atlantic and considered degraded creoles, into a messy, still fluctuating field of increasingly racialized difference only then emerging as a tool to create hierarchies within the British Empire. At the time that metropolitans first adopted this figure of the Indian to signify the British colonies in North America, conceptions of racial difference between Native Americans and Europeans were still evolving and unstable. When Europeans had initially encountered Native Americans in the sixteenth century, they did not consider Natives racially different. In fact, much British colonial writing of the seventeenth and early eighteenth centuries refers to Native Americans as white.[24] Despite this apparent color blindness, though, most Europeans considered Native American culture and religion to be barbarous. In textual and visual records of early colonization, Europeans delineated the cultural boundaries between barbarous Natives and civilized Europeans through apparel and ornament—a feathered headdress, a tomahawk, moccasins—that marked the Native inferior to the European. Nonetheless, early explorers, missionaries, and settlers often believed that these boundaries could be crossed and that Native Americans could be elevated to civilized status with the proper education.[25] Over the course of the eighteenth century, as the availability of land decreased and colonists coveted Native land and resources, Europeans increasingly marked Native Americans as racially different by categorizing them as "red." Not until near the end of the century, after the conclusion of the War of American Independence, would redness and the supposed irredeemable inferiority that accompanied it become the justification for denial of Native sovereignty and for westward expansion.[26] In their use of the figure of an Indian to depict the colonists as creoles, metropolitans employed many of the same discourses of racial difference with which both colonists and metropolitans justified imperialism toward Native Americans. By overwriting white creoles with red Indians, they united the two collectives of very different cultures, as well as disparate positions within the structure of empire, under one symbol. However, these political prints depicted "white" colonists as "red" by means of the same pictorial strategies that were being more and more often deployed to depict Native Americans, themselves once considered "white," as different and inferior.

British prints published in response to the Stamp Act initiated the use of the figure of the Indian to construct the metropolitan government as unjustly oppressing the colonies. Through these prints, it would be metropolitans, rather than colonists, who first visualized colonial resistance to imperial policy. In the process of stimulating public debate over the structure of empire, the figure of the Indian developed a transatlantic currency among both metropolitans and colonists. *The Deplorable State* was immediately followed by a flurry of prints that similarly utilized the figure of the Indian to decry the Stamp Act as harmful to the empire. London prints like *The Great Financier, or British Economy for the Years 1763, 1764, 1765* and *The State of the Nation: 1765, etc.* rely on the Indian to depict a British economy trending downward toward ruin as a result of its North American colonial policies. Even though these prints were produced at the metropole, they were exported and sold in the colonies, as evidenced by Philadelphia advertisements for *The State of the Nation: 1765, etc.*[27] These political prints were part of a public protest so successful that in 1766 Parliament repealed the Stamp Act. That year metropolitan prints such as *The Balance, or America's Triumph, The New Country Dance, and The Triumph of America* celebrated the repeal. As their titles alone indicate, these prints convey a sense of victory for the colonial political body against the metropolitan Parliament. At the same time, their continued use of the figure of the Indian racially reinforced the cultural inferiority of colony to metropole.

Following the repeal of the Stamp Act, the Indian temporarily receded as an emblematic figure in British political prints, appearing in only one print, *The Triumvirate, or Britannia in Distress*, published in London in 1769. Rather than focusing on intra-imperial trade or colonial sovereignty, this print primarily debated political events at the metropole and protested the exclusion of John Wilkes from Parliament that year. The appearance of the Indian in this print demonstrates the figure's continued currency as a symbol of the colonies, yet the scarcity of the figure during this period suggests that despite the colonial outrage against statutes like the Townsend Acts passed from 1767 to 1768, metropolitans did not feel compelled to depict the colonies as a distinct political body. However, this decline reversed sharply following Parliament's passage of the so-called Coercive Acts in 1774. Parliament passed these four acts (the Boston Port Act, the Massachusetts Government Act, the Administration of Just Act, and the Quartering Act) partly in retaliation for the Boston Tea Party in December 1773, itself a colonial response to Parliament's passage of the Tea Act earlier that year.[28] By tightening imperial authority over colonial self-government even further, the Coercive Acts stimulated a new wave of metropolitan political prints that featured the Indian, an iconological trend that soon reached across the Atlantic Ocean, once again, to the colonies.

Such prints criticize the Coercive Acts through words and images of escalating interracial violence. One of the earliest of these, the engraving *The Able Doctor, or America Swallowing the Bitter Draught* (figure 8.3), makes clear to viewers that it refers to the Boston Port Act through three textual references to Boston. This first of the acts closed the Port of Boston to trade as retribution for the Tea Party. First published in the *Gentleman's Magazine* in London in April 1774, this print depicts the colonies as an Indian Princess restrained on the ground by members of Parliament. Lord Mansfield holds her arms to the ground, while Lord Sandwich holds

Figure 8.3. *The Able Doctor, or America Swallowing the Bitter Draught.* Engraving. Published in the *London Magazine*, vol. 43, 1774. British Museum. © Trustees of the British Museum.

her feet, lifts her skirt and leers. Prime Minister Lord North pours liquid, presumably tea, judging by the shape of the pot, down her throat. France and Spain stand at right, amused at the spectacle. Britannia covers her eyes in disgust at the behavior of her ministers.[29] Even though she is restrained, the Indian Princess nonetheless resists by spouting the tea back into Lord North's face.

This engraving metaphorically constructs the Tea Act and the Boston Port Act as means of forcing the colonial consumption of metropolitan goods. In this context, the engraving espouses the cause of the colonists who protested the Tea Act. By depicting the Indian Princess as a sexual victim resisting the advances of Parliament, the engraving characterizes this forced consumption as a metropolitan act of economic rape. Like many political prints published following passage of the Coercive Acts, *The Able Doctor* relies on satire to criticize the British Empire. As a visual medium, these prints function through what one art historian describes as "the deployment of a pictorial negative."[30] As a genre, satirical prints like *The Able Doctor* picture the current state of the British Empire, which they ridicule, as they seek to stimulate social change. In *The Able Doctor*, Britannia's need to avert her gaze from the rape of her daughter cues metropolitan viewers to sympathize with the colonists across the Atlantic with whom they are similarly related by blood. The print constructs parliamentary acts like the Boston Port Act and the Tea Act as a contradiction to the legitimate structure of empire.

Political prints published in the years preceding the American Revolution, like *The Able Doctor*, are often interpreted to support American independence because they favor the rights of the colonies. In *Playing Indian*, for example, Philip Deloria cites *The Able Doctor* as an example of how "colonial propaganda . . . adapt[ed]" the figure of the Indian "in order to convey revolutionary messages."[31] While this print clearly advocates colonial rights, viewers would not necessarily perceive its "message" to be "revolutionary." Describing *The Able Doctor* as an instrument of the revolutionary cause elides its complex iconological origins in the metropolitan imagination and obscures the structure of empire that this print advocates. Prints such as *The Able Doctor* would indeed eventually become instruments of revolution, yet as generated by metropolitans they focused on terms of colonial inclusion and subordination, not independence. In its composition and iconology, *The Able Doctor* draws on patterns of representation employed in European prints of the early modern period that depicted the American continents through the emblematic figure of the Indian Queen, such as Theodor Galle's influential print *Vespucci Discovering America* and the widely disseminated engraving of Galle's painting by Jan Van der Straet (figure 8.4). This 1600 engraving, which would be reproduced throughout the eighteenth century, depicts the Indian Queen as inviting European sexual conquest. Clad in only a feathered skirt and headdress, she looks in wonder before the commanding gaze of Vespucci, who stands fully clothed before her. This sexualization of the Indian Queen metaphorically portrays the Americas, and implicitly its indigenous people, as inviting European conquest.[32] *The Able Doctor*, with its Indian Princess supine and nearly naked at center, surrounded by standing, fully clothed Europeans, bears remarkable iconographical and compositional similarities with *Vespucci Discovering America*.

We can see from these similarities that the allegorical imagery of *The Able Doctor* is derived from a visual tradition that already depicted imperial identity as grounded in exploitation. This tradition erased the violence of imperialism by portraying European conquest of the Americas as a consensual sexual act between Europeans and colonists. Analogously, the exploitation of metropole by colony would certainly be permissible. The representation of the colonies as red authorizes such exploitation.

Figure 8.4. Jan Van der Straet, *Nova Repurta: Vespucci Discovering America.* Engraving. Antwerp, 1600. British Museum. © Trustees of the British Museum.

Thus, *The Able Doctor* does not protest either the exploitation of the colonies by the metropole or the subordination of colonists. The first part of the engraving's title condones a hierarchical relationship between metropole and colony by comparing Lord North to a doctor and the colonies to a patient. Instead of protesting an inappropriate relationship between doctor and patient, this print protests parliamentary mismanagement by depicting Lord North as a doctor who abuses his patient. *The Able Doctor*, then, does not criticize colonial exploitation per se, but rather the degree to which the metropole has exploited the colonies. The problem is not exploitation itself, but rather that Parliament has driven the colonies to resist by being overly oppressive. As pictured in this illustration, metropolitan oppression exceeds *even what is allowable to an Indian*. The satire of the title *The Able Doctor* is conveyed by the word "Able," not "Doctor." A doctor's purpose, in the context of this engraving, is to restore the empire to its thriving position before the imposition of the Stamp Act, which included metropolitan extraction of wealth from the colonies. The problem shown in the image is that these members of Parliament are not "Able"—instead of acting in the interests of the empire, these doctors abuse their power. Therefore, *The Able Doctor* simply advocates a recalibration of imperial exploitation to acceptable levels. While *Vespucci* illustrates a solitary emblematic figure of Europe as a consensual partner, *The Able Doctor* depicts the Indian Princess surrounded by multiple European figures. By depicting emblems of the empires of Spain and France lingering and watching, *The Able Doctor* articulates the anxiety that this intra-imperial oppression has made the British colonies, and by extension the British Empire, vulnerable to inter-imperial aggression. The print argues that without changes to the structure of empire, Britain might be forced to share the economic spoils of her once consensual conquest of the colonies. It uses the figure of the Indian to advocate the repeal of the Coercive Acts in the hope that in doing so the empire can return to the consensual exploitation of colony by metropole.

As the conflict between colony and metropole escalated, metropolitans used the figure of the Indian to register open colonial rebellion.[33] Metropolitan printmakers continued to represent the colonies primarily as a female Indian, but ceased to depict this Indian as exploited and enslaved. The titles of these prints, such as *Bunker's Hill, or the Bless'd Effects of Family Quarrels* (1775), *When Fell Debate and Civil Wars Shall Cease* (1775), and *The Parricide. A Sketch of Patriotism* (1776), show how even as the American crisis developed into outright civil war, metropolitans invoked familial likeness between Britons on both sides of the Atlantic. Rather than lying prone as in *The Able Doctor*, this Indian was portrayed more and more frequently by artists as "standing up" to emblematic symbols of the metropole in a fight for liberty. *The Female Combatants* (1776), for example, depicts a nearly naked Indian Princess with feathered skirt and headdress and hair at her shoulders. She is tattooed and of slightly darker complexion than Britannia, who sports a stylish gown and coiffed hair. This artist has depicted the Indian Princess as engaged in a boxing match with Britannia, who calls the Indian Princess a "slut." The engraver thereby makes a pun to negatively conflate sexual liberty with political liberty and criticize calls for colonial autonomy as licentious and extravagant.[34] While the artist has used clothing, tattoos, and skin tone to emphasize the cultural inferiority of creoles to metropolitans, the two figures' horizontal alignment suggests a measure of equality in terms of their political strength. The artist depicts the Indian Princess with a relatively light skin tone, in contrast to the dark skin of the Indian Princess in prints like *British Resentment* (figure 8.2). The engraver thereby partially mitigates her redness, even though she remains racialized in the form of her feathers and tattoos. Kinship is explicitly invoked in the Indian

Princess's reference to Britannia as her "mother." At the same time that this metropolitan artist depicts violence between colonist and metropole, he downplays the civil war's bloodshed, and its potential to tear apart the empire, by depicting the conflict as a sporting boxing match. Prints such as the *Female Combatants* suggest a longing for a reunion between the family unit of colony and metropole. Indeed, prints of this type have ceased to focus their satirical criticism on parliamentary policy and instead communicate a public yearning for a reconciliation that will draw the colonies back within the fold of the empire.

Colonial Prints and the Imperatives of Diaspora

The use of the figure of the Indian as a symbol of the colonies originated with metropolitans as a means to racially mark colonists as creoles within the empire. However, between the Stamp Act and the War of American Independence, this allegorical figure would become so integral a vehicle for transatlantic debate over imperial policy as to be employed in prints produced by colonists themselves. Such prints remain heavily derivative of metropolitan prototypes. Often these prints directly reproduced their metropolitan models, as in Paul Revere's 1774 copy of *The Able Doctor*. At other times colonial engravers slightly modified the iconography of London prints as a response to metropolitan thought, as in the case of John Singleton Copley's iteration of *The Deplorable State of America* (1765). Indeed, the dearth of colonial innovation in these political prints emphasizes the extent to which metropolitans dominated the visual discourses constructed through the figure of the Indian.

The tensions between colonial efforts to copy and to alter these metropolitan originals illustrate the vexed position of creoles within the British Empire. Facing westward from the center of imperial power, metropolitans pictured creoles as alien and inferior by racializing them as red savages. Facing east toward their homeland, however, creoles desperately desired to assert their oneness with the metropole. As members of what Leonard Tennenhouse has called an English diaspora, creoles sought to assert continuity with the metropole in order to reinforce their bonds with their homeland.[35] In cultural terms, this desire manifested in the form of literary and visual works that reproduced metropolitan forms. This would be especially true in the case of the political prints protesting the Stamp Act, which required that creoles demonstrate their expertise in the terms of the debate at the metropole. However, participation in this debate demanded that creoles reproduce a cultural form that racially marked them as others. Paradoxically, asserting their purity as English subjects required colonists to picture themselves as savages.

Nonetheless, colonists modified these illustrations in ways that demonstrate their own resistance to the imperial ideologies embedded in this visual signifier. The first colonial print to employ the figure of the Indian was Boston artist John Singleton Copley's modification of the London print *The Deplorable State of America*. Copley produced his version in November 1765, eight months after the metropolitan original appeared.[36] Copley's iteration emulates the metropolitan engraver's composition but reconfigures some of its iconology. Whereas the London original portrays a dark-skinned male Indian standing with bow and arrow mounted on his back, Copley depicts a female Indian with lighter skin lying on the ground, with bow and arrow at her side. Copley's change to a prone female figure holding no weapons reasserts a near totality of colonial subordination lost to the London original. Copley's Indian is a defenseless victim of metropolitan policies.[37] However, by lightening the skin tone of the Indian to match that of the other figures in the print, Copley erases one of the figure's most prominent bodily markers of racial inferiority. His decision to place the bow and arrow at the Indian's side, rather than on her body, further separates his Indian from objects that symbolically constructed creoles as savages inferior to Europeans. In mitigating the redness of his Indian, Copley proclaims the Stamp Act to be an act of imperial oppression by metropolitans against fellow white Englishmen.

Following the passage of the Coercive Acts, colonial prints remained closely tethered to metropolitan originals. The most frequently reproduced metropolitan print, the 1774 London engraving *The Able Doctor* (figure 8.3), would be republished in several subtly different versions. While these prints continued to criticize the Coercive Acts within imperial frameworks, they advocated divergent responses to imperial oppression. Seven months after its London prototype, Paul Revere engraved a copy of *The Able Doctor* to be published in *The Royal American Magazine; or, Universal Repository for Instruction and Amusement*. Revere's version, like much of the meticulous engraver's work, is almost an exact copy of the London version, except that Revere adds the word "TEA" to the pot.[38] Revere's insertion demonstrates at least measured support for the Boston Tea Party and for colonial resistance. In response to Revere's print, the Philadelphia broadside iteration that followed just two months later distanced itself from any revolutionary message. The anonymous artist of this engraving also copied the metropolitan original, but retitled the broadside *The Persevering Americans, or the Bitter Draught Return'd*.

This title directs attention toward the Indian Princess's metaphoric rejection of the Tea Act and the Coercive Acts. However, by characterizing the Indian Princess as "Persevering," the print portrays the colonies as laboring to bear imperial oppression until it could be corrected from within the imperial government.[39] In this sense the Philadelphia reproduction tempers any support for insurrection implied in Revere's version.

Not until 1775, following the Battles of Bunker Hill and Lexington and Concord, would colonists explicitly incorporate the figure of the Indian into their calls for breaking the bonds that tethered colony to metropole. Late that year, Timothy Green of New London printed a crude woodcut relief of *The Able Doctor* as the frontispiece of his edition of *Freebetter's New England Almanac of the Year 1776*. Green's iteration mirrors his metropolitan prototype by exactly copying and reversing the original. However, Green uses *The Able Doctor* to mediate an anonymous revolutionary poem embedded in stanzas across the top pages of the almanac's interior. By placing the Indian Princess in dialogue with this poem, Green transforms the Indian Princess from a figure that divided the British Empire into two collectives to a symbol of American nationalism. This poem subverts the filial conventions that positioned the Indian Princess as the daughter of Britannia by offering Greece and Rome as alternative "parent state[s]" to the colonies, which are identified under the umbrella of "America."[40] After first identifying America as the heir to ideals of liberty and resistance to tyranny that originated in Greece and Rome, the poem next depicts America's rise to its own imperial status before any mention of Britain. The poem depicts the ascent of America as a moment when the ideals of American liberty can enlighten the world:

> "Hail! happy day, while patriotic fire
> Glows in the breast of the noble mind t'inspire
> Flame'd by this spark *America* will shine
> And lighten distant worlds with rays benign.

Such lines advocate and celebrate American independence to an extent unrealized in *The Able Doctor* as an individually circulating illustration. In its glory America emulates Rome, compared with whom "No human granduer e'er appear'd so great; / Spread its vast wings to earth's extreamest point, / And sea and land to pay low homage join'd."[41] Lines like these reproduce tropes common among revolutionary-era poems that celebrate "The Rising Glory of America" by poets such as Philip Freneau and Timothy Dwight.[42] Through these stanzas the poem thereby depicts America as reaching prominence as a global empire that will expand across the globe.

Moreover, this poem counteracts *The Able Doctor*'s depiction of Britannia as a maternal force sympathetic to colonial oppression. When Britannia finally appears, she enters as a force of "TYRANNY," who "alarms / freedom's true son, and forces to arms." The poet emphasizes the loyalty of the colonists to the mother country, asking rhetorically, "Did we the parent whence we sprung disgrace? And show ourselves a mean degen'rate race?" This last clause demonstrates the poet's awareness of metropolitan accusations that colonists had degenerated into creole savages and rhetorically asserts their falsity. While the engraving *The Able Doctor* pictures Britannia averting her gaze from the rape of the colonies, this poem describes Britannia as having been transformed into a "tyrant" who, "having taught them to be free and brave, Would her own breast her offspring enslave!" According to this poet, British tyranny has forced the colonies to fight for freedom from metropolitan slavery. The use of the figure of the Indian as the cover for the almanac that contains this poem shows that, by 1775, at least New England colonists had begun to redeploy the allegorical figure of the Indian as a symbol of the colonies in works that advocated American independence.[43] Through this combination of image and text, this edition of *Freebetter's Almanac* adopts redness as a marker that racially differentiates American liberty from British tyranny.

Redness and the Emergence of U.S. Empire

Whether privileging colonial or metropolitan perspectives, political prints that employ the figure of the Indian invite questions about the structure of the British Empire through a narrative of racial difference. Engravings that rely on the figure of the Indian to symbolize the colonies posit differences between whiteness and redness (and accompanying cultural qualities of civilization and savagery) as baseline beliefs shared by British subjects on both sides of the Atlantic. Copley, as we have seen, sought to diminish prominent markers of racial difference between colonists and metropolitans when in his Stamp Act–era reproduction of *The Deplorable State of America* he made the skin of the Indian lighter than it was in the metropolitan original. At the same time, metropolitan prints such as *The Female Combatants* depicted the colonies as an Indian Princess with fair skin in their effort to portray racial consanguinity between empire and colony. A survey of seventy-seven prints shows that almost 60 percent of metropolitan prints depict the Indian with darker skin than the emblematic figures that accompany them, while only 18 percent of political prints produced by colonists do so. Analogously, 68 percent of metropolitan prints marked the Indian as other through stereotypical accessories such as feathers or bow and arrows, while just 27 percent of colonial prints conformed to this convention.[44] This trend shows that colonists and metropolitans alike agreed that redness could serve as a means to racially mark peoples as culturally inferior to white Europeans and thereby unfit for sovereignty. Most likely it was the very scarcity of signifiers of redness in the metropolitan original of *The Able Doctor* that enabled Timothy Green to appropriate it as a call for revolution in his 1775 edition of *Freebetter's Almanac*.

In the process of deploying the figure of the Indian to mark creoles as different and inferior, metropolitans contributed to the growing sense among the colonists that they constituted a collective political body rather than thirteen individual colonies. At the time of the Stamp Act, colonists living in the diverse colonies from Massachusetts to Maryland to Georgia did not think of themselves as possessing a shared colonial identity. While they first and foremost identified themselves as Virginians or Carolinians, they also identified themselves primarily with the British metropole and seldom with creoles of neighboring colonies. When the metropolitan Andrew Burnaby noted in his travels that "fire and water are not more heterogeneous than the different colonies of North America," he articulated this lack of a common identity among colonists. The 1755 print *British Resentment* (figure 8.2) used the two separate Indian Princesses, physically similar and equally subordinate to Britannia, to signify distinct political entities under imperial authority. Political prints published in response to the Stamp Act visualized, for the first time, the colonies as sharing the hardships caused by metropolitan aggression, using the single figure of an Indian.[45] Perhaps ironically, this signifier of colonial unity originated at the metropole to keep the colonies firmly subordinate to the empire. Creoles considered themselves distinct from their neighbors in other colonies when Burnaby observed them during his tour of North America. But the fact that in 1765 and afterward creoles reproduced metropolitan prints that visualized the colonies as one political body suggests that the colonists began to think of themselves as sharing a common identity, even if this was portrayed by a symbol that, despite their diasporic desire for continuity with the metropole, represented colonists as distinct and alien.

The colonists of British North America at first emulated, and later adopted, the same evolving racialized discourses of redness that metropolitans had developed not only to justify imperialism against Native

Americans, but also to subordinate and differentiate white colonists of their transatlantic empire. This phenomenon recalls the problem that Gilroy identifies in scholarship about black culture in the transatlantic world. Gilroy apprehends that theorists of black identity tend to reify Euro-American absolutist understandings of the racial purity of the nation by placing a disproportionate importance on blackness as a determinate of national identity among diasporic Africans. He warns against the tendency among scholars of black nationalism to conclude "based on over-integrated conceptions of pure and homogenous culture . . . that black political struggles are automatically expressive of the national or ethnic differences with which they are associated."[46] In examining how race structured the eighteenth-century British Empire, scholars have made just the opposite mistake. For decades scholars have studied how Britons, as well as the colonists of what would later become the United States, developed race to construct the transatlantic boundaries that linked populations within the empire through racial homogeneity and excluded Native Americans through racial difference. This focus has obscured the extent to which metropolitans used this same discourse of redness to racially manage whites at the margins of the empire. This metropolitan deployment of race as a formulation of racial inclusion became expressive of racial differences that allowed colonists to conceive of themselves as possessing a shared ethnic identity distinct from that of metropolitans. Yet when white colonists dressed as red Indians at the Boston Tea Party, they did not necessarily do so in celebration of their uniquely American character. Instead, their performance registers the vexed process whereby colonists adopted the figure of the Indian as a symbol of their own emergent imperial nation: a symbol that acted as a racialized marker of their own creole degeneration, expressed through an iconological tradition initially developed by British metropolitans as a means to debate the terms of colonial dependence following the Stamp Act of 1765.

On a broader level, these transformations in the use of the figure of the Indian between the French and Indian War and the War of American Independence reveal tensions between the British nation and empire. The formation of national identities depends on the ability of a group of people to imagine themselves as a homogeneous cultural community. At the same time, empire is predicated on the expansion of the nation into new geographical territories. In some cases, such an extension of borders stimulates the formation of national identities by placing the nation in conflict with racial or ethnic others, as Colley argues that imperial conflict with France stimulated the unification of the British nation. But such expansion might also require the empire to incorporate populations formerly outside the boundaries of the nation or, as in the case of the British colonies in North America, disperse national populations across geographies that require innovations in the political and economic structure of the empire. During the colonial era, British metropolitans employed the figure of the Indian as a means to racially subordinate their own diasporic populations within the empire. In doing so, they unwittingly reconfigured British national expansion into a transnational movement. In this sense the figure of the Indian registers a rupture in the compatibility of nation and empire.

Notes

1. Tamara Hunt, *Defining John Bull: Political Caricature and National Identity in Late Georgian England* (Burlington, VT: Ashgate, 2003), 12. On the use of emblems in political prints, see Lester C. Olson, *Emblems of American Community in the Revolutionary Era: A Study in Rhetorical Iconology* (Washington, DC: Smithsonian Institution Press, 1991).

2. E. P. Richardson, "Stamp Act Cartoons in the Colonies," *Pennsylvania Magazine of History and Biography* 96.3 (1972): 277–284.

3. Scholars interpret the Stamp Act as a "prologue" to American Independence that set colonists on a "road to revolution." Mercy Otis Warren advanced this narrative in her *History of the Rise, Fall, and Termination of the American Revolution* (1805). For one of the earliest iterations of this idea in modern historical thought, see Edmund S. Morgan and Helen M. Morgan, *The Stamp Act Crisis: Prologue to Revolution* (Chapel Hill: University of North Carolina Press for the Institute of Early American History and Culture at Williamsburg, Virginia, 1953). For a more recent and one of the most frequently cited versions, see T. H. Breen, *The Marketplace of Revolution: How Consumer Politics Shaped American Independence* (New York: Oxford University Press, 2004).

4. On the development of a collective American memory of the Tea Party in the early nineteenth century, see Alfred F. Young, *The Shoemaker and the Tea Party: Memory and the American Revolution* (Boston: Beacon Press, 1999), esp. 85–180. In the most recently published history of the Boston Tea Party, Benjamin Carp writes that when worn by British colonists, Indian "disguises celebrated the uniquely American identity of the white colonists." Benjamin L. Carp, *Defiance of the Patriots: The Boston Tea Party and the Making of America* (New Haven, CT: Yale University Press, 2010), 157. Philip Deloria characterizes the Boston Tea Party as "a catalytic moment" and an "origin story." "For the next two hundred years," he writes, "white Americans molded similar narratives of national identity around the rejection of an older European consciousness and an almost mystical imperative to become new." Philip Deloria, *Playing Indian* (New Haven, CT: Yale University Press, 1995), 2.

5. Benedict Anderson, *Imagined Communities: Reflections on the Origin and Spread of Nationalism* (London: Verso, 1993), 44.

6. Edward Larkin, "Nation and Empire in the Early U.S.," *American Literary His-*

tory 22.3 (2010): 3. In reference to Anderson's theories, Ed White has argued that in the case of the colonies of British North America "the overarching imagined community is the *empire*, imagined as a complicated community of hierarchies and relations, an encompassing system whose viability hinges on the careful construction, regulation, and maintenance of certain smaller collectivities." Ed White, "Early American Nations as Imagined Communities," *American Quarterly* 56.1 (2004): 67, emphasis in original. Timothy J. Shannon studies debates over colonial rights and governance in terms of empire in *Indians and Colonists and the Crossroads of Empire: The Albany Congress of 1754* (Ithaca, NY: Cornell University Press, 2000).

7. Anderson, *Imagined Communities*; Paul Gilroy, *The Black Atlantic: Modernity and Double Consciousness* (London: Verso, 1993); Linda Colley, *Captives: Britain, Empire, and the World, 1600–1850* (London: Johnathan Cape, 2002).

8. Gilroy, *Black Atlantic*, 30.

9. The concept of creolization describes a syncretic process wherein the culture of the colonies in North America deviated from European norms. This essay employs the term *creole* to describe "an imperial discourse of colonial difference" that justified metropolitan authority over colonies in North America. See Ralph Bauer and Jose Antontio Mazzotti, "Introduction," in *Creole Subjects in the Colonial Americas: Empires, Texts, Identities*, ed. Ralph Bauer and Jose Antonio Mazzotti (Chapel Hill: University of North Carolina Press for the Omohundro Institute in Early American Culture, 2009); also Sean Goudie, *Creole America: The West Indies and the Formation of Literature and Culture in the New Republic* (Philadelphia: University of Pennsylvania Press, 2006), 7–9. Scholarly discussions of creolization remain heavily indebted to the work of Benedict Anderson, especially in *Imagined Communities*, 22–33.

10. Olson, *Emblems of American Community*, 8–9.

11. Amelia Rauser, *Caricature Unmasked: Irony, Authenticity, and Individualism in Eighteenth-Century Political Prints* (Newark: University of Delaware Press, 2008), 30–31. As early as 1739, London itself supported 551 coffeehouses, 207 inns, and 447 taverns. By the time of the War of Independence, most British towns with even a few thousand residents boasted at least one coffeehouse that might subscribe to print sellers. Troy O. Bickham, *Making Headlines: The American Revolution as Seen through the British Press* (Dekalb: Northern Illinois University Press, 2009), 39.

12. Hunt, *Defining John Bull*, 12.

13. Olson, *Emblems of American Community*,75.

14. Colley, *Captives*, 171–174.

15. Timothy J. Shannon analyzes this print as a vehicle for structuring the British Empire in *Indians and Colonists*, 56–63. Shannon argues that the Indians in this print might with equal facility signify actual Native Americans or colonists. While I agree with Lester Olsen and other scholars who argue that these Indians represent colonists, Shannon's argument emphasizes the ambiguity of racial boundaries between creoles and Native Americans in the metropolitan imperial imaginary.

16. Michael Gaudio, *Engraving the Savage: The New World and Techniques of Civilization* (Minneapolis: University of Minnesota Press, 2008), xii.

17. E. McClung Fleming, "The American Image as Indian Princess, 1765–1783," *Winterthur Portfolio* 2 (1965): 68.

18. Ibid., 67.

19. For further discussion and examples of such prints see Hugh Honour, *The New Golden Land: European Images of America from the Discoveries to the Present Time* (London: Allen Lane, 1975), 84–117.

20. Ibid., 109.

21. Bauer and Mazzotti, "Introduction," 41.

22. Anderson, *Imagined Communities*, 57–60; Bauer and Mazzotti, "Introduction," 22–32.

23. Anderson, *Imagined Communities*, 58.

24. Nancy Shoemaker, *A Strange Likeness: Becoming Red and White in North America* (New York: Oxford University Press, 2004), 129–130, 136–137. See also Alden T. Vaughn, "From White Man to Redskin: Changing Anglo-American Perceptions of the American Indian," *American Historical Review* 87.4 (1982): 919–927.

25. Shoemaker, *A Strange Likeness*, 37.

26. Ibid., 137–139.

27. Richardson, "Stamp Act Cartoons in the Colonies," 288.

28. For a summary of the provisions of these acts and the logic behind their passage, see Carp, *Defiance of the Patriots*, 190–200.

29. See M. Dorothy George, *English Political Caricature to 1792: A Study of Opinion and Propaganda* (Oxford: Clarendon Press, 1959), 150–151.

30. Mark Hallett, *The Spectacle of Difference: Graphic Satire in the Age of Hogarth* (New Haven, CT: Yale University Press for the Paul Mellon Centre for Studies in British Art, 1999), 10.

31. Deloria, *Playing Indian*, 30.

32. See Peter Hulme, *Colonial Encounters: Europe and the Native Caribbean, 1492–1797* (New York: Routledge, 1992), 1–2; Gaudio, *Engraving the Savage*, xiv–xv. Deloria notes a connection between these two engravings, yet reads the *Able Doctor* as a contrast, rather than a continuation, of the sexualization and subordination of the colonies in *Vespucci Discovering America*.

33. Following the Battles of Lexington and Concord and the Battle of Bunker Hill in 1775, British metropolitans realized that they were now involved in "a military action." Gordon S. Wood, *The American Revolution: A History* (New York: Modern Library, 2002).

34. See Rauser, *Caricature Unmasked*, 80–83.

35. Leonard Tennenhouse, *The Importance of Feeling English: American Literature and British Diaspora, 1750–1850* (Princeton, NJ: Princeton University Press, 2007), 1–12.

36. Copley's version would itself be copied and slightly revised by an artist identified only as Wilkinson. This copy was published in the *Pennsylvania Gazette* in January 1766. For a detailed discussion of the multiple versions of this print and their symbolism, see Richardson, "Stamp Act Cartoons in the Colonies." See also Vincent Carretta, *George III and the Satirists from Hogarth to Byron* (Athens: University of Georgia Press, 1990), 105–110.

37. Carretta, *George III and the Satirists*, 105.

38. Olson, *Emblems of American Community*, 112.

39. Ibid., 113.

40. Nathan Daboll, *Freebetter's New England Almanack, for the Year of Our Lord 1776* (New London, CT: Timothy Green, 1775).

41. Ibid.

42. For an analysis of such poems within the paradigm of British diaspora, see Tennenhouse, *The Importance of Feeling English*, 12–18.

43. After 1776, *The Able Doctor* circulated as a transfer print on powder horns carried by soldiers of the Continental Army. See Lester C. Olson, "Pictorial Representations of British America Resisting Rape: Rhetorical Re-Circulation of a Print Series Portraying the Boston Port Bill of 1774," *Rhetoric and Public Affairs* 12.1 (2009): 25.

44. Olson, *Emblems of American Community*, 109.

45. T. H. Breen has argued that colonial boycotts of metropolitan goods following passage of the Stamp Act contributed to the unity of the American colonies. Breen, *The Marketplace of Revolution*.

46. Gilroy, *The Black Atlantic*, 31.

ZACHARY MCLEOD HUTCHINS

AFTERWORD: CORPORATISM AND THE STAMP ACT CRISIS

IF, AS THE FOREGOING chapters have suggested, the Stamp Act Crisis was an event that fractured more than fomented national identity, it was, nevertheless, a moment in which individuals from disparate backgrounds regularly banded together. Groups of colonists took joint action in temporarily and contingently unified bodies. Each corpus ranged in size, from the handful of Rhode Island elites who supported parliamentary power and signed their anonymous editorials on hemp and flax production with the pseudonym "O.Z.," to the teeming mobs that gathered to threaten the life and property of Andrew Oliver and other stamp men. These bodies, regularly represented and racialized in the London prints discussed by Clay Zuba (chapter 8), acted in concert on economic questions of production and consumption, a reality acknowledged visually in *The Able Doctor* (see figure 8.3) as the Indian Princess rejects tea forced down her throat. Concerned that North American colonists might cut off their food supply, the inhabitants of St. Kitts and Nevis rioted in protest against the Stamp Act, while the slave owners of Jamaica and Barbados sought to protect their investment in human labor by accepting a tax on paper. Shared legal and economic interests led families, neighbors, and business partners into cooperative attempts to articulate and defend their collective right, as colonists, to representation in the legislative process and consent in its economic decrees.[1]

These fleeting moments of economic cooperation sometimes masked deep political disagreements over the privileges and responsibilities of British subjects, as Alex Jablonski attests in chapter 6. The wavering uncertainties and inconsistencies of Gilbert Gigliotti's singular, anonymous poet (chapter 3) hint at the difficulty, in this political identity crisis, of achieving constitutional conviction and moral clarity as an individual, let alone as a collective; in 1765, the coordination of production and consumption, of riots and boycotts, did not necessarily signal ideological unity or a shared political vision. When colonists did come together to oppose the Stamp Act as a corpus, a unified body, they prioritized mutual economic interests above a national identity derived from shared government, ethnic background, or geographical origins. As T. H. Breen argues, "[T]he claims of nationalism—whatever its character at that moment—were always woven into a complex web of other loyalties."[2] During the Stamp Act Crisis, protesting colonists elevated local commerce and corporate priorities above national or ethnic allegiances, deploying commercial affiliations and relationships to serve political ends.[3] As Barbara Clark Smith writes, "[N]etworks of mutual obligation," in which "each household in a neighborhood was likely to be in debt to some of its neighbors and a creditor to others," forged a sense of economic solidarity within colonial communities resisting imperial taxation and oversight.[4]

Resistance to the Stamp Act, as noted by Molly Perry (chapter 2) and Todd Thompson (chapter 7), was first modeled on the example of the Spitalfields weavers and then stoked by the consensus-building power of North American printers, whose nearly unanimous opposition reflected an understanding that the Stamp Act would be bad for the industry, regardless of the political views espoused by any individual printer. Both of these groups are in keeping with our modern, commercial understanding of the corporation as "a trade-guild" or a company of craftsmen engaged in a shared business venture.[5] Pauline Maier recollects the influence "of those artisans who filled the ranks of the Sons of Liberty (and whose Committee of Mechanics gradually replaced the Sons of Liberty as a separate entity in New York politics after 1774). On occasion the interests of merchants, seamen, and artisans (or of special interest groups within those larger categories) conflicted, but firm economic bonds also linked them together" in advocating for their collective, corporate rights.[6] Of course, the word *corporation*, true to its Latin roots, also signified a more general collection of "persons united, or regarded as united, in one body," whether or not they shared the economic interests of leather-aproned artisans. In historical usage this definition from the *Oxford English Dictionary* most frequently applied to the members of a church, a reminder that shared religious beliefs were alleged to have sparked collective economic and political action during the crisis, as Patrick Mullins explains in chapter 1. And this religious sense of the word *corporation* is also, simultaneously, a prompt inviting us to acknowledge that corporatism is once again, a quarter millennium after the Stamp Act's passage, on the rise in North America.

Recent decisions by the U.S. Supreme Court, most notably in *Citizens United v. Federal Election Commission* (2009) and *Burwell, Secretary of Health and Human Services, et al. v. Hobby Lobby Stores, Inc., et al.*

(2014), have upheld the right of corporations to free speech and religious freedoms. This trend suggests that the American Revolution, in establishing individual rights, did not necessarily abolish "corporate group rights and representation by estates," as Howard Wiarda and others have suggested.[7] In the *Hobby Lobby* decision, Justice Samuel Alito, writing for the Court, states that in the Religious Land Use and Institutionalized Persons Act of 2000 (RLUIP) Congress deployed the "familiar legal fiction" whereby a corporation is treated as a person to support the extension of "rights, whether constitutional or statutory . . . to corporations."[8] Justice Ruth Bader Ginsburg, in her dissent, contends that this support for corporate rights is an innovative misreading that departs from legal and cultural precedents. Ginsburg argues that the RLUIP "amendment in no way suggests that Congress meant to expand the class of entities qualified to mount religious accommodation claims" to include corporations.[9] However, the attribution of collective rights and responsibilities to groups of people with shared economic interests is an American tradition with through-lines from the Stamp Act Crisis to the Roaring Twenties and presidential candidate Mitt Romney's widely panned 2011 campaign declaration, "Corporations are people, my friend."[10]

Ironically, the most famous advocate of American corporatism was also a professional hermit whose cultural cachet is predicated on his status as an individual. Henry David Thoreau, a man known primarily for living in relative isolation at Walden Pond, identifies the corporation as a locus of civic rights and responsibilities in "Civil Disobedience," urging like-minded business partners to raise their collective, corporate voice in objection to raw materials and goods derived from chattel slavery. In his tirade against the Mexican-American War and Northern complicity in the evils of slavery, Thoreau declares that "the opponents to a reform in Massachusetts are not a hundred thousand politicians at the South, but a hundred thousand merchants and farmers here, who are more interested in commerce and agriculture than they are in humanity, and are not prepared to do justice to the slave and to Mexico, cost what it may"—a complaint reminiscent of the Whiggish, slaveholding hypocrites criticized by J. Hector St. John de Crèvecoeur (chapter 5). It is a Northern commercial collective that Thoreau condemns for the evils of slavery and a Northern commercial collective that he exhorts to action because he sees the corporation as a political entity with greater moral potential than a democratic majority.[11] "To act collectively," Thoreau declares in *Walden*, "is according to the spirit of our institutions."[12]

Like the men—and women, as Caroline Wigginton helpfully reminds us (chapter 4)—who elevated shared, local economic interests and moral responsibilities above a transatlantic national identity in their opposition to the Stamp Act, Thoreau questions a hierarchy that places national allegiance above corporate conscience. Majority rule is potentially tyrannous and virtual representation may be immoral, Thoreau argues, because

> a government in which the majority rule in all cases cannot be based on justice, even as far as men understand it. Can there not be a government in which majorities do not virtually decide right and wrong, but conscience?—in which majorities decide only those questions to which the rule of expediency is applicable? Must the citizen ever for a moment, or in the least degree, resign his conscience to the legislator? Why has every man a conscience, then? I think that we should be men first, and subjects afterward. It is not desirable to cultivate a respect for the law, so much as for the right. The only obligation which I have a right to assume is to do at any time what I think right. It is truly enough said that a corporation has no conscience; but a corporation of conscientious men is a corporation with a conscience.[13]

In his vision of representative government's failures and his description of a corporation with a conscience, Thoreau recalls the moral (not merely economic) outrage of Spitalfields weavers and colonial printers even as he prophetically anticipates Alito's understanding of Hobby Lobby.[14] Thoreau advocates what Manuel Luis Martinez calls a "corporatist individualism" in which the anarchic potential of atomistic independence is constrained by the discovery of shared sentiments and a desire for collective action.[15] Corporations—"persons united, or regarded as united in one body"—thus stave off a descent into the Hobbesian state of nature even as they more closely align with the individual conscience than a national body politic.

The corporatism so recently defended by Alito is familial and reflects the earlier understanding of James Otis, who posited that the nation is not simply an aggregation of individuals but a collection of small corporations that have banded together in a communal enterprise. Alito specifies that publicly held companies cannot exercise religious freedoms precisely because, religiously speaking, they are not corporations—unified groups. Instead, his ruling applies to "closely held corporations, each owned and controlled by members of a single family, and no one has disputed the sincerity [or unity] of their religious beliefs."[16] Otis first articulated this familial basis for American corporatism in his 1764 attack on the authority that Parliament claimed over the colonies in the Sugar

Act and subsequently exercised in the Stamp Act. In *The Rights of the British Colonies*, Otis declares that God "has made it *equally* necessary that from *Adam* and *Eve* to these degenerate days, the different sexes should sweetly *attract* each other, form societies of *single* families, of which *larger* bodies and communities are as naturally, mechanically, and necessarily combined, as the dew of Heaven and the soft distilling rain is collected by the all enliv'ning heat of the sun. *Government* is therefore most evidently founded *on the necessities of our nature*."[17] In this preemptive assault on the Stamp Act, Otis positions the family—and communities constructed out of familial alliances—at the heart of society; family groups, not merely individuals, authorize the actions and benefit from the protections of government. The nation is, thus, a servant of the family as well as the individual, and Alito's opinion accords corporations or close-knit organizations the same protections offered to individuals inasmuch as they demonstrate familial cohesion of the sort that drew Adam to Eve.[18]

A chorus of voices has warned against this new wave of corporatism, but some critics have understated or misrepresented the historicity of this claim to communal or collectively held rights. In a critique of policies that treat corporations as people, for example, Robert Reich attributes the popularity of "this anthropomorphic fallacy" to "the false impression that corporations pay it [the corporate income tax], and therefore they should be entitled to participate in the democratic process under the old adage 'no taxation without representation.'" Reich correctly points to the Stamp Act Crisis and taxation debates of the 1760s as the genesis of modern American corporatism, but he brushes off the weight of history too easily, without fully acknowledging its relevance. Reich resists Thoreau's call for conscientious corporations and the logic underlying Otis's characterization of government, warning, "Companies are not patriotic. To believe that they should be—even could be, under the logic of supercapitalism—is to further anthropomorphize the corporation, and confuse the set of legal contracts that comprise a company with rights and responsibilities of citizenship that only people can exercise."[19] Corporatism is, to Reich, irreconcilable with liberalism and the defense of individual rights, notwithstanding assurances from Thoreau and Alito that any construction of corporate citizenship rests in the rights and responsibilities of the individuals who unite as a closely knit community: a collaborative or familial liberalism.[20] Treating a corporation as a person is, as Reich alleges, an act of fantasy; however, the acknowledgment of corporate, collective rights is a tradition every bit as venerable as honoring the "fantasmatic" authority of nations.[21]

Joint action asserting collective rights, during the Stamp Act Crisis, preceded and eventually enabled a liberal emphasis on individual freedoms during the American War of Independence. Even the means by which individual colonies expressed their will to Parliament, through the use of an agent, speaks to the corporate self-understanding of those colonists who would eventually found the United States of America. As Edwin Tanner explains, the colonial agent's duty was to "pull wires, exert influence, bring pressure to bear. In fact, he was what we might call a general lobbyist" of the sort that now pressures Congress on behalf of businesses and special interest groups. An agent's work was to argue for "corporate independence."[22] In many respects, individual North American (and Caribbean) colonies, often competing with each other to influence the policies of a legislature in which they were not represented, bore a closer resemblance to modern corporations than to the states they would become after the Revolution. Parallel to the long-standing emphasis, within the United States, on individualism, is an alternative, largely forgotten tradition of North American corporatism and the promotion of corporate, collective rights.

In October 1774, when the First Continental Congress finally assembled in Philadelphia, their opening act was to form a Continental Association that enshrined the rights and responsibilities of local economic cooperatives. The delegates declared that this association, the first formal embodiment of a coalition that would eventually become the United States of America, would bind their constituents to respect non-importation and non-consumption resolutions. Adherence to the association would be monitored by a committee "chosen in every county, city, and town, by those who are qualified to vote for representatives in the legislature, whose business it shall be attentively to observe the conduct of all persons touching this association." These local economic watchdogs were to ensure that their neighbors did not drink tea or purchase other banned products and to guarantee that local "venders of goods or merchandize will not take advantage of the scarcity of goods, that may be occasioned by this association, but will sell the same at the rates we have been respectively accustomed to do, for twelve months last past"—a key protection afforded by eighteenth-century corporatism, which posited a popular right to affordable foodstuffs.[23] "It was on this level," Breen writes, the level of local committees protecting collective commercial rights, "that ordinary men and women declared their independence."[24]

Although this tradition of corporatism waned after the War of American Independence, it did not disappear.[25] Jon Gjerde writes that the new nation "jettisoned most of its corporatist elements," but the belief in collective rights and responsibilities that undergirded colonial action during the Stamp Act Crisis lingered, evolving to meet the demands of new republican realities.[26] The prominence of Freemasons and Freemasonry in early American politics speaks to the ways in which gentlemen transformed the craft guild into a vehicle for promoting the political interests of social elites, as Margaret Jacob has noted.[27] And Edward Countryman and Gregory Nobles have demonstrated that an anxiety "to form organizations centered on their occupations" persisted among the citizens of the new republic as "the private or voluntary, association emerged as the dominant form of social organization" in the "new corporatism" of the early 1820s. Fifty years after the American War of Independence, many North Americans continued to organize "collective identity according to private interests rather than communal will" or individual rights.[28] The corporatism that animated colonial protests continued, in new forms, to have an impact on life in the early Republic.

If, as so many have asserted, the colonial fight for rights during the Stamp Act Crisis was a prologue to revolution and American nationalism, it may also serve as a precedent upholding the Supreme Court's recent corporatist turn. Although this volume questions the wisdom of causally linking the War of American Independence to the transatlantic taxation debates of the 1760s, the two events are clearly related; the Stamp Act must play some part in any account of evolving colonial understandings of the rights that the inhabitants of North America would eventually claim as their own in the Declaration of Independence. In celebrating this originary moment with liberal, nationalist accounts of the Stamp Act Crisis, a coexisting corporate emphasis on collective rights and responsibilities has too often been forgotten, an outcome lamented by both Smith and Quentin Skinner: "As with our cultural heroes, so with many of our values and practices: they too are liable to become buried in the sands of time, and stand in need of being excavated and reconsidered."[29] Today, 250 years after the Stamp Act's passage and in the wake of several Supreme Court decisions citing the act or promising to re-enshrine corporate rights, seems an appropriate moment to dust off this important piece of legislation and ask: What have you done for me philately?

Notes

1. Barbara Clark Smith suggests that eighteenth-century understandings of legislative representation entailed "sharing fundamental interests with one's constituents"; economic solidarity was a prerequisite of effective representation. Even after colonists

voted for their representatives, they reserved the right to disregard laws passed by those representatives. Colonists conceived of their disobedience to statutes such as the Stamp Act as a form of political liberty whereby "the workings of the law might sometimes be modified by the giving or withholding of 'after the fact' consent." Barbara Clark Smith, *The Freedoms We Lost: Consent and Resistance in Revolutionary America* (New York: New Press, 2010), 90, 42.

2. T. H. Breen, "Interpreting New World Nationalism," in *Nationalism in the New World*, ed. Don H. Doyle and Marco Antonio Pamplona (Athens: University of Georgia Press, 2006), 46. Breen, painting with deliberately broad strokes, describes nationalism and collective protest "in the name of an imagined community, in other words, of a country of the mind" as the primary fuel for colonial fervor during the 1760s. It would be foolhardy to allege that corporate ties ever commanded complete allegiance. But surely, between the "imperialist nationalism" and "Revolutionary nationalism" described by Breen, there was a period after colonists began to be disaffected with Great Britain and before they imagined a continental alliance of states, when loyalty to local communities and occupation-based economic networks predominated (44–45). See also Pauline Maier, *American Scripture: Making the Declaration of Independence* (New York: Alfred A. Knopf, 1997), 59–69.

3. Edward Countryman characterizes eighteenth-century corporatism as "a collective expectation that men of power and wealth would act to remedy problems of popular concern"; it entails a belief that the common people hold certain rights (the right to reasonably priced food and fuel; freedom from extortionate lending) collectively and might act collectively to seize those rights from those in power. Edward Countryman, *A People in Revolution: The American Revolution and Political Society in New York, 1760–1790* (Baltimore: Johns Hopkins University Press, 1981), 56. See also Allan Kulikoff, *The Agrarian Origins of American Capitalism* (Charlottesville: University Press of Virginia, 1992), 104.

4. Smith, *The Freedoms We Lost*, 59. See also Allan Kulikoff, *From British Peasants to Colonial American Farmers* (Chapel Hill: University of North Carolina Press, 2000), 203–54.

5. Smith suggests that colonial artisans preserved a strong sense of their collective rights: "Though English guilds did not put down roots in the colonies, the knowledge and very identity of artisanship still passed from tradesman to apprentice. The 'misteries' of trade encompassed not only specific skills and techniques but also expectations about the length of the workday, standards of work and workplace conditions, and the appropriate relationships among apprentices, journeymen, and masters of the trade." Smith, *The Freedoms We Lost*, 16.

6. Pauline Maier, *The Old Revolutionaries: Political Lives in the Age of Samuel Adams* (New York: Alfred A. Knopf, 1980), 66.

7. Howard J. Wiarda, *Corporatism and Comparative Politics: The Other Great "Ism"* (Armonk, NY: M. E. Sharpe, 1997), 97.

8. Samuel Alito, "Opinion of the Court," *Burwell, Secretary of Health and Human Services, et al. v. Hobby Lobby Stores, Inc., et al.* http://www.supremecourt.gov/opinions/13pdf/13-354_olp1.pdf, p. 18 (accessed 12 December 2014).

9. Ruth Bader Ginsburg, "Ginsburg, J., dissenting," *Burwell, Secretary of Health*

and Human Services, et al. v. Hobby Lobby Stores, Inc., et al. http://www.supremecourt.gov/opinions/13pdf/13–354_olp1.pdf, p. 10 (accessed 12 December 2014).

10. Michael J. Hogan reviews many of those twentieth-century through-lines in "Corporatism," *Journal of American History* 77.1 (1990): 153–60.

11. Henry David Thoreau, *"Walden," "Civil Disobedience," and Other Writings* 3d ed., ed. William Rossi (New York: W. W. Norton, 2008), 281. The corporation possesses greater moral potential for Thoreau because it is a step closer—by virtue of its smaller size—to individual sovereignty: "The progress from an absolute to a limited monarchy, from a limited monarchy to a democracy, is a progress toward a true respect for the individual. Is a democracy, such as we know it, the last improvement possible in government? Is it not possible to take a step further towards recognizing and organizing the rights of man? There will never be a really free and enlightened State, until the State comes to recognize the individual as a higher and independent power, from which all its own power and authority are derived, and treats him accordingly" (299). Thoreau's view of the corporation, as a group of like-minded men, approaches this ideal more nearly than the nation.

12. Ibid., 92.

13. Ibid., 278.

14. In characterizing Hobby Lobby as a corporation of conscience, Alito notes: "Hobby Lobby's statement of purpose commits the Greens [owners] to '[h]onoring the Lord in all [they] do by operating the company in a manner consistent with Biblical principles.' App. in No. 13-354, pp. 134–135 (complaint). Each family member has signed a pledge to run the businesses in accordance with the family's religious beliefs and to use the family assets to support Christian ministries. 723 F. 3d, at 1122. In accordance with those commitments, Hobby Lobby and Mardel stores close on Sundays, even though the Greens calculate that they lose millions in sales annually by doing so. *Id.*, at 1122; App. in No. 13–354, at 136–137. The businesses refuse to engage in profitable transactions that facilitate or promote alcohol use; they contribute profits to Christian missionaries and ministries; and they buy hundreds of full-page newspaper ads inviting people to 'know Jesus as Lord and Savior.'" Alito, "Opinion of the Court," 14.

15. Manuel Luis Martinez, *Countering the Counterculture: Rereading Postwar American Dissent from Jack Kerouac to Tomás Rivera* (Madison: University of Wisconsin Press, 2003), 94.

16. Alito, "Opinion of the Court," 29.

17. James Otis, *The Rights of the British Colonies Asserted and Proved* (Boston: Edes and Gill, 1764), 8.

18. Alito's acknowledgment of familial cohesion as a source of legal protection is in keeping with at least one colonial American law described by Smith, which "made it a crime for a victim to 'smother' a theft—that is, hush up the matter once the stolen goods had been privately recovered—unless the thief turned out to be a member of the immediate family." Smith, *The Freedoms We Lost*, 20.

19. Robert B. Reich, *Supercapitalism: The Transformation of Business, Democracy, and Everyday Life* (New York: Alfred A. Knopf, 2007), 216–17, 220.

20. Unfortunately, the speech rights granted to corporations in the *Citizens United*

decision are not contingent on the familial or ideological unity of corporate ownership, a reminder that this new corporatism is emerging somewhat chaotically, on an ad hoc basis through individual judicial decisions.

21. Jacqueline Rose, *States of Fantasy* (New York: Oxford University Press, 1996), 9.

22. Edwin P. Tanner, "Colonial Agencies in England During the Eighteenth Century," *Political Science Quarterly* 16.1 (1901): 33–34.

23. "The Association," in *Select Charters and Other Documents Illustrative of American History*, ed. William MacDonald (New York: 1899), 365–66.

24. T. H. Breen, *The Marketplace of Revolution: How Consumer Politics Shaped American Independence* (New York: Oxford University Press, 2004), 326.

25. Michael Merrill suggests that Alexander Hamilton and the Federalists, by undermining the barter economy that sustained local economic networks and empowered groups of artisans or farmers, subverted the corporate bent of the American Revolution. See Michael Merrill, "The Anticapitalist Origins of the United States," *Review* 13.4 (1990): 465–97.

26. Jon Gjerde, *The Minds of the West: Ethnocultural Evolution in the Rural Middle West, 1830–1917* (Chapel Hill: University of North Carolina Press, 1997), 11.

27. Margaret C. Jacob, *Living the Enlightenment: Freemasonry and Politics in Eighteenth-Century Politics* (New York: Oxford University Press, 1991), 50. On the role of Freemasonry in the Revolution and early Republic, see Steven C. Bullock, *Revolutionary Brotherhood: Freemasonry and the Transformation of the American Social Order, 1740–1830* (Chapel Hill: University of North Carolina Press, 1996).

28. Countryman, *A People in Revolution*; Gregory Nobles, "The Rise of Merchants in Rural Market Towns: A Case Study of Eighteenth-Century Northampton, Massachusetts," *Journal of Social History* 24.1 (1990): 17. See also Peter Dobkin Hall, *The Organization of American Culture, 1700–1900: Private Institutions, Elites, and the Origins of American Nationality* (New York: New York University Press, 1982), 53–54.

29. Quentin Skinner, *Liberty Before Liberalism* (New York: Cambridge University Press, 1998), 111.

ABOUT THE CONTRIBUTORS

Gilbert L. Gigliotti is Professor of English at Central Connecticut State University and teaches the literatures of early America, Greece, and Rome, as well as popular culture. His somewhat schizophrenic research and publication history include topics in both the neo-Latin poetry of colonial and revolutionary America and that iconic Hollywood couple Frank Sinatra and Ava Gardner.

Zachary McLeod Hutchins is Assistant Professor of English at Colorado State University, where he teaches courses in early American literature and culture. He is the author of *Inventing Eden: Primitivism, Millennialism, and the Making of New England* (Oxford University Press, 2014) and is currently completing a second book on representations of slavery in eighteenth-century American newspapers.

Alexander R. Jablonski is a PhD candidate in early American history at Binghamton University. His research considers the political, religious, and cultural problems of defining British subjecthood in the century between the Glorious and the American Revolutions.

J. Patrick Mullins is Associate Professor of History at Marymount University. He received his PhD in history from the University of Kentucky in 2005, and his field of specialization is the intellectual and cultural history of colonial and revolutionary America. His book manuscript on the political thought and activism of Jonathan Mayhew is presently under editorial review.

Molly Perry is a PhD candidate at the College of William & Mary and a lecturer in the history department at Christopher Newport University. Her current project, “Influencing Empire: Protest and Persuasion in the Plantation Ports of the British Empire,” examines how, during the period of reform following the Seven Years’ War, local communities attempted to shape the course of the British Empire using a spectrum of persuasive techniques, including metropolitan lobbying, theatrical street protests, aggressive petition campaigns, and new strategies of consumer protest. Her research focuses on the experience of the residents of British port cities in the greater Caribbean, including sailors and slaves.

Todd Nathan Thompson is Associate Professor of English at Indiana University of Pennsylvania, where he also serves as coordinator of the Master's in Literature and Master's in Composition and Literature programs. He is the author of *The National Joker: Abraham Lincoln and the Politics of Satire* (Southern Illinois University Press, 2015). Thompson's work on political satire and American literature has also appeared in *Scholarly Editing*, *Early American Literature*, *ESQ*, and elsewhere.

Caroline Wigginton is Assistant Professor of English at the University of Mississippi, where she specializes in the study of gender, race, and sexuality in the early Americas. She is the co-editor of *Transatlantic Feminisms in the Age of Revolutions* (Oxford University Press, 2012) and is completing her first book, *In the Neighborhood: Women's Publication in Early America* (University of Massachusetts Press, 2016).

Clay Zuba is a PhD candidate in the Department of English at the University of Delaware, where he is completing his dissertation, "Printing Indians and the Imperial Contest in America." His research has been supported by the Smithsonian American Art Museum and the Winterthur Museum and Library.

INDEX

Note: Page numbers in *italics* refer to illustrations.